The Girl's Own

The Girl's Own

*Cultural Histories of the
Anglo-American Girl, 1830–1915*

Edited by Claudia Nelson
and Lynne Vallone

The University of Georgia Press
Athens and London

© 1994 by the University of Georgia Press
Athens, Georgia 30602
All rights reserved
Designed by Betty Palmer McDaniel
Set in ten on thirteen Sabon
by Tseng Information Systems, Inc.
Printed and bound by Thomson-Shore, Inc.
The paper in this book meets the guidelines for
permanence and durability of the Committee on
Production Guidelines for Book Longevity of the
Council on Library Resources.

Printed in the United States of America
98 97 96 95 94   C   5   4   3   2   1

Library of Congress Cataloging in Publication Data
The Girl's own : cultural histories of the Anglo-American
    girl, 1830–1915 / edited by Claudia Nelson and
    Lynne Vallone.
        p.   cm.
    Includes bibliographical references and index.
    ISBN 0-8203-1615-6 (alk. paper)
        1. Teenage girls in popular culture—United States—
    History—19th century.   2. Teenage girls in popular
    culture—England—History—19th century.   I. Nelson,
    Claudia.   II. Vallone, Lynne.
    HQ798.G55   1994
    305.23'5—dc20   93-29651

British Library Cataloging in Publication Data available

For Laura Baxter Dickson (born 1899)
—C.N.
For Hilda LeClaire Stever White (born 1905)
—L.V.

Contents

Acknowledgments

This collection includes two essays that have appeared in somewhat different form elsewhere. We are grateful to their publishers for permission to reprint versions of the following:

Sherrie Inness, " 'It Is Pluck, But Is It Sense?': Athletic Student Culture in Women's College Novels, 1895–1910," *Journal of Popular Culture* 27.1 (1993).

Martha Vicinus, "What Makes a Heroine? Nineteenth-Century Girls' Biographies," *Genre* 20 (Summer 1987).

Lynne Vallone is grateful to the Department of English at Texas A&M University for its help with the manuscript's production, and to the members of the Interdisciplinary Group for Historical Literary Studies of Texas A&M University for their enthusiastic support for this book. I am grateful, as well, to the 1992–93 IGHLS steering committee—Larry J. Reynolds, Jeffrey N. Cox, and Mary Ann O'Farrell—for release time that enabled me to focus on this project. I would also like to thank my colleague Pamela R. Matthews for her advice and suggestions on this book and on other matters. I am especially grateful to Howard Marchitello, my husband and colleague, who has cheerfully and ably assisted this project in ways too numerous to list.

Both editors would like to express their thanks to Nancy Grayson Holmes, formerly of the University of Georgia Press, for her never-flagging enthusiasm for this project; to Judith Plotz and the other reviewer of the manuscript, for their kind words and helpful suggestions; to the many scholars who helped by providing encouragement and putting us in touch with possible contributors; to those who submitted essays and bore with us patiently through the publication process; and above all, to each other for a fruitful and always enjoyable process of collaboration and discovery.

The Girl's Own

LYNNE VALLONE AND
CLAUDIA NELSON

Introduction

But the mother of the little woman-child sees in her the born queen, and, at the same time, the servant of home; the daughter who is to lift the burden of domestic cares and make them unspeakably lighter by taking her share of them; the sister who is to be a little mother to her brothers and sisters; the future wife and mother in turn, she is the owner of a destiny which may call on her to endure much and to suffer much, but which, as it also bids her love much . . . is well worthy of an immortal creature.—*The Mother's Companion* (1887); quoted in Gorham 5–6

With a flash of laughing defiance, the girl bares her wrist, throwing into relief muscles like harpstrings. "I can row six miles without fatigue," she says, "and walk ten. I can drive and swim, and ride twelve miles before breakfast on a trotting horse. I eat heartily three times a day, and sleep soundly for eight hours out of the twenty-four. . . . Do I ever have headaches? Once in a while, but not so often as do my collegian cousins. Hysterics? No; nor the blues!"—"What Shall We Do with Our Daughters" (1876); quoted in Cogan 27

In her 1837–38 correspondence with Caroline Wells Healey, her classmate at Joseph Hale Abbot's Boston school, the thirteen-year-old Ednah Dow Littlehale vigorously debates the Woman Question with her fifteen-year-old friend. Resentful of what she understands to be the slavery resulting from woman's social, economic, legal, and political inequality with man, Ednah issues a rallying cry for all American women: "Stand up, and assert your rights, be *slaves* no longer; or at least spurn your *tyrants;* grant them no favor; let them not lead you to the *altar* of *matrimony,* until you are allowed your full political rights; the rights of free women" (McFadden 843). The somewhat superior Caroline (she notes that Ednah is "so much younger than myself") responds by invoking the separate-sphere argument that locates woman's rights and duties in the home. She dismisses Ednah's assertions as nonsense: "What mean you, by the political rights of women? for here it is that you become *nonsensical*. Are you a friend of Harriet Martineau's, would you wish your husband to stay at home, and take care of your children? for you to go to Caucus? No! You do not know what you are saying" (844). At the close of her next letter, Ednah charmingly and childishly replies to her friend's philosophy and chastisement by putting Caroline in her place: "If you don't think women have as good a right to vote as men you ought to be ducked in the *frog pond*" (845).

Margaret McFadden's recent publication and discussion of this series of letters on women's rights exchanged by the schoolfellows (each of whom became an active participant in women's issues and social reform as an adult) reveals that both the terms and the spirit of key feminist arguments of the nineteenth century were part of girls' culture. That the two friends, identically educated and coming from similar class and religious backgrounds, could espouse such different positions on the Woman Question likewise briefly demonstrates that girls' culture was not monolithic but multivocal. *The Girl's Own: Cultural Histories of the Anglo-American Girl, 1830–1915* explores some of the "voices" of the Girl's cultural history—those voices that seek to define and contain her, as well as her own voice—in a variety of forums and formats. The institutions, practices, and literatures discussed in these essays reveal the ways in which the Girl expressed her independence, as well as the ways in which she was imagined, presented, manufactured, and controlled.

Thus, for instance, the outspoken Ednah stoutly defends herself in the face of Caroline's dismissiveness, when she resists Caroline's labeling her a "ninny": "You may call me a *ninny*, but I call myself Ednah" (845). The pejorative "ninny" participates in the attempt (here joined by a girl herself) to define girls as objects: silly, brainless, and unable to recognize their own best interests. The refusal to admit or own anything other than her given—and accepted—name, however, posits a subjectivity that declares for the Girl a name and a voice of her own, and that actively seeks to deny the inadmissible objectification dedicated to the denial or even annihilation of her place and her part.

Objectified yet demanding subjectivity, sexualized but not always sexual, girls were both fascinating and troubling for those Victorian commentators who wrote about women. The Girl's relation to the world, established through familial relationships, domesticity, work, reading, and so forth, was always understood to be inseparable from her gender. Yet for these understandings, "gender" signified the maternal or the religious rather than the sexual or the erotic. The Girl existed as raw potential, for she could embody either virtue (as wife/mother or spinster/sister) or a kind of depraved independence and sexual freedom (as "fast girl" or "New Woman"). There was, for example, considerable debate about the place of girls in society waged within nineteenth-century periodicals. Such articles as Eliza Lynn Linton's "The Girl of the Period" (*Saturday Review* 1868), M.A.E.L.'s "The Girl of the Future" (*Victoria Magazine* 1870), and Sarah Grand's "The Modern Girl" (*North American Review* 1894) expressed or responded to the anxiety over the Girl's potential as a suffragist, a "fashionable" or "advanced" woman, or even a barren woman, unable to bear children because her body had been taxed by overeducation. Girls themselves sometimes took part in this debate, as in the eighteen-year-old Gertrude Hemery's call for worldly wisdom and sexual knowledge on the part of the young (*Westminster Review* 1894).

The anxiety surrounding Victorian commentary on girlhood seems to have arisen in part from the Girl's refusal to be categorized. "Adolescence," for instance, was a new and often disquieting concept in the late nineteenth century; in particular, the adolescent girl was disturbing because she might equally well act out what women were supposed to be—and what they were not. Depending not only upon her age but also upon her class, educational attainments, and marital or biological status, a "girl" might be what Charlotte Yonge termed a "home daughter" in her early twenties, a wife and mother aged seventeen, or a self-supporting member of the workforce at twelve. Increasingly, girls' energies might be directed not only toward making home happy but also toward activities as disparate as serving as a military nurse on the battlefields of the Crimea or the American South, earning a university degree, or (warned reformers) dragging out a miserable existence as prostitute or factory hand.

It is emblematic of the Victorian ambivalence toward girlhood that for much of the period (until the passage of the Criminal Law Amendment Act of 1893), British law set the age of consent at thirteen: if upper-class girls were supposed to be the embodiment of purity, their working-class counterparts were acknowledged to be sexual beings at puberty. The tension between "young lady" and "young person," between home daughter and home help, recalls the perennial Victorian tension between private and public spheres. Nor was class the only problem ruffling the placidity of commentators on girlhood; as journalist Eliza Lynn Linton fulminated again and again, the middle-class "girl of the period" was alarmingly ready to covet the freedom and earning power she thought she saw in her poorer sister. Many Victorians defined a girl as an unmarried young woman who was financially dependent, confined (more or less willingly) to the home, and sexually innocent. But the great number of exceptions to this stereotype—in all classes of society—was perennially disturbing.

Although she is clearly a significant figure in the Victorian controversy surrounding female sexuality and behavior, the adolescent girl as represented in contemporaneous cultural productions—conduct manuals, diet books, institutions, novels, periodical literature, photographs, paintings—remains today relatively unexplored. *The Girl's Own* seeks to find its place alongside other recent treatments of the figure of the adolescent girl, including Patricia Marks's *Bicycles, Bangs and Bloomers: The New Woman in the Popular Press* (1990), Sheila Rowbotham's *Good Girls Make Good Wives: Guidance for Girls in Victorian Fiction* (1989), Frances B. Cogan's *All-American Girl: The Ideal of Real Womanhood in Mid-Nineteenth-Century America* (1989), Deborah Gorham's *The Victorian Girl and the Feminine Ideal* (1982), J. S. Bratton's *The Impact of Victorian Children's Fiction* (1981), Joan N. Burstyn's *Victorian Education and the Ideal of Womanhood* (1980), and Carol Dyhouse's *Girls Growing Up in Late Victorian and Edwardian England* (1981) and *Feminism and the Family in England, 1880–1939* (1989). In building upon these discussions of girlhood and related topics, *The Girl's Own* seeks to expand the current interest in female sexuality and social history to include more fully the young woman's participation in the formation of nineteenth-century culture in England and the United States.

For despite the many obvious differences in the two nations' approaches to child-rearing and family life in this period—for example, in education, manners, the caste system, and women's power to earn and control money—British and American constructions of girlhood were in many ways strikingly similar. A shared language led to a shared literature, for one thing; such American chroniclers of girlhood as Louisa May Alcott, Susan Coolidge (Sarah Chauncey Woolsey), and Susan Warner (Elizabeth Wetherell) were tremendously popular in Britain, which in turn exported the productions of Charlotte Yonge, Juliana Ewing, and many others. Although it is impossible to quantify such influence, its importance nonetheless demands acknowledgment. Another key likeness lies in the two countries' understanding of female sexuality. British and American physicians often quoted each other across the miles, demonstrating a shared belief in all the "shoulds" surrounding young womanhood that so many of the young women themselves were ready and eager to reject. The lives of real girls doubtless differed radically from one location to the next (and, of course, regional variations within each country, together with the contrasts between the urban and the rural, would also have been important); nevertheless, the range of ideals of girlhood obtaining in Britain had much in common with that characterizing the United States—as the essays contained in *The Girl's Own* help to demonstrate.

Girls, Dinah Mulock commented in 1857 (with exclusive reference to the monied classes), are usually not given anything to do; they are "papa's nosegay of beauty to adorn his drawing-room. He delights to give them all they can desire—clothes, amusements, society; he and mamma together take every domestic care off their hands; they have abundance of time and nothing to occupy it" (274). As the contributors to this volume suggest, however, Victorian visions of girlhood in both Britain and the United States were far more varied than this picture of conspicuous consumption would indicate. At once females and children, girls were doubly removed from the rough-and-tumble of the marketplace or the Empire—but by virtue of the moral influence with which both women and children were credited, their very otherness lent them an oppositional power over the public sphere from which they were supposed to be excluded.

This ambiguity, as we have already suggested, made the Girl a significant focus for Anglo-American cultural anxieties. Commentators were unsure where to place her—as the light of the home? the potential academic or professional rival of her brother? the (a)sexualized object of male desire? And having thus classified her, they had no guarantee that she would stay in her pigeonhole. Constructing girlhood entailed a constant struggle for dominance as girls simultaneously proffered their own interpretations of the role, interpretations that both drew upon and added to the multiple meanings possible for this social group. The protean quality of the Girl as simultaneous subject, object, and opponent of cultural classification is evident throughout the essays here collected.

In positioning the articles within the volume, we have tried to bear in mind the Girl's own "position" within each chapter. Together, the essays sketch a roughly chronological trajectory that follows her from domestic activities such as cooking or shopping or reading, to her canonization or condemnation by nineteenth-century society for her ability or inability to embody the virtues demanded by the Victorian cult of True Womanhood, to her own incursions into the public spheres represented by school or work, and finally back "home" once more, as turn-of-the-century social activists did their best to come to terms with a girlish figure who had acted in ways that should have been impossible to the ideal girl of Victorian prescription and imagination. As will quickly become evident, however, such rebelliousness and refusal to be labeled is by no means confined to the last years of the period or to the United States alone. Ultimately all of us who study Victorian girls of any decade must come to terms with the tensions between real and ideal, virtue and vice, public and private, body and soul, and subject and object—as the Victorians themselves were usually well aware. Nineteenth-century constructions of the Girl as present or potential influence for good or evil, indeed, typically drew their energy from precisely these irreconcilable dichotomies.

The place of the "home girl" in scientific housekeeping—the function from which feminine influence was often thought to flow—is the subject of the articles by Claudia Nelson and Judith Pascoe. Nelson's examination of dietary theory as instrument of social change focuses on girls' novelist Louisa May Alcott as at once product and promulgator of an ideology of housekeeping that stressed for both genders a set of "feminine" virtues that Alcott nonetheless found it necessary to reclaim from the male domain and retheorize in "feminist" terms. Pascoe discusses the "one-man literary business" of Philadelphia writer/publisher Timothy Shay Arthur, whose constructions of girlhood in the context of virtuous and economical house-keeping placed girls above the consuming passions and the passion for consuming that typified Arthur's vision of mid-century American society. Whether as the central site of domestic-based social improvement or as the virtuous "other" suggesting an alternative expression of domesticity itself, the Girl in Alcott's and Arthur's visions simultaneously was empowered through housekeeping and empowered housekeeping in her turn.

In their contributions to this volume, Martha Vicinus and Julia Court-ney discuss the relationship between girls and the didactic entertainment afforded them by literature. Vicinus's examination of biographies' expli-cation of the possibilities for female heroism demonstrates the extent to which biographies of such Victorian "saints" as Florence Nightingale or Grace Darling validated nontraditional, nongendered virtues: obstinacy, initiative, public success. (Later biographies, she suggests, were more "Vic-torian" than the Victorians in downplaying women's independence and emphasizing romance as a value.) Courtney provides insight into girls' as-similation of improving literature through her description of a manuscript magazine, the *Barnacle,* written by a group of young women as a response to their reading of narratives by Charlotte Yonge. In the stories, travel ac-counts, poems, illustrations, and other components of the *Barnacle,* we can trace the preoccupations and concerns of girls who later exerted significant influence on female education in Britain. These two essays' examinations of histories for and by girls suggest that such texts served not only to encourage conformity to a particular ideal but also to liberate readers chafing under their enforced conformity to a rival model of femininity.

But efforts at liberation were often profoundly disturbing to onlookers, who discerned in such strategies the incipient destruction of the ideal by the anti-ideal. The erotic energy of the Girl, Christina Boufis argues, was at the heart of the mid-Victorian anxiety over the "Girl of the Period" as described in hostile fashion by Eliza Lynn Linton and sympathetically by sensation novelists such as Rhoda Broughton. Linton's and Broughton's complementary visions of the Girl as a full participant in the market economy, even insofar as the latter also governed sexuality, "may be seen as a focal point for fears of class dissolution and societal changes," just as her regulation through literature may be seen as emblematic of an English struggle for "national self-definition."

The marketplace, Leslie Williams observes in her essay on John Everett Millais, was a driving factor in the creation of sentimentalized representations of girlhood for both painter and consumer of images. While in his iconic paintings of girlhood Millais learned to meet his audience's desires for comfort and caution, Williams argues, his works also testify to the Girl's "complicated symbolic value." As Carol Mavor's essay on Lewis Carroll's photographs of little girls makes clear, assumptions about girlhood were sometimes undermined even while they were celebrated; simultaneously eroticized and pure, fetishized and individual, Carroll's girls afford troubling glimpses not only into the Victorian objectification of girlhood but also into that of our own day.

The paradoxes at work in girlhood's representation also functioned within its theoreticization. Social progress could be inseparable from earlier, "repressive" ideals of femininity, public life inextricable from domesticity, as Joyce Senders Pedersen's contribution to this collection indicates. In her analysis of the stances of British "liberal feminists," many of them the founding mothers of women's education in the mid-Victorian years, Pedersen notes the interplay of family politics and larger social issues, the extent to which the hopes for domestic, academic, and national success coincided with and reinforced one another. The model for girlhood, indeed, could serve as a model for British society in general, in which "the principled pursuit of high ideals" essential to the individual's or country's well-being depended at once on the self-sacrifice usually associated with femininity and the self-discipline often linked to masculinity; the two principles come together in the girls' schools envisioned by the liberal feminists.

Sherrie Inness and Sally Mitchell likewise focus on the acknowledgment that girls' place might no longer be the home. In her examination of the treatment of athletics and athletes in American women's-college fiction, Inness argues that in contrast to the gymnastic exercises sanctioned by college administrators, team sports provided an opportunity for girls to empower themselves by creating a common culture in which they would establish the mores. Like Pedersen's liberal feminists and pioneering teachers, Inness's student athletes bend conservative ideals of femininity to their own purposes. Mitchell's documentation of the intrusion of the work ethic into the middle-class feminine ideal (as seen especially in girls' magazines) also explores the creation of a culture of girlhood that rejected traditional domesticity. She contends that the perception that young women could—in fact, should—be self-supporting helped to reverse earlier British norms by defining girls in terms of their ages and career-mindedness rather than their class. Working-class validations of self-assurance, ambition, and distance from the home circle penetrated upward at the turn of the century to bring about a radical shift in the characteristics deemed acceptable for girls of the bourgeoisie. For working girls and college athletes alike (as for readers of biographies or Alcott novels), self-sacrifice could seem to go hand in hand with self-actualization.

None of the girls discussed in these essays appears content to occupy the role assigned her by the conventions of her culture. In the final chapter in this volume, Lynne Vallone comments upon the erotic girl (the unwed mother), who becomes a source of tension as a being "out of place." Vallone's essay on the organization of the National Florence Crittenton Mission in turn-of-the-century America details the attempt to reintegrate "fallen" girls into a type of family, the better to restore the vanished innocence essential to the construction of Victorian womanhood. Such reforming efforts bring us full circle, back to the stifling or liberating purity of the nineteenth-century home. But for the Crittenton workers as for their contemporaries and predecessors, there seemed no certain way to induce the Girl to remain within the domestic pigeonhole.

Perhaps still more for the Victorians than for ourselves, girlhood was a time of liminality. Poised not only between childhood and adulthood but also between purity and desire, home and market, tradition and change, nineteenth-century Anglo-American girls at once symbolized, experienced, and in some degree forwarded the cultural crisis into which they were born. As the essays in this volume variously suggest, it is unwise to read the Victorian Girl simply, whether as a creature of patriarchal repression or as a late-twentieth-century teenager in period costume. Often, indeed, it is difficult to separate repression from empowerment, given the fluidity with which one nineteenth-century theorist's constrictive stereotypes of angelic femininity may become another's liberating vision of goddesslike strength.[1]

In our own day, which has witnessed the gradual shrinking of the category of "girl" to exclude all but the prepubescent, we may have trouble seeing girlhood as significant to social change. But as we have already observed, and as the essays included in this collection show, in defining "girls" the Victorians tended to be specific as to class and vague as to age, so that a "girl" could be any unmarried female of genteel family background between the ages of, say, five and twenty-five. In contrast, of course, our own practice reverses that custom, instead drawing precise age boundaries around a category that has little to do with income levels. Much of the tension surrounding the Girl that these essays identify clearly emanates from her ambiguity of position: by virtue of her status (position, inexperience, presumed purity, and so forth) she is a girl—but what if these status indicators were absent? In other words, what happens if femininity turns out to be learned rather than innate? This very tension becomes not only a motive for the cultural controlling of girlhood, but also an energy source enabling girls—as they moved over into the category of "young women"—to gain a measure of control on their own part. Without the Victorian girl, then, the contemporary woman becomes in some ways unimaginable.

NOTE

1. Nor can we define the Girl merely as the opposite or the pale copy of the Boy. To be sure, his gender, just as much as hers, was continually under construction in this period, as he moved from comparative androgyny to hypermasculinity; but boyhood and girlhood seemed to most Victorians to have little in common, and an understanding of the one sheds only faint light on the other.

WORKS CITED

Bratton, J. S. *The Impact of Victorian Children's Fiction.* London: Croom Helm, 1981.

Burstyn, Joan N. *Victorian Education and the Ideal of Womanhood*. London: Croom Helm, 1980.

Cogan, Frances B. *All-American Girl: The Ideal of Real Womanhood in Mid-Nineteenth-Century America*. Athens: U of Georgia P, 1989.

Dyhouse, Carol. *Feminism and the Family in England, 1880–1939*. Oxford: Basil Blackwell, 1989.

———. *Girls Growing Up in Late Victorian and Edwardian England*. London: Routledge and Kegan Paul, 1981.

Gorham, Deborah. *The Victorian Girl and the Feminine Ideal*. Bloomington: Indiana UP, 1982.

Grand, Sarah. "The Modern Girl." *North American Review* 158 (June 1894): 706–14.

Hemery, Gertrude. "The Revolt of the Daughters: An Answer—by One of Them." *Westminster Review* 141.6 (June 1894): 679–81.

Linton, Eliza Lynn. "The Girl of the Period." *Saturday Review* 25 (14 March 1868): 339–40.

McFadden, Margaret. "Boston Teenagers Debate the Woman Question, 1837–1838." *Signs: Journal of Women in Culture and Society* 15 (1990): 832–47.

M.A.E.L. "The Girl of the Future." *Victoria Magazine* 15 (September and October 1870): 440–57, 491–502.

Marks, Patricia. *Bicycles, Bangs and Bloomers: The New Woman in the Popular Press*. Lexington: UP of Kentucky, 1990.

[Mulock, Dinah Maria]. "A Woman's Thoughts about Women: Something to Do." *Chambers's Journal of Popular Literature, Science and Arts* 7 (2 May 1857): 273–75.

Rowbotham, Sheila. *Good Girls Make Good Wives: Guidance for Girls in Victorian Fiction*. Oxford: Basil Blackwell, 1989.

CLAUDIA NELSON

Care in Feeding: Vegetarianism and Social Reform in Alcott's America

In Britain and North America alike, the nineteenth-century obsession with social reform was predominantly an obsession with personal reform. Thus the problems of the lower working class might be cured by sending poor urban children to farm life in rural England or the western United States, there to learn from foster families the virtues of domesticity and outdoor activity; prostitutes might best be saved individually, through the concern of a W. E. Gladstone; and while governments sought to extirpate by law or by force venereal disease, slavery, and a host of additional social evils, reformers knew that moral regeneration could only come from within. As Dr. William A. Alcott reminded young husbands in 1839, "Who does not see, that if each father were to succeed in nothing more than in converting, by a right moral influence, his own household, the millennium could not be distant?" (103).

Likewise, many reformers agreed with Alcott that "right moral influence" was to a large extent dependent upon right eating. The most eminent American physician of the Revolutionary period, Benjamin Rush, had noted that mental illnesses were susceptible to menu change; Rush recommended a stimulating diet of meat, wine, hot spices, and opium in cases of hypochondria (101–3) and a "low diet" of vegetables for mania and excessive sexual appetite (193, 352).[1] The latter prescription—and the linkage of overstimulated digestion, madness, and desire—was popularized in the 1830s by Sylvester Graham, who held that the "reciprocity of influence" between the three major systems of the body, the nutritive, reproductive, and mental, ensures that "extraordinary and undue excitements" inflicted upon any one of these systems will affect the "organs and functions" of any other (17). Such a systemwide breakdown is likely especially to involve the stomach, which, "more largely supplied with nerves and blood-vessels than any other organ in the body . . . more directly and powerfully sympathizes with the genital organs, in all their excitements and affections" (48). Through "high-seasoned food; rich dishes; the free use of flesh; and even the excess of aliment," young men may "increase the concupiscent excitability and sensibility of the genital organs, and augment their influence on the functions of organic life, and on the intellectual and moral faculties" (18–19). Those who do not act on their desire are no better off than those who do, as "those LASCIVIOUS DAY-DREAMS, and *amorous reveries*" to which all young people—and especially the wrongly fed—are liable "are often the sources of general debility, effeminacy, disordered functions, and permanent disease, without the actual exercise of the genital organs!" (25).

While historians today often dismiss Graham as a crank who, as Joseph Jones suggests, sold greater intellects than his own a "bill of groceries," the connection between diet and desire that he helped to articulate had widespread influence. From the establishment of Oberlin College on Grahamite principles in 1836, to the 1863 vision that led Ellen G. White to found the Seventh Day Adventists, to Dr. J. H. Kellogg's "cornflake crusade" for healthy eating and pure living, manifestations of vegetarian morality had significant effect over the course of the century. Gerald Carson reports that "between 1830 and 1890 no less than eighty-five popular health magazines appeared in the United States, many with Grahamite affiliations" (58), while Hillel Schwartz observes the connection between Grahamism and such contemporaneous phenomena as the hydropathic spa and dress reform (59). Those social reformers who took a dietary stance included Henry David Thoreau (whose Walden experiment, as Daniel Dombrowski notes, combined the minimum of meat, tea, and coffee with the maximum of chastity), Elizabeth Blackwell (who connected premature sexuality in girls with "coffee, hot bread, mingled butter or molasses, rich or highly spiced dishes, pickles, wine, [and] pastry" [132]), Robert Dale Owen (who linked his teetotalism and vegetarianism with his virtue in "never [having] entered a brothel in his life" [qtd. in Walters 23]), and the abolitionist Theodore D. Weld.

But for all the prominence of men in this effort to purify America's palates, the food-reform movement relied upon its appeal to women. If William Alcott advises "the young husband who wishes to avoid every improper feeling of every description . . . to avoid, with the utmost care, all exciting food or drink. . . . [to] keep his blood and all his fluids in as pure a state as he possibly can" (*Husband* 289), he also admits that it is to the young wife that God has assigned the duty of "the physical education of herself and of those around her" (*Wife* 174). Indeed, Alcott notes, the housewife is of greater moral importance than any lawyer, legislator, or clergyman, as she functions on a more private and personal—and hence more influential—level than is possible for a public functionary: "What can a minister do for a person who . . . is drenched, daily, with hot, compound, or over-stimulating drinks; or fed with hot, oily, indigestible or poisonous food; and whose very solids and fluids, in every 'nook and corner,' are, as it were, defiled?" (*House-Keeper* 37). It is woman who commonly controls food, and thus woman who may cleanse society.

Woman, indeed, "is the divinely appointed teacher of man" (*House-Keeper* 316)—not only as his cook, since Alcott hopes by simplifying American diet to emancipate her from the kitchen, but also because of the implication that she is less liable than her husband to sin. As Alcott reminds his male readers in an attempt to dissuade them not merely from illicit sex but also from nonprocreative marital sex, "Wherever impurity can be found, man is, directly or indirectly, the cause. He is ever, at least since the days of the first pair, the grand seducer" (*Husband* 249). Given this thoroughly Victorian location of desire within the specifically male body, it is difficult to avoid reading the hot, overstimulating, drenching poisons defiling unspecified bodily nooks and corners as semen.[2] It is no coincidence that social purity and women's rights were so often espoused in tandem in both the United States and Britain; as numerous commentators have observed, the frequently perceived asexuality of woman served not only as the excuse for keeping her out of the public sphere, but also, ironically, as the primary aperture through which she might enter this public life. Diseased and passionate, men were at the mercy of their uncontrollable desires; pure and selfless, women had the morals and personal influence essential to reform. When the reform in question was dietary, furthermore, only women were likely to have the domestic skills necessary to enact it.

Given the Victorian perception that the most successful reforms were those imposed upon the young, who, their feet early set in paths of righteousness, would live temptation-free lives and produce offspring as pure as themselves to populate a new Eden, a key figure in the food-reform ethos becomes that of the middle-class girl. The present subjects of dietary discipline and the future wielders of dietary power, girls stood in a dual relation to food in vegetarian families: learning self-control at their mothers' tables, they could grow up to enforce for their husbands a regimen of plainly cooked, unspiced, vegetable foods in place of the fried meats, overstimulating condiments, and morally dangerous pastries that were at the root of American alcoholism and abuse of sexuality. Husbands, free of the corrosive effects of pernicious desire, would rise to new heights of accomplishment; children, born to parents not enervated by excess, would populate a newly vigorous republic; and women, no longer prisoners of bedroom or kitchen, would at last take their place as the moral equals (at least) of men. But before that utopian vision could be enacted, girls had to be properly trained in reformist housekeeping.

In this connection, the children's books of Louisa May Alcott are particularly notable—not simply because of her focus on girlhood and family utopias but also because she herself was a product of a Grahamite childhood, the sometimes unwilling subject of vegetarian reform who grew up to espouse a (celibate) feminist reform in turn. Her juvenile fiction, notably *An Old-Fashioned Girl* (1870) and the Rose Campbell duo of *Eight Cousins* (1874) and *Rose in Bloom* (1876), at once reconstructs and deconstructs her upbringing and larger social conditions. As the daughter of William Alcott's cousin, sympathizer, and youthful best friend, she wrote on one level, as Karen Halttunen observes, "to extend Bronson Alcott's perfectionist cult of domesticity and his creed of self-restraint to a generation of middle-class Americans" (251), while on another level—her children's books mirroring her Gothic shockers—she wrote to undercut the idea that "domesticity and self-restraint" should be both beginning and end of women's existence.

Most literary critics discuss Alcott's feminist rebellion primarily with regard to her melodramas and/or her first best-selling novel for girls, *Little Women* (1868). Judith Fetterley's pathbreaking article "*Little Women:* Alcott's Civil War," for instance, argues that the novel's interest derives from a tension "between its overt messages and its covert messages" (370), a presentation of submission as simultaneously women's only choice and women's doom that Alcott eventually repressed, as in "the tedious sentimentality of *A Rose in Bloom* [sic]" (371).[3] However, as such critics as Veronica Bassil have noted, the tensions in Alcott's work extend throughout her novels for girls, far from being negated by her depictions of domesticity; domesticity in fact serves as the locus for "anger, sorrow, and destruction" (193). I will contend that a major source of this ambivalence toward the home is to be found in the peculiar dynamics of the Bronson Alcott household, in which the power that William Alcott (echoing prevailing Victorian belief) sought to arrogate to women was in fact situated in Bronson himself. In her domestic novels, then, Alcott at once provides girls with standard reformist prescriptions as to the desirability of establishing a new society based on a particular set of female values and warns them that control of this society, too, may be denied them. And to a great extent, in Alcott's literature as in her life, the battleground for this struggle is gastronomic.

Charles Strickland observes that Bronson's views on raising the perfect child centered on the point "that gentle means must be used to promote ascetic ends, a view which made the burdens of childhood peculiarly intense," since a naughty child was not merely an irritant but a contradiction in terms, even a crime against nature ("Father" 9). Closer to the divine than any adult could be, children should be in full control of the appetites comprising their lower natures—and if they need help achieving such control, an appeal to their guilt feelings can provide it. The keynote of Bronson's strategy in dealing with his children is struck in his advice to three-year-old Anna: "Give up your want to Father's, and then you will begin to love me *more*. And the more you do so, the more you will go on to love me, till, by and by, you will love me well enough to *give up* your want always" (qtd. in Bassil 189). For children if not for father, virtue means self-abnegation; those children who refuse to abandon appetite are not simply self-willed but unnatural, unable to love their father.

The "wants" Bronson asked his children to relinquish were frequently dietary, whether in occasional tests of willpower such as seeing whether the toddlers Anna and Louisa could refrain from stealing apples left out to tempt them (they couldn't), or in daily fare on the Alcott table. In her satirical sketch of life in Bronson's utopian "consociate family" at Fruitlands in 1843, "Transcendental Wild Oats" (1876), Alcott recalls, "Unleavened bread, porridge, and water for breakfast; bread, vegetables, and water for dinner; bread, fruit, and water for supper was the bill of fare ordained by the elders" (157). As Bronson's contemporary Robert Carter summed up the Alcott rationale:

> He maintained . . . that the evils of life were not so much social or
> political as personal, and that a personal reform only could eradicate
> them; that self-denial was the road to eternal life, and that property
> was an evil, and animal food of all kinds an abomination. No animal
> substance, neither flesh, fish, butter, cheese, eggs, nor milk, was al-
> lowed to be used at "Fruitlands." They were all denounced as pollution,
> and as tending to corrupt the body, and through that the soul. (qtd. in
> Sears 38–39)

As "Transcendental Wild Oats" makes clear, however, Bronson's strictures against animal substances were not shared by his wife, Abba. While Alcott's sketch depicts her father as a saintly idealist at the mercy of Fruitlands' cofounder, the English vegetarian Charles Lane, Abba appears throughout as "unconverted but faithful to the end" (150)—too practical, hard-working, humorous, and devoted to her children to care for theory, too loyal and responsible to abandon her helpless husband. (She is, indeed, the only true adult at Fruitlands.) In "Wild Oats" Abba rebels against the colony's rejection of leather shoes and animal-fat lamps, as the former are necessary to her children and the latter to her fulfillment of motherly duties; in real life she rebelled as well against Bronson's vegetarianism, slipping bits of meat to her daughters.

Young Louisa's wilfulness and her "carnivorous" personality (she accepted the meat with delight) seemed to Bronson two sides of one coin: "I am not sure but that her untameable spirit derives something of its ferocity from the nature of her diet," he mused in "Observations on the Spiritual Nurture of My Children." "The Spirit is, perhaps, clogged in its functions, from having to dispose of so much animal matter, in the way of organic association, digestion, etc. . . . Think of a young being, compelled to lug about, in the very seat of its Spiritual life, a burden of flesh!" (qtd. in Strickland, "Father" 32). The bond between the two strong-minded women—eaters of forbidden food, rebels against the "inner light," brunettes in a family in which blondness represented spiritual grace—often confounded Bronson, who commented in an 1846 journal entry, "Two devils, as yet, I am not quite divine enough to vanquish—the mother fiend and her daughter" (qtd. in Halttunen 235).

In the Alcott marriage, then, it was Abba who was cast as sensualist, worker, and financier, Bronson who acted as idealist, moralist, and shaper of his daughters' characters. The description of Mr. March at the beginning of *Good Wives* (1869) as "the household conscience, anchor, and comforter" (8) is suggestive; he is, indeed, another version of Beth, a male Angel in the House. As Rena Sanderson notes, Bronson's coopting of the persona that Victorian practice would normally have assigned to Abba may have put pressure on his daughter to accept the male role of breadwinner, since "her father's idealism and anti-materialism already pre-empted the 'morally superior' feminine role which the unruly Louisa suspected she could never attain" (44). Equally significant, it seems to have been the cause of marital strain between Bronson and Abba.

Sarah Elbert suggests that a major source of the friction at Fruitlands was the restructuring of the Alcott family into the larger consociate family whose heads were not Bronson and Abba but Bronson and Charles Lane. By creating a family based not on kinship of blood but kinship of spirit and by demoting Abba from partner to housekeeper, Lane "undermined the authority Abba exercised in her own sphere" and minimized her influence (56). As Elbert points out, it was the men who made the decisions about diet, household schedule, and certain aspects of child-rearing that would normally have fallen to Abba (70); Abba's resentment at her loss of power was shared by her second daughter, whose Fruitlands diary contains such entries as "Father and Mr. L. had a talk, and father asked us if *we* saw any reason for us to separate [break up the community]. Mother wanted to, she is so tired. I like it, but not the school part [Lane was their principal teacher] or Mr. L." (entry of 20 November 1843; Sears 110). In this context, Fetterley's point that in *Little Women* the women seem to have no role that the men can't fill better ("War" 375) suggests not the incapacity of women but the encroaching nature of men, whose appetite for dominance extends even to the household.

Indeed, at Fruitlands the reversal of nineteenth-century convention extended into the bedroom. The English vegetarian community of which Lane had been a member had aimed (not always successfully) at celibacy, perhaps as a result of their reading of Graham and William Alcott, and Lane and Bronson determined that celibacy would be the practice also at the new community. Abba, however, was less extreme; while she was later to lecture "on the dangers of unchecked fertility, the advantages of . . . sexual continence" (Elbert 94), she appears to have resented the imposition of strict asceticism on her marriage and especially Lane's role in making this decision. Natania Rosenfeld recounts also that "during times of sexual abstinence, Bronson Alcott became jealous of the physical affection Marmee gave her children" (10). As a beneficiary of Abba's demonstrativeness (and as a girl who feared that her thoughts and actions would never approach the spiritual perfection her father demanded), Alcott sided with her mother.

"Transcendental Wild Oats," for instance, casts Abba as a beleaguered earth mother. The celibate paradise of the men—who, "pledged to the spirit alone . . . anticipate no hasty or numerous addition to their numbers" (149)—seems ultimately sterile; so idealistic are these farmers that none of their crops can bear fruit, "as manure was not allowed to profane the virgin soil" (159).[5] In contrast, it is Abba, as "Sister Hope," who stands for what Elbert terms "abundance and comfort, 'the bread and wine of a new communion'" (75); nor can Bronson/"Abel Lamb" be saved except through his role as husband and father, which finally imbues him with responsibility and the work ethic. The asceticism of "Abel," in other words, imposes impossible burdens on his family; the humanity of "Hope" legitimates her children's inevitable wants and simultaneously reinstates her as the true moral center of the Fruitlands community.

In this context, in which reform is simultaneously longed for and unattainable, a means of male control and a way for women to achieve a specifically female power, Alcott's reform writings for girls alternately embrace her father's ideals and condemn his constrictiveness. What had seemed in her own family a male-dominated drama becomes in her work a process in which women, whether as fictional characters or as author, have the last word. For all her endorsements of self-restraint, a reformist catchword Bronson and the social purity workers (often women) held in common, what her books for girls prize most highly is a value that seems to emanate from women: love. In *Eight Cousins* and *Rose in Bloom*, however, Alcott hints at the problems that may arise when men control not only child-rearing but romance.

These two novels describe the girlhood and young womanhood of Rose Campbell, an orphaned heiress who lives with her great-aunts Plenty and Peace in a house known as the "Aunt-hill" because of its proximity to the four Campbell sisters-in-law and their numerous male progeny. Each aunt, as Strickland observes, represents a different school of American motherhood: severity (Jane), morbid clucking (Myra), obsession with fashion (Clara), ineffectual sweetness (Peace), outdated lavishness (Plenty), and common sense (Jessie) (*Domesticity* 126); so incompatible are most of their attitudes toward Rose's upbringing that Rose is pleased to find a foster father in her bachelor uncle, Alec. A physician and reformer, Alec has strong views on dress reform, exercise, education, and diet, all of which he puts into practice with Rose. By the end of *Eight Cousins* Rose has vindicated his methods by developing from a morose, peaked, "unchildlike" girl into a healthy and happy young woman; by the end of the sequel, she has indicated her love for him still further by avoiding marriage to the most dashing and dissolute of her cousins and choosing instead Alec's namesake and stand-in, Mac, just as at the end of *Eight Cousins* she has chosen to live with Alec—"who I love best, [and] who I'm happiest with" (290)—rather than with any of her aunts. On the face of it, then, the Campbell series describes a consummated Electra complex that seems to enjoy its creator's full approval.

In fact, however, the real story may be more complicated, Rose's health and happiness more apparent than real. First, it seems evident that if any character here represents Alcott herself, it is not Rose but the foundling maid-of-all-work, Phebe, whose dark hair, talent (in singing), competence, and lack of family ties suggest also the orphaned heroines of Alcott's Gothic thrillers. As Jane Van Buren has noted, these heroines' "orphanhood . . . provided freedom from family domination" (290); likewise, Bassil comments, they tend to be "threatened, often sexually, by an evil older man" who stands in the place of the father (191). Given this pattern, we may hypothesize that if Alec's relationship to Phebe (whom he regards as "the finer girl of the two" [*Cousins* 52]) is neither controlling nor sexually charged, this may merely be because of the presence of Rose—who, blonde, undistinguished artistically, less forceful than Phebe, and tied to Alec by blood and sentiment, would seem to represent the docile sisters in the Alcott family constellation. The bond between Rose and Alec, then, for all its overwhelming importance to both participants, may not strike Alcott herself as entirely beneficial.

Alec's reformism is the focus of the novel's ambiguity toward him. Since Rose has effectively "given up her want" (in Bronson's phrase) in order to please her uncle, she is both mentally and physically under his control; as he puts it, she is his "pet and plaything" (*Cousins* 162). Alcott implies that while the physical effects of Alec's reformism are wholly good, the state of being entirely dominated—however benevolently—may lead to discontent even while it ensures that such a feeling may never be expressed. Thus when Alec asks Rose to choose between the fashionable walking suit that Aunt Clara has bought for her and his own recommendation, a rational Bloomer-type outfit, she responds, having previously "resolved [she] would [like it], just to please uncle,"

> "Why, I take this one, of course, uncle. The other is fashionable, and— yes—I must say I think it's pretty—but it's very heavy." . . . Rose spoke gently but decidedly, though there was a look of regret when her eye fell on the other suit which Phebe had brought in; and it was very natural to like to look as other girls did. (*Cousins* 214)

The principal difference between the two dresses is that Clara's is designed for a young lady (whose main function is to look appealing rather than to move freely), Alec's for a young girl; as *Rose in Bloom* makes clear, Rose's acceptance of Alec's reforms must end not only in health but also in endogamy. For all that Alec "do[es] not approve of cousins marrying" (*Rose* 49), his desire "to choose her society carefully and try to keep her unspoiled by the world" (44–45)—enforced in part by his choice of unfashionable clothes for her and by his reluctance to allow her to socialize with eligible non-Campbells—ensures that only a Campbell, and indeed only a Campbell who shares Alec's reformism, will be sufficiently well acquainted with Rose to love her. It is striking, given Alec's purported disapproval of marriage between first cousins, that when he and his brother-in-law discuss possible mates for Rose, none of those mentioned is *not* her cousin. Since the other weddings in Rose's circle are notably exogamous, her cousin Archie marrying the nameless Phebe despite strong Campbell opposition, her future brother-in-law Steve marrying Kitty Van Tassel (who worries about how little she has in common with Steve's parents [*Rose* 202]), and her friend Annabel engaging herself to the Chinese student Tokio Fun See, Rose's union with Mac emphasizes her inability to look beyond Alec or Alec's stand-ins for emotional satisfaction.

Rose's exercise, too, pits body against mind to show the extent to which she is governed by Alec rather than by herself. While the narrator makes much of the connection of physical activity to health and of health to beauty, and while it is clear that Rose would have been entirely sedentary without Alec's influence, this influence is not always physically salutary, precisely because Rose gives herself over to him too completely. First, following her uncle's recommendation that despite her terror of horses she learn to ride, Rose gallops desperately up to impress him and falls off, spraining her ankle. Afraid to mention the injury to him lest her effort to please him be undermined by her failure to stay on the horse, Rose tries to keep the sprain a secret and goes untreated, exacerbating the damage. Similarly, toward the end of *Eight Cousins* Rose's reluctance to let her own judgment override her uncle's brings her close to death from pneumonia. Alec has foolishly encouraged her to go skating one wintry afternoon because Myra's hypochondria has annoyed him, and Mac, Rose's skating date, doesn't show up because his mother finds it too cold for him. Instead of going home or seeking Mac, Rose waits for hours in the cold. The narrator fixes the blame not on Rose's lack of enterprise, which is after all a product of her upbringing, but on Alec and his double.

That the fate Rose suffers in this episode is torture by cold seems related to her desire to achieve Alec's approval whatever the cost; it is suggestive that neither Myra nor Jane, for all that they are the least obviously motherly of the aunts, believes in exposing young people to frigid temperatures. For all Alec's passionate interest in Rose's upbringing, he seems more concerned at times with proving the worth of his system than in doing what is best for his adopted daughter. Thus while his teaching of her emphasizes physiology above any other academic discipline, he talks her out of going to medical school, despite the narrative's endorsement of female doctors: "Uncle thought it wouldn't do to have so many M.D.'s in one family, since Mac thinks of trying it" (*Rose* 11). The only career possible to Rose, then, is that of philanthropy—and even there her role is confined to giving the money she has inherited from her biological father to the charities recommended by her foster father. Their practice here, it transpires, is that Alec "suggest[s] the idea and [gives] Rose all the credit of it" (230), while reminding his niece, "If you do this thing for the sake of the gratitude, then it *is* a failure" (228).

Since emotional satisfaction proves difficult to achieve when Rose can expect neither control over the projects nor thanks, she mourns toward the end of the novel that she is not "contented. . . . I'd like a little fun and fame" (288), and eventually she accepts Mac's proposal with the fear "that you will fly too high for me to follow, because I have no wings" (307). Hence Alec's recommendation that Rose practice "the art of living for others . . . patiently and sweetly" (288) seems double-edged, even though she subsequently accepts his point of view under the emotional duress of his life-threatening illness; that she has lived only for others without ever achieving the sense of self that Phebe has had from the beginning is precisely her problem. Phebe's simultaneous achievement of artistic and personal success suggests that true womanhood can come through other methods than that of "giving up your want always," while that each of the mothering strategies the aunts represent encourages the development of a variety of female "want" suggests that even flawed women understand a truth impenetrable by even the best men. Jessie, the best of the aunts, warns Alec that "she feels the need of what none of us can give her,—a mother. . . . I think you *will* need me, for, wise as you are, you cannot understand a tender, timid little creature like Rose as a woman can" (*Cousins* 40). A mother's function, at least in terms of the Campbell saga, is clearly to legitimate female aspirations toward some sort of power.

The area in which female power is most fully expressed in the Campbell saga is that of food and drink. To be sure, it is Alec who controls Rose's diet, forbidding her coffee, "hot bread and fried stuff" (*Cousins* 33), and flinging her patent medicines out the window; his endorsement of oatmeal porridge and brown bread likewise recalls William Alcott, who describes brown bread as "a very tolerable sort of food" (*House-Keeper* 129). Clearly Alec means to protect Rose from the overstimulating foods that horrified diet-reform circles, not only for the sake of her physical health but also as a way of bringing her will under his benevolent control (significantly, he makes her oatmeal himself). Similarly, Alec—like Alcott—has strong views against alcohol,[6] and intemperance is specifically linked in *Rose in Bloom* to sexual incontinence: Charlie's inability to control his drinking seems akin to his predilection for "fast and fashionable damsel[s]" (79),

while "the weakness that makes a man a brute" ends the romantic understanding that was on the point of blooming between himself and Rose
(145). "Like a commander issuing orders" to "a well-drilled private obedi-
ently receiving them" (149), Alec instructs Rose not to love Charlie until
the latter has gained the self-control essential to a woman's happiness; well
disciplined herself by diet and education,[7] Rose agrees that her feelings for
Charlie are by no means so strong that she cannot put them aside at Alec's
behest.

On the other hand, food reform takes second place in *Eight Cousins* to
food as affectional bond. Rose's path toward health, obedience, and con-
tinent marriage may be paved with the brown bread, oatmeal, and cold
water of the Fruitlands regime, but her enjoyment of familial love and abundance is punctuated by food too rich and flavorful to have passed Bronson's
ascetic scrutiny. Thus Alec's respect for bread and his guilt over having
entirely absorbed Rose's affections lead him to sign Rose up for cooking
lessons with Aunt Plenty so that the child may learn to bake "a handsome, wholesome loaf" (*Cousins* 183). But despite Alec's comment that he
would rather that Rose "learned how to make good bread than the best pies
ever baked" (183), Plenty, longing for her great-niece's companionship,
puts bread-making last on the curriculum, behind such antireform fare
as tarts and pickles (both pastry and condiments are consistently singled
out by writers with Grahamite sympathies as stimulating to the passions).
Plenty endears herself to her family with her delectable cakes, well iced and
covered with sugar roses, while the first jolly family supper Rose enjoys
with the boys features marmalade, plum cake, lemon pie, tarts, and frit-
ters—indeed, the only food on the table that would win William Alcott's
approval is the dish of baked pears. Even Alec first woos Rose with a "spicy
box of Oriental sweetmeats" (*Cousins* 64). Love within the Campbell clan
seems inseparable from a busy kitchen, and it is the aptly named Plenty
who is at once the most demonstrative and the best cook of the family.

Mac's tendency to what Rose dismisses as "the vegetarian mania"—his
diet consists of "bread and milk, baked apples, and potatoes" (*Rose* 5)—
and his rejection of tea as lacking in nourishment (219) establish him as
more hard-line even than Alec with regard to foodstuffs. This self-discipline
ensures both his right to Rose and his need of her: unlike Charlie, he can
channel his sexual desire into making his way in the world, proving that he
will be both a responsible husband and a considerate one, but at the same
time he needs someone to provide him with an emotional center. It is Rose
rather than any innate talent who turns him from a medical student into

a poet; her role in their marriage will continue to be that of inspiration, he tells her, promising, "My little gift [for versifying] will celebrate your greater one [for love]" (307). In this capacity, indeed, Rose will effectively serve as food both for Mac and for his work as a writer. Fortunately, her training in creating domestic comfort, which Alec terms "one of the most beautiful as well as useful of all the arts a woman can learn" (*Cousins* 181), ensures that this "food" will be continually self-replenishing—a skill she could not have learned from Alec, but only from other women. Love, Alcott suggests, is women's particular forte (the affectional relationships that include women as one or both of the partners are both more demonstrative and more influential than those comprising only men), and it is love that gives women whatever measure of power they may achieve.

If food sometimes serves as a way of characterizing love, it may also serve as a metaphor for characterizing the printed word. What Alec terms the "food we give that precious yet perilous thing called imagination" (*Rose* 170) is a perennial concern for Alcott, who worries about boys' reading and girls' reading alike. That bad reading may have the same effects as bad food in undermining self-control and encouraging excess is evident from Alcott's consistent linkage of the two. For instance, *Little Men* (1871) has Mr. Bhaer warning the bookish Demi, "You are greedy also, my son, and you like to stuff your little mind full of fairy tales and fancies, as well as George likes to fill his little stomach with cake and candy. Both are bad" (47). Likewise, in *Eight Cousins* Alec compares his nephews' move from sensation stories and "Oliver Optic" to more down-to-earth fare to "going from raspberry tarts to plain bread and butter"—a move that will "probably save them from a bilious fever" (202). The young Rose's depredations on her father's library contribute as much as her coffee-drinking and failure to exercise to her "pale, heavy-eyed, and listless" look (3); and when she dips into a French novel in *Rose in Bloom*, Alec proves to her that its content—which "won't bear putting into your innocent mind" (169)—is the literary equivalent of "French bonbons with . . . poisonous color on them" (171).

The metaphor of poisoned sweets originates in Alcott's work as a description of Jo's sensational writings, which Professor Bhaer compares first to whiskey and then to "put[ting] poison in the sugar-plum, and let[ting] the little ones eat it" (108). The reference, of course, is to the practice of some nineteenth-century confectioners of diluting white sugar with cheaper substances such as arsenic (William Alcott, for instance, mentions a case in which a New York family nearly died from eating frosting "pronounced

by eminent chemists to be ONE FIFTH RANK POISON" [*Mother* 191]),
but the concern is less with physical illness than with mental corruption.
Researching her stories, Jo falls victim to her own wares:

> unconsciously, she was beginning to desecrate some of the womanliest
> attributes of a woman's character. She was living in bad society; and,
> imaginary though it was, its influence affected her, for she was feed-
> ing heart and fancy on dangerous and unsubstantial food, and was fast
> brushing the innocent bloom from her nature by a premature acquain-
> tance with the darker side of life, which comes soon enough to all of us.
> (*Wives* 103)

Unknown to Jo, her sensational reading is a form of mental masturbation, and she risks corrupting other young people through her own writings. As one might suppose, the original source of the infection is not the
innocent Jo but the male editor for whom she writes, who—concerned
with profit rather than with healthy spiritual influence—demands something "short and spicy, and never mind the moral" (102). Mr. Dashwood
is not even an honest businessman, since he cares nothing for the literary
(let alone ethical) quality of his product and takes advantage of Jo's inexperience to underpay her (102). The "food" that finally establishes Jo as
a writer, predictably, is her membership in her family—what one might
term her daily bread. The love of kindred, rather than the desire for fame,
is the stuff of women's talent, and just as Phebe launches her singing career
with "Home Sweet Home," Jo's masterpiece is firmly based in women's
domestic power.

The Grahamite interconnection of digestion, intellect, and sexuality is
especially threatening because wrongdoing in any of the three systems will
have repercussions in one or more of the others. While Graham and his
followers could only suggest that each system be stimulated as little as
possible (food being limited to little more than graham crackers and cold
water, education making minimal demands, and sexuality confining itself
to procreation), Alcott places her emphasis differently, implying—as we
have seen—that the purifying power of domesticity and women's love may
provide channels through which strong feeling, strong-mindedness, and
strong food may safely flow. For women to be the subjects of domestic
theory may have its dangerous side (only Alec's obvious love for Rose
makes his control of her in the least tolerable), but when women properly
wield domestic power, Alcott indicates, they may contravene the rules of
theory without damage. Hence Plenty's dietary munificence; hence, too,
some aspects of *An Old-Fashioned Girl*.

While the latter novel adapts Grahamite principles to the same extent that the Campbell tales do, it differs from them in that the messenger of reform is not a father figure but the young heroine, Polly Milton, in whom domestic and feminist principles coexist. If Alec Campbell, like Mr. March, Professor Bhaer, and Bronson Alcott, disturbs us by usurping the prerogatives of the "true woman" to control the aspirations of the "little woman," Polly creates no such tension, demonstrating instead how prerogatives and aspirations may combine to entitle women not only to domestic bliss but also to careers and the full rights of citizens. Domesticity, however, must come first, and Alcott explains in her preface that Polly is intended "as a possible improvement upon the Girl of the Period, who seems sorrowfully ignorant or ashamed of the good old fashions which make woman truly beautiful and honored" (v–vi). The reference to Eliza Lynn Linton's 1868 *Saturday Review* essay, which accuses fashionable women of immodesty and unfemininity, sets the course for the novel: *An Old-Fashioned Girl* will provide a corrective to frivolity, not only because the latter encourages sexual license but also—as Strickland notes—because it degrades women by giving them nothing meaningful to do (*Domesticity* 92).

Polly is "old-fashioned" because she is rural rather than urban, a minister's daughter rather than a businessman's, and has been brought up along Bronsonesque lines rather than in conformity to the careless permissiveness of the "new-fashioned" parent. Her difference is evident when she visits the Shaws, a rich family in the city (presumably Boston) that forms the only environment we ever see her occupying. While Polly is polite to her elders and particularly to Mr. Shaw's neglected mother, is modest in dress and speech, and comes from a close-knit and loving family, the three Shaw children (Fanny, Tom, and little Maud) are disrespectful, dismayingly adult, and quarrelsome; nor do they have much feeling for their father, who is absorbed by business, or their mother, a hypochondriac. Polly's first visit serves to put the Shaws temporarily on a better track and to convince Polly herself for all time of the hollowness of wealth and fashion; her second encounter with them, when she moves to the city six years later to work as a music teacher, enables her to continue her project of reform, see the Shaws safely through Mr. Shaw's bankruptcy, and marry Tom. The adult Polly's conformance to vegetarian precepts is significant: what she accomplishes with regard to the Shaws, teaching them simultaneously to moderate their consumption and to control their behavior, is essentially a dietary reform.

Food has three aspects in *An Old-Fashioned Girl*: that of fashion, that of domesticity, and (most radically) that of feminism. In its fashionable guise, food represents its own opposite, being at once unwholesome and

unsustaining; indeed, it follows Grahamite principle in acting as a simu-
lacrum for illicit sexuality. Thus Polly, following Fanny in trepidation to the
"fashionable ice-cream saloon" where Fanny and her schoolmates ("girls
of the period" all) habitually lunch, finds not only that she must abandon the "honest" gingerbread old Mrs. Shaw has provided and attempt
instead "to satisfy her hearty appetite on one ice and three macaroons"
(22), but also that the "saloon" serves as a rendezvous enabling Fanny to
conduct a flirtation with a boy of whom Mr. Shaw disapproves. Likewise,
Fanny's fondness for school depends on the opportunities it provides the
pupils to spend their time "eating confectionery" and discussing the scandalous elopement of a sixteen-year-old classmate with her Italian music
teacher (20).

Here the evils of "confectionery" precisely match those upon which
William Alcott dilates in *The Young Mother:*

> The *moral* results, to the young, of using confectionery, are still more
> dreadful [than the physical or intellectual]. . . . Just in proportion as we
> gratify our propensity for excitement at the confectioner's shop, just in
> the same proportion do we expose ourselves to the danger of yielding
> to temptation, should other gratifications present themselves. (193)

The temptation in question is twofold, to sex on the one hand and selfishness on the other, for the candy eater rapidly becomes insensible to "duty
to himself or others" (193). And indeed it is Fanny's impropriety (her flirta-
tions, her enjoyment of risqué French theatrical pieces) and her lack of any
sense of family responsibility that disturb Polly. In the Shaws' fashionable
set, even little Maud's infant friends are liable to dietary and romantic dis-
sipation—the children's parties, much to old Mrs. Shaw's disgust, furnish
enough wine to get the boys "tipsy," and every five-year-old is expected to
have a "beau," which Polly thinks "ridiculous and unnatural" (136, 46). In
the view of all the Alcotts, such practices can only end in disaster, for the
one indulgence, be it in alcohol, sexual precocity, or sweets, presupposes
the others; in William Alcott's words, "The young of both sexes who are
in the use of confectionery, are on the high road to gluttony, drunkenness,
or debauchery; perhaps to all three" (*Mother* 193).

If the fashionable world's endorsement of candy is one indicator of its
moral ills, confectionery serves also as a metaphor for those moral ills as
a whole. Hence Polly's life at the Shaw home, where "she had nothing
to do but lounge and gossip, read novels, parade the streets, and dress,"
quickly makes her "as heartily sick of all this, as a healthy person would be

who attempted to live on confectionery" (35). The aptness of the comparison depends not only on its association with ill health, whether physical or moral, but also on the fact that these "poisonous French bonbons" are products not of the home kitchen but of the public marketplace. The domestic economy—if it has not been polluted by outside influences—is sound; the ice-cream saloon, on the other hand, where food is a commercial venture rather than a labor of love, is merely a subgenre of the saloon in general. One problem with the fashionable world, then, is that money has become divorced from real work (that which is based on love), so that the leaders of fashion have "nothing to do" but talk or stare, as far from the real stuff of life as confectionery is from the main course. It is inevitable in such a world that Mr. Shaw will go bankrupt, since money is no longer tied to value; his "failure" is also, of course, the Shaw family's only hope of real success.

In contrast to the unpalatable and dangerous food of the fashionable dystopia is the food associated with Polly, which is at once reformist and domestic. Not only does she prefer to eat food associated with home (such as old Mrs. Shaw's "honest, brown cookies" [22]), but she also makes food as a way of making the home, as when she attempts through cooking molasses candy with the Shaw children to bring the siblings closer together. Each of the three main characters in the novel is associated with a particular food—Fanny with sweets (the confectionery of the first half of the story shading into the more acceptable cake of the second half), Tom with peanuts (whose unmodishness and packaging—as individual units surrounded by unpalatable shells—reflect his distance from the rest of his family), and Polly with country products such as brown bread, honey from her own hives, and apples. Polly's fare is thus the only one to enjoy a family connection, a fact inseparable from its country origin and unexciting nature.

Significantly, Polly never covets any food distasteful to diet-reform circles: just as (like the Alcott girls) she keeps a diary intended for her parents' perusal, so that she can be sure of thinking no thoughts they would be disappointed to see, she desires no food they would be disappointed to have her eat.[8] The molasses candy she makes for the Shaws was considered a healthful sweet by all but the most stringent theorists, the gingerbread she prefers to the more fashionable ices and macaroons passes William Alcott's scrutiny as "not highly objectionable" (*House-Keeper* 114), and her statement as an adult that "my habits are so simple; a bowl of bread and milk night and morning, with baked apples or something of that sort, is all I want" (149–50) establishes her as free from fashionable vices and

thoroughly in control of her own wants. The adult Polly shuns parties, refuses an attractive marriage, and teaches the newly impoverished Fanny
how to do without new dresses. That she prefers "a country supper" and
"a good country breakfast" (of brown bread and baked beans) to more
stimulating urban viands (160, 182) suggests that her continued rural innocence depends on her failure to develop new tastes and desires. Moreover,
she is able to import rural housekeeping values to the city, transforming
Maud into an ersatz country girl whose favorite social occasions are the
johnnycake and baked-apple parties hosted by Polly and the studious Will
Milton and who is overjoyed at Mr. Shaw's bankruptcy because it means
that the family will move to a smaller house where Maud may do the housekeeping. Domesticity, reform, and the influence of the "true woman" are
clearly inseparable.

But Polly's self-control is also what makes it possible for her to earn her
own living; one reason she refuses to go to parties is that she sees fashionable life as incompatible with her work as a music teacher, telling Fanny,
"I've come to work, not play; to save, not spend; and parties will be quite
out of the question for me. . . . I shouldn't be fit to give lessons if I was up
late" (153–54). Her independence demands her ability not to "spend"—a
word whose sexual connotations for the nineteenth century make it particularly apropos here. As Angela Estes and Kathleen Lant have observed
of *Little Women*, "each sexual coming-of-age is a blow to the foundations
of the female community" (107), for self-reliance and the ability to earn
money for the family become more difficult in a context of licensed desire.

The point in the novel at which desire—and specifically feminine desire
at that—is ratified is its overtly feminist episode, during which Polly intro-
duces Fanny to a female bohemian community of artists, sculptors, and
writers. Dedication to talent and the choice of a life's work render even
sexuality nonthreatening; for instance, the "Boston marriage" of Rebecca
Jeffrey and Lizzie Small, who "live together, and take care of one another in
true Damon and Pythias style . . . [and who are] as happy and independent
as birds" (255), is to continue after Lizzie's more conventional marriage the
following spring, just as Lizzie will also retain her career (262). Similarly,
the independence of the ideal woman (whom Becky is immortalizing in a
statue) will make it possible for her to "stand alone, and help herself," "be
something more than a nurse [and wife and mother]," and have "earned the
right to use" her artistic and housewifely talents via the ballot-box (258–
59). Although the present-day advanced women tend to be "frail-looking"
or "sick, tired, and too early old" as the "heavy price" demanded for "a

little money and success" (256, 263), it is nonetheless not their desire but society's anger at that desire that is wearing them down—for the woman of the future, which each working woman is "helping, by her individual effort and experience," to bring about (263), is to be "strong-minded, strong-hearted, strong-souled, and strong-bodied . . . larger than the miserable, pinched-up woman of our day" (258).

In this context of worthy work and loving sisterhood, appetite loses its danger, as it serves to promote women rather than to degrade them. Appropriately enough, then, the meal the group shares—to which each working member contributes equally—combines reformist foods such as oranges and crackers with less-approved foods such as sardines and cheese. Nor does any of this food depend on women's labor (even Polly buys the nuts, jam, and cake that she donates for herself and Fanny); artists, who "in spite of their independence . . . are womanly" (261), have the ability to achieve power through other means than domesticity alone. Within the normal nineteenth-century pattern in which men earn money and women turn that money into family well-being, Fanny realizes that "money can't buy" the talent, independence, and respect for which she longs (261); her only hope is to become a homemaker. But within a purely feminine economy in which women both earn the money and use it to create a sisterly community, independence and dedication make all things possible: "each cherished a purpose, which seemed to ennoble her womanhood, to give her a certain power, a sustaining satisfaction, a daily stimulus" (261). Where stimulation is danger in the fashionable world, the feminist community transforms it into a type of health food.

Readers of Alcott will recall further variations upon the themes described here—how the self-denial of the March girls in giving up their Christmas breakfast to a poorer family (again, one headed by a husbandless woman) is rewarded by still more luxurious additions to their Christmas dinner, relinquishment legitimating appetite at last; how Jo Bhaer gives little Daisy an operational toy kitchen so that Daisy may cook herself back into the hearts of her brother and her brother's friends, producing treats much richer and more stimulating than the bread-and-milk suppers normally served at reformist Plumfield. The central image, however, is one of control, whether over the self or over another. "Treat your stomach like a well governed child," Graham had written (qtd. in Schwartz 31), and Alcott extends the simile—and the power available to women—by defining women not only as consumers but also as providers. As Schwartz notes of Graham, his "theory of diet was also a theory of domestic relations and a social program" of which mothers were the linchpin (25) while in Alcott's own family both diet and domestic relations were dominated by the father, in her fictional families she restores the centrality of women. Even as the digestion was to be disciplined, limited as to experience, trained to purity and to a decent lack of appetite—in short, treated as female—it was also to be given back into the control of women themselves. And by controlling their appetites as girls, women might gain the right in certain contexts to express them at last as adults.

NOTES

An earlier version of this paper appears in Susan R. Gannon and Ruth Anne Thompson, eds., *The Child and the Family: Selected Papers from the 1988 International Conference of the Children's Literature Association* (Pace University, 1988); another version was delivered at the 1992 Modern Language Association meeting in New York City. I am grateful to Alfred David, Anne Morey, and Lynne Vallone for their insightful comments over the course of the essay's evolution.

1. Rush was of course by no means the first to link mind and digestion. Bronson Alcott, for one, took Pythagoras as a dietary model, and the Fruitlands experiment had much in common with Jean-Jacques Rousseau's advocacy of vegetarianism as part of a general return to nature and espousal of moderation in every aspect of daily life. It is also worth noting that the American vegetarian movement had much in common with its British counterpart, which indeed, in 1838, established a school named after Bronson Alcott—ironically, at Ham Common in Surrey. Space limitations, however, preclude discussion of dietary reform outside the American context.

2. This parallel may help explain why women such as Abba Alcott's cousin Miss Robie felt secure combating menstrual cramps with exactly that food seen as most sexually dangerous. In a letter of 6 December 1841, Robie recounts a visit to the Alcott household: "As it was time for me to expect a headache, I did not dare to go to Concord without carrying tea and coffee and cayenne pepper,—and a small piece of cooked meat, in case my wayward stomach should crave it" (qtd. in Sanborn 10). Typically, Bronson—for whom, as we shall see, women rather than men were the principal subjects of appetite—pressured Robie into abandoning all these specifics save the tea and disapproved of her indulgence even in that.

3. See also Estes and Lant, Gaard, and Keyser for similar approaches to the March saga, and Fetterley ("Impersonating"), Sanderson, and Van Buren for feminist discussions of Alcott's thrillers.

4. Herein lies the radicalism of Bronson's approach to social reform—not that he sought to control thoughts and words as well as deeds, or that he saw wrong

diet as one of the principal causes of wrong thinking, but that he saw appetite as a predominantly female problem rather than something imposed on women by men. For all his support of William Alcott's argument that women must be freed from the kitchen ("No hope is there for humanity," warned Fruitlands' founders in a letter published on 8 September 1843 in the *Herald of Freedom*, "while Woman is withdrawn from the tender assiduities which adorn her and her household, to the servitudes of the dairy and the flesh pots" [qtd. in Sears 48]), in his own family circle Bronson cast himself as the morally advanced being. Furthermore, as his admirer Dr. F. L. H. Willis observed, in practice he seemed "indifferen[t] to the domestic burden that was resting upon his devoted wife" (qtd. in De Puy 50).

5. This stance (not satirical invention but actual Fruitlands practice) is another reflection of what Elbert calls Bronson and Lane's fear "that the body's befoulment, its excrement and dirt, might infect the soul"; the evils caused by the consumption of fertilized vegetables were akin to those caused by eating meat (75). The position "Sister Hope" takes, which Alcott as narrator implicitly endorses, is rather one of natural and unaffected practicality.

6. Temperance points are also made in *Good Wives* (1869), *Jo's Boys* (1886), and *Jack and Jill* (1881), among other works; as Elbert notes, Alcott was a "founder of the Concord Women's Temperance Society" (262). This concern was common among nineteenth-century feminists, who feared that drunkenness led to violence against women and to children marked by their fathers' excesses.

7. Strickland notes cogently that Alec's insistence that Rose gain "a thorough understanding of 'morals' and physiology [is] an oblique reference to what later generations would call sex education" (*Domesticity* 127); Alec's disquisition on the body to Rose and Mac may more specifically be a warning against the consequences of masturbation (*Cousins* 220–21). As we have seen, Rose's upbringing is nothing if not conducive to self-control of every kind.

8. Not content merely to know what his daughters were thinking, Bronson Alcott would remove diary entries of which he disapproved, such as Anna's more unhappy notations about life at Fruitlands (Elbert 65)—functioning as a sort of externalized superego.

WORKS CITED

Alcott, Louisa May. *Eight Cousins, or The Aunt-Hill.* 1874. Boston: Roberts Brothers, 1876.

———. *Good Wives: A Story for Girls.* 1869. London: Blackie and Son, Limited, 1900.

———. *Little Men.* 1871. New York: Airmont, 1969.

———. *An Old-Fashioned Girl.* 1870. New York: A. L. Burt Company, n.d.

———. *Rose in Bloom.* 1876. New York: Dell, 1986.

———. "Transcendental Wild Oats: A Chapter from an Unwritten Romance." 1876. Rpt. Sears. 145–74.

Alcott, William A. *The Young House-Keeper, or Thoughts on Food and Cookery.* Fourth Stereotype Edition. Boston: George W. Light, 1839.

———. *The Young Husband, or Duties of Man in the Marriage Relation.* 1839. New York: Arno, 1972.

———. *The Young Mother, or Management of Children in Regard to Health.* Third Stereotype Edition. Boston: George W. Light, 1838.

———. *The Young Wife, or Duties of Woman in the Marriage Relation.* 1837. New York: Arno, 1972.

Bassil, Veronica. "The Artist at Home: The Domestication of Louisa May Alcott." *Studies in American Fiction* 15.2 (Autumn 1987): 187–97.

Blackwell, Elizabeth. *The Laws of Life, with Special Reference to the Physical Education of Girls.* New York: George P. Putnam, 1852.

Carson, Gerald. *Cornflake Crusade.* New York: Rinehart, 1957.

De Puy, Harry. "Amos Bronson Alcott: Natural Resource, or 'Consecrated Crank'?" *American Transcendental Quarterly* n.s. 1.1 (March 1987): 49–68.

Dombrowski, Daniel A. "Thoreau, Sainthood and Vegetarianism." *American Transcendental Quarterly* 60 (June 1986): 25–36.

Elbert, Sarah. *A Hunger for Home: Louisa May Alcott's Place in American Culture.* New Brunswick: Rutgers UP, 1987.

Estes, Angela M., and Kathleen Margaret Lant. "Dismembering the Text: The Horror of Louisa May Alcott's *Little Women.*" *Children's Literature* 17 (1989): 98–123.

Fetterley, Judith. "Impersonating 'Little Women': The Radicalism of Alcott's *Behind a Mask.*" *Women's Studies* 10.1 (1983): 1–14.

———. "*Little Women:* Alcott's Civil War." *Feminist Studies* 5.2 (Summer 1979): 369–83.

Gaard, Greta. "'Self-Denial Was All the Fashion': Repressing Anger in *Little Women.*" *Papers on Language & Literature* 27.1 (Winter 1991): 3–19.

Graham, Sylvester. *A Lecture to Young Men.* 1834. New York: Arno, 1974.

Halttunen, Karen. "The Domestic Drama of Louisa May Alcott." *Feminist Studies* 10.2 (Summer 1984): 233–54.

Jones, Joseph. "Transcendental Grocery Bills: Thoreau's *Walden* and Some Aspects of American Vegetarianism." *Texas Studies in English* 36 (1957): 141–54.

Keyser, Elizabeth Lennox. "Alcott's Portraits of the Artist as Little Woman." *International Journal of Women's Studies* 5.5 (November/December 1982): 445–59.

Rosenfeld, Natania. "Artists and Daughters in Louisa May Alcott's *Diana and Persis.*" *New England Quarterly* 64.1 (March 1991): 3–21.

Rush, Benjamin. *Medical Inquiries and Observations upon the Diseases of the Mind.* 1812. New York: Hafner, 1962.

Sanborn, F. B. *Bronson Alcott: At Alcott House, England, and Fruitlands, New England (1842–1844).* Cedar Rapids: Torch Press, 1908.

Sanderson, Rena. "*A Modern Mephistopheles:* Louisa May Alcott's Exorcism of Patriarchy." *American Transcendentalist Quarterly* n.s. 5.1 (March 1991): 41–55.

Schwartz, Hillel. *Never Satisfied: A Cultural History of Diets, Fantasies and Fat.* New York: Doubleday, 1986.

Sears, Clara Endicott, comp. *Bronson Alcott's Fruitlands.* 1915. Boston: Houghton Mifflin, 1942.

Strickland, Charles. "A Transcendentalist Father: The Child-Rearing Practices of Bronson Alcott." *History of Childhood Quarterly* 1 (Summer 1973): 4–51.

———. *Victorian Domesticity: Families in the Life and Art of Louisa May Alcott.* University: U of Alabama P, 1985.

Van Buren, Jane. "Louisa May Alcott: A Study in Persona and Idealization." *Psychohistory Review* 9.4 (Summer 1981): 282–99.

Walters, Ronald G., ed. *Primers for Prudery: Sexual Advice to Victorian America.* Englewood Cliffs: Prentice-Hall, 1974.

JUDITH PASCOE

Tales for Young Housekeepers: T. S. Arthur and the American Girl

In the thriving publishing center of nineteenth-century Philadelphia, Timothy Shay Arthur represented something of a phenomenon, a one-man literary business devoted to defining proper behavior in a world made tempting by the increasing availability of material goods. Arthur's propagative success was such that in the decade of the 1840s, six percent of all the native fiction published in the United States was written by his hand; over his lifetime he produced more than two hundred titles. This number included several long-running periodicals, the most successful of which was *Arthur's Home Magazine,* a monthly compendium of moralistic fiction and miscellaneous advice ranging from "How to Keep from Drowning" to "How Women Can Earn Money." [1]

Arthur's literary barrage occurred between approximately 1840 and 1885, but what small enduring fame he achieved came from just one work, the 1852 temperance novel *Ten Nights in a Bar-Room,* which by 1900 had sold an astounding one million copies. Possibly the most famous fictional girl of the nineteenth century was the stoic Mary Morgan, who, in Arthur's novel and William W. Pratt's stage adaptation, saves her inebriated father from physical and spiritual deterioration, standing firm against a projectile bar glass and her father's delirium tremens. In provincial theaters up until at least the 1920s and in provincial school libraries even later, the brief life and elongated death of Mary Morgan, like that of Harriet Beecher Stowe's Little Eva and Charles Dickens's Little Nell, elicited an enjoyable orgy of sentimental tears from the audience, a response orchestrated by Arthur for the political end of drumming up support for temperance legislation. [2]

Mary Morgan is probably the most normative embodiment of a Victorian stereotype: the angelic, martyred girl child. But she resides within a larger body of work by Arthur that represents a considerably more complex response to the exigencies of Victorian womanhood. Writing at a time when America was going through an economic and psychic transformation, a change from a local to a national economy—or from, as one historian characterizes it, an ethos of self-denial to a cult of self-realization—

Arthur creates a fictional world in which the acquisition of material goods is both a central preoccupation and one repeatedly allied with female character, usually that of wives and mothers (Lears 4). In Arthur's tales, the girl or daughter stands caught between a heroic potentiality and a seemingly inevitable fall into invalidism and misdirected materialism. Arthur fashions a vision of a new girl worker, appropriate offspring of an increasingly industrial society, who represents a healthy acquisitiveness based on hard labor that contrasts with the decadent materialism associated in these stories with speculative business concerns. These fictional girls also serve, perhaps, to mediate Arthur's concerns about his own status as a publisher and author reliant on female purchasing power; they operate within a home marketplace without being corrupted by the consuming passions of the grown women who figure there.

Philip Fisher suggests a parallel between the process by which popular forms come to work on the public imagination and the therapeutic process schematized by Sigmund Freud, claiming that both involve recognition, repetition, and working through. Fisher writes:

> Popular forms are frequently repetitive, and they are frequently read almost obsessively, as detective novels, westerns, romances, and pornography are, becoming part of what might be called a diet of reality that returns again and again to the same motifs so that they might not slip away. (7)

Arthur's contribution to this "diet of reality" was a story formula that might be characterized as "Keeping Up with the Joneses." In this formula, which Arthur repeated over and over again in his novels and magazine stories, male characters are what they earn—or rather, they are what they manage to purchase with what they earn. A story called "Where the Money Goes" serves as a representative example of the mode. The story pits Mr. Barnaby, a small businessman with annual receipts of $2,000 a year, against Mr. Malcolm, who only earns $1,500 a year but who somehow has more to show for his earnings. The story's dilemma is posed by Mrs. Barnaby, who measures her own household against that of her neighbors the Malcolms:

> I'm sure we don't indulge in any extravagances. We haven't bought an article of new furniture during the year; while the Malcolms have had a beautiful sofa, a set of candelabras, a large mahogany rocking-chair, and a dressing bureau for which they paid twenty-five dollars. (8)

As the story proceeds, Mr. Barnaby reveals himself to be pound-wise but penny-foolish. In the course of a day, he purchases on impulse a bunch of flowers, preserved tomatoes, out-of-season strawberries, toys for his children, and "a quarter of a dollar's worth of buns" for tea. Mr. Barnaby eventually learns from Mr. Malcolm, who lived with a shrewd old farmer as a boy, that these pennies add up; he resolves to cease his petty spending in the interest of amassing more substantial wealth.

The moral of this story, and many others like it, is not that one should deny oneself in the interest of saving money or of fostering a more spiritual existence, but that one should save in small ways so that one can buy bigger-ticket items: nice furniture, for example, or a larger house. The point is not to be happy with less, although this might be necessary in the short run, but rather to learn how to acquire more. As Mr. Barnaby's story ends, he resolves to give up dessert, situating his household and bodily economy in parallel:

> I don't believe I would have a dyspeptic symptom, if I did not touch puddings, pies, sweetmeat, nuts and raisins, blanc-manges, floating-islands, and a hundred and one other things that my good wife prepares for our gratification, and which I eat after my appetite has been satiated on plain and more substantial food. (24)

Although Mrs. Barnaby has, until this point in the story, played no role in the quotidian extravagance judged to make the difference between the Barnabys and the Malcolms, she is finally held responsible for the household's "bad" economy; her kitchen stands as a production plant flooding a glutted market, creating a demand for products with supplemental (taste) rather than use (nourishment) value.

Although the Barnabys' saga was published in *Stories for Young Housekeepers* (1854), part of a series entitled "Library for the Household," and thus would seem to target a female audience, one wonders whether women were really the readers of choice for a volume that so determinedly allies the female with a destructive counter-economy, reserving a redemptive role for the master of the house. That husbands might actually be the readers Arthur had in mind when penning these stories is additionally suggested by the nod he gives to a gendered reader assumed to share with the author a superior ability to reason: "We think the reader will be at no loss to 'figure out' the matter, after we enlighten *him* a little as to the mode in which the financial affairs of the family were conducted" (emphasis added, 9).

Over and over in Arthur's stories, women are associated with a profligate materialism; the culinarily excessive Mrs. Barnaby stands as just one representative of a fictional realm in which wives are usually found wanting in both senses of the word. In "A Bad Habit Cured," Mrs. Armand has a propensity for borrowing her neighbor Mrs. Lovell's nicest belongings, a "very fine light blue cashmere" baby's cloak, for example, or a Britannia-metal coffee-pot. Mrs. Lovell despairs as time after time the borrowed objects are returned damaged, most gallingly in the case of the coffee-pot, which is part of a set:

> She remembered her Britannia coffee-pot as a beautiful piece of ware, without a scratch or bruise, and bright as silver. But this was as dull as pewter . . . the mouth of the spout had received a disfiguring bruise, and the little jet knob on the lid was entirely broken off! (38–39)

While the profligate Mrs. Armand is clearly the most glaring example of selfish acquisitiveness in this story, even the much-abused Mrs. Lovell is tainted by her affection for nice things. Before the story is resolved, the women's husbands, both clearly above such trivialities as ruined tea sets, intercede and smooth things over. While in the terms of the narrative Mrs. Lovell's dissatisfaction is justified, she emerges from the story seeming petty in comparison to the two men, perhaps overly concerned with inconsequential objects such as her teapot's little jet knob.

If not always as exploitative as Mrs. Armand, female neighbors generally assert an unhealthy influence in these stories, serving as models of conspicuous consumption. When in "Agreeable Neighbors" Mrs. Sunderland comes into contact with Mrs. Henley, Mr. Sunderland finds it more expedient to change houses than to let his wife continue in this new alliance. The contrast between Mrs. Sunderland before and after associating with her neighbor is characterized by way of housekeeping excess:

> She used, every fall, to put up a few jars of preserves—and these were generally confined to peaches and plums, the cost of which did not exceed five dollars. But this, the first season of her acquaintance with Mrs. Henley, she was visited with a regular preserving mania. Quinces, peaches, pears, plums, pine-apples, watermelon-rinds, and dear knows what all! were boiled down in the best double-refined loaf sugar, and sealed up in glass jars, the number of which I will not pretend to give. (84)

Interestingly, the "preserving mania" of Mrs. Henley parallels the describing mania of Arthur's text. Arthur so lovingly and exactingly elaborates upon the material excesses of his characters that the descriptions threaten to supersede the putative morals of these tales. For stories that set out to steer young housekeepers away from an error most often represented as an excessive affection for material things, they derive a great deal of their narrative energy from lengthy descriptions of these desirable objects.

Nowhere is this more true than in *Window-Curtains,* in which the titular objects become personified enactments of consumer desire. In this story Hiram Melchor, who, in accordance with Arthur's usual formula, is characterized by way of his finances ("My salary was nine hundred dollars per annum"), is tempted by a fellow clerk's more sumptuous housekeeping, by the contrast between his own green Venetian blinds and his co-worker Baldwin's handsome window curtains. Arthur takes his favorite theme to extravagant emotional heights in this story; when Melchor's wife suggests that curtains like the Baldwins' might be had for forty dollars, Melchor admits to "an instinct of danger—a sense of approaching evil" (32). As the story proceeds, Mrs. Melchor is allied with a female penchant for window dressings. As Mr. Harvey, the cashier with whom Melchor works, states categorically: "Most women have a weakness in the line of window-curtains. I know how it is with my wife. If she's said 'curtains' to me once since we were married, she's said 'curtains' more than a hundred times" (36).

Even more ominously, the curtains, once purchased, take on a personality of their own, mirroring the story's wives in their demands. Melchor's new curtains are hostile to the other furnishings of his living room: "Curtains would not be at peace with cane-seat and ingrain. They carried themselves haughtily; threatening at last, to abandon the parlor if such plebeian associates were not removed" (102). Mr. Harvey observes, "You'll have to match them in the end. Curtains are terribly exacting" (36).

Arthur's association of women and material desire reaches its most extreme realization as the objects of consumer passion in this story take on the personalities of desiring women; in his new curtains Melchor additionally acquires a dissatisfied wife.[3] That women should be so closely allied with conspicuous consumption in Arthur's stories reflects their evolving status in an increasingly bourgeois society, their involvement in what Stuart Culver has described as a "new domestic labor of consumption" (112). In Arthur's Philadelphia, women at mid-century were just beginning to come to the downtown area to shop (Geffen 312). According to Culver, the new household required an artistic homemaker who could envision the home as both a stage for social "performance and a collection

of objects expressing the personality and power of the absent male owner"
(112). Arthur provides an oblique commentary on this kind of domestic
theater in *Window-Curtains*. As the Melchors' living room is increasingly
dominated by objects selected purely for their aesthetic appeal, for their
ability to match the splendor of the curtains, the room becomes increasingly less functional: the Melchors eventually avoid entering the room, let
alone tarrying there. The one room of the house associated primarily with
nonproductive activities—sitting, entertaining, relaxing—comes to domi-
nate the household, but what little use value it has is further eroded by its
transformation into a purely decorative realm.

Just as the family parlor becomes a decadent representation of its former
self, the wives in Arthur's stories, orchestrators of households increasingly
devoted to display, seem unable to strike the correct balance between labor
and leisure. In a piece entitled "Health of Women," published in *Arthur's
Home Magazine* in 1884, the health of housekeepers correlates directly
with the number of servants they retain: "Those who have but one servant
are, as a rule, in the enjoyment of a good share of bodily vigor, while those
who keep two servants, and in consequence do little or no stirring work
in the household, are ailing a great deal of the time" (666). This association between brisk labor and female vigor is not borne out by the many
Arthur tales in which female housekeepers are made sick by excess work.
In "Saving at the Spigot," a wife who decides to dispense with a servant
falls ill as a result of laboring over a hot iron all day. Her effort toward
greater domestic economy turns out to be misconceived, as it takes her
several days to recover from the ironing siege.

Standing in contrast to enfeebled wives and mothers like the one in
"Saving at the Spigot" is the Arthurian girl, who is most typically lauded
for her capacity to work. Stories about girls in Arthur's canon tend to be
stories about girls learning to take on their mothers' work. "Little Anna,"
in the 1843 story by that name, assumes the task of sewing, washing, and
ironing her father's handkerchief when her mother's head hurts. In *The
Prattler*, an 1876 publication aimed at children, girls gain kudos for completing their mother's chores. Blossom, in "Blossom's Baby Shower," enter-
tains her baby brother while her mother is sick. Three-year-old Brownie
struggles to dress herself since "she knew baby kept mamma awake nights,
and that she did not feel very well" ("Brownie" 238). Over and over in
these stories, girlish labor is compared with womanly languor. In "My First
Summer in the Country," the female narrator recalls going to the country so that her mother could recuperate; motherly convalescence provides

an opportunity for daughterly enterprise. The narrator describes her own apple-picking adventures:

> It was mounting the ladder and climbing the trees that made this work so enjoyable to me. I soon learned to do it readily; I was so much smaller and lighter than the others that I could venture farther out on the limbs to reach the fruit, besides my short skirts being less likely to get entangled in the branches. It soon became a settled thing that I should do the climbing. (42)

Although not all the girls in *The Prattler* are lauded for their intrepidity, girlhood for Arthur seems to represent a privileged state, a healthful potential for productive labor. That this positive status depends on girlhood's distinction from full womanhood, on daughters' differences from their mothers, is underscored by another class of girl who figures prominently in the bourgeois families around which Arthur's stories revolve— that is, the working-class girl.

Servant girls in stories published under Arthur's editorial aegis frequently serve as a mirror against which the foibles of their mistresses can be seen to greatest advantage. In "Good for Nothings," that Mrs. Veasie has gone through ten girls in a year leads the reader to conclude that the fault is in the mistress and not the servant. Similarly, in "The House-Cleaning," another tale in Arthur's *Stories for Young Housekeepers,* a wife's unwillingness to hire supplemental servants for spring cleaning causes an uprising among her regular servants that, in the terms of the story, is clearly justified. While female employers in these stories are ostensibly training their hired "girls," they are in reality being trained by these girls in the proper modes of household management; recalcitrant servants in story after story insist on a more reasonable distribution of household duties.

But if the wives in these stories are set in opposition to their laboring employees, their daughters have more in common with these other girls than with their ineffectual mothers. In "Janet's Way," a story by Sydney Dare published in *Arthur's Home Magazine* in 1884, the daughter of the title takes over for her family's housekeeper when the woman needs some time off, and far outstrips the servant in terms of efficiency. In contrast to the wife in "Saving at the Spigot" who goes into a decline after taking on a day's worth of ironing, Janet eventually supplants the servant, finding the woman another post so that she can continue running the household in this new, improved way. Furthermore, she pockets the servant's salary, earning herself the right to buy "a new book or a bit of music or anything else" (395).

As Janet's plans for spending her money suggest, the contrast between wives and girls in Arthurian stories is not one between consumerism and spartanism; girls, like their mothers, are defined in terms of acquisitiveness. In a piece entitled "Give Boys a Chance," taken from the *Decorator and Furnisher* and reprinted in the *Home Magazine* in 1884, girls' bedrooms are described as training grounds for future consumers: "Girls have the best room in the house, they have good carpets and furniture, they are allowed to keep birds and plants, and are permitted to have many pretty little kickshaws on their tables and what-nots" (208). In contrast, complains the piece, boys' rooms contain "no fire, no gas, no paper, a strip of worn carpet, a plain linen curtain [and] . . . a table given up by the girls on being presented with a better one" (208). If girls are surrounded by luxuries from birth, this is not necessarily a bad thing—the piece goes on to argue that a boy will never become a "man of taste" unless he is granted a few of the accouterments usually reserved for girls (for example, "a few good prints"). What seems to make the difference between the materiality of girls and the decadence of women, in Arthur's fictional worlds, lies in the former's propensity for thrift and hard work. Girls in these stories are more discerning and more deserving shoppers.

As noted earlier, Arthur seems not so much to object to an increasingly dominant consumer ethos as to decry those who do not function within this new ethos in a fiscally responsible way. His advice to young women is not to forgo worldly possessions but rather to acquire them at a good price. In "Getting Along," published in *Arthur's Home Magazine* in 1884, a young female receives this advice: "Go to the second-hand stores and pick up bargains in china and small things. You can get straw matting for twenty-five cents a yard and cheese-cloth for window-curtains for five cents a yard. Japanese ornaments make a beautiful show and cost only a few cents" (Harvey 472).

The message of Arthur's publications, taken as a whole, can be paraphrased as follows: buy only what you can afford, but by all means buy. It is entirely appropriate that the model wife of the aforementioned *Window-Curtains*, a saga of domestic spending that spans twelve issues of *Arthur's Home Magazine*, is a shop girl, the perfect wife for the self-made and honest Martindale, who provides a counter for Hiram Melchor. Having fled the "evil eyes" of his own window curtains, Melchor gazes through the

Martindales' window upon "the very face of a home-angel," before coming finally to the sad realization: "Better patience, economy and self-denial for a few years, and assured success at the end, than dash and extravagance and the failure that is almost sure to come" (695).

Although equally didactic in impulse, Arthur's *Ten Nights in a Bar-Room* would seem to be engaged with a different kind of moral battle, one identical to that of hundreds of other temperance tracts seeking to demonstrate an association between drinking and decay. But Arthur's most famous novel can be read as one more literary manifestation of a preoccupation with economic health. Drinking, in this novel, is on a par with the consuming passions of the householders of the monitory domestic tales. In fact, Arthur makes this association explicit in *Window-Curtains,* writing:

> Window-curtains . . . are like the strong drink that perverts a man's appetite. Afterward he tipples through sofas, mirrors, Brussels, brocatelle, silk damask, tapestry, velvet, pictures and vases, until he loses himself in the drunkenness of social rivalry, and sinks to ruin in the end. (36)

The liquor business, for Arthur, is just one more example of consumption run amuck, and Mary Morgan, his most rarefied character, underscores the crucial status of the girl as a mark of value in Arthur's text.

Ten Nights in a Bar-Room records the events of the narrator's ten separate visits to Slade's tavern, a cheerful drinking establishment that deteriorates over time into a prototypical den of iniquity in which mayhem eventually reigns supreme. Arthur's critique of the liquor business places as much emphasis on the unhealthiness of the business as on the beverage. The decline of Slade's tavern is directly related to its participation in an unhealthy system of exchange, one in which money is expended for a product with no real value. As one of the bar's customers describes Slade's enterprise: "He does not add to the general wealth. He produces nothing. He takes money from his customers, but gives them no article of value in return—nothing that can be called property, personal or real" (119). While Slade does supply a consumable product, this product, like the dessert that the husband in "Where the Money Goes" decides he is better off without, has no nutritional value. Like the increasingly extravagant window curtains, which are many times removed from the practical Venetian blinds they replace, the liquor Slade sells is several times removed from its original unprocessed value as corn or barley. A value based on nutrition is supplanted by a value based on pleasure; the state of intoxication produced

by the liquor parallels a hedonistic, equally insatiable pleasure produced
by increasingly sumptuous draperies.

As in Arthur's economic cautionary tales, the female in *Ten Nights* represents a site of contest; the girl is set against models of mature womanhood
that are inevitably subsumed by unhealthy systems of exchange. Even when
the narrator of the novel is claiming that women are paragons of an inherent morality that renders them more hostile than men to the liquor
business, he provides a lengthy and striking anecdote of a woman who is
the exception to the rule he has just laid down, one who insists on opening
a dram-shop against her husband's better impulses:

> And what was the result? The husband quit going to church. . . . Next
> he began to tipple. Soon, alas! the subtle poison so pervaded his sys-
> tem that morbid desire came; and then he moved along quick-footed
> in the way to ruin. In less than three years, I think, from the time the
> grog-shop was opened by his wife, he was in a drunkard's grave. (56)

This story seems an extraneous interruption to the saga of Slade's tavern, in which Mrs. Slade is an unwilling participant. But even though she is
opposed to her husband's project from the beginning, she is less an embodiment of a correct moral stance than a shadowy illustration of the errors of
her husband's ways. An ineffectual presence at the beginning of the story,
by the end she is a ghost of her already insubstantial self. When the visitor to
Slade's bar encounters her during his seventh sojourn, she presents "a pale,
shrunken countenance, hollow, lustreless eyes, and [a] bent, feeble body"
(164). By the end of his stay, she is suffering from "repeated hysterical and
fainting fits" (191).

The wives and mothers in the novel slink about on the edges of the main
action, unable to exert a healthy influence over the proceedings. Even as
Mrs. Hammond, the mother of one of the denizens of the bar, exclaims to
her son, "Your mother will protect you," he dies in her arms, enabling one
of the novel's most melodramatic moments: "One long scream of horror
told of her convictions, and she fell, lifeless, across the body of her dead
son!" (170). The phlegmatic nature of other adult women is emblematized
in a decadence that manifests itself as bad housekeeping. When the narrator returns to the inn for his fifth visit, he is struck immediately by the
change in standards of cleanliness: "Then the room was as sweet and clean
as it could be; the sheets and pillow-cases as white as snow, and the furniture shining with polish. Now all was dusty and dingy, the air foul, and
the bed linen scarcely whiter than tow" (109).

In the midst of this spiritual and physical decline, only daughters in the novel remain impervious to the forces of decay. Of Slade's daughter Flora, situated within the slovenly chambers described above, the narrator comments: "In her alone, of all that appertained to Simon Slade, there was no deterioration" (112). The daughters in the novel seem to represent a transcendent value outside the system of bad exchange represented by the bar. An interesting gloss on their unique status is provided by a curious piece in *Arthur's Home Magazine* railing against the practice of allowing paper currency to remain in circulation for protracted amounts of time. The piece begins by lauding the Bank of England for its habit of paying out new notes on all checks and destroying all notes that are returned to the bank, before going on to express an abhorrence of worn paper money:

> Some of the notes, especially those of smaller denominations, are offensive to the smell as well as to the sight. You cannot touch them without having an odor of dirt left upon your fingers. Why may not infectious diseases be communicated through this means? Doubtless they often are. ("Filthy" 213–14)

The paper currency is a mere marker of the value vested in gold and silver. The more it is circulated, the more it is distanced from the precious metals it represents as its inferior material status becomes more and more transparent. In an economy in which symbols of value are exchanged instead of substances of inherent use value, to circulate is to be diminished. In the barroom economy (in which nothing useful is produced and in which foodstuffs are, through distillation, stripped of nutritional value) the only way to avoid diminishment is to stay outside this system of exchange. The girl, by virtue of her otherness—she is outside the barroom economy but also outside a sexual economy that aligns women with their corrupted husbands—is able to intercede in this bad business and exert a force for change.

In the most melodramatic moment in the novel, Mary Morgan gets hit by a bar glass flung at her father, whom she is trying to remove from Slade's tavern. Significantly, however, it is not the blow that leads to her demise, but rather a kind of wasting illness that sets in after the fact and allows the kind of protracted death also found in novels by Dickens. In a macabre twist, the dying girl acts as nurse to her father, who is in the throes of delirium tremens. She is consumed by fever but also by her father's neediness as he calls on her to save him from his delusions.

Both in successfully removing her father from Slade's tavern and in succoring him through his alcoholic illness, Mary Morgan carries out roles that seem more appropriate for a wife than for a daughter. Her crazed father ultimately finds his only solace from frightening apparitions in his daughter's bed, and she expends a considerable amount of her last breath on luring him back into her arms: " 'Here, father! Here!' Mary called to him, and he sprung into the bed again; while she gathered her arms about him tightly, saying, in a low, soothing voice,—'Nothing can harm you here father' " (87). Deborah Gorham, in her study of the Victorian girl, describes the sexually charged nature of Victorian portrayals of the father/daughter relationship, suggesting that the image of the good daughter was used "to transcend some of the problems inherent in portraying the sexuality of the feminine Victorian woman" (41). In Arthur's novel, Mary is as much wife as daughter. While Mrs. Morgan rather ineffectually offers her husband strong coffee, Mary's bed acts as a magnet to which the raving man is repeatedly drawn, although the attraction is carefully attributed to ethereal forces. Over and over, in the bedroom scenes, her unearthly status is underlined; it is her "angel-look" that drives her father's demons from the room (87). Harvey Green, one of the denizens of the bar, further attests to her liminal position when he corrects someone who suggests that Simon Slade, the thrower of the bar glass, will stand trial for manslaughter. Green replies with a "cold, inhuman chuckle, 'No—girl-slaughter,' " making clear that the universalizing use of the word "man" is inadequate to describe the otherness of Mary Morgan (97).

While Arthur went to great lengths to establish the otherworldly aspect of his girl protagonist in the deathbed scenes of the novel—"This is Mary's room; and she's an angel," her father exclaims—the spectacle of a father jumping in and out of his daughter's bed apparently did not meet late-century standards of propriety (78). The erotic potential of the deathbed scenes in Pratt's stage version is muted somewhat, although these scenes take up a larger fraction of the play than of the novel. Additionally, in the transformation of the novel for the stage, Mary Morgan was supplemented by a new girl character, Mehitable Cartright, who provides a new and safer focus for desire.

Writing of the change that took place in cultural forms in the late part of the nineteenth century, Martha Banta describes an alteration of the balance between show and tell: "The earlier compulsion to expound moral tales to a people who were nervous over not being moral enough was replaced by expanded methods for giving the public the shows that entertain" (609). The somber cautionary tale provided by the death of Mary Morgan in Arthur's novel is still present in the stage version, but it is inflected by the addition of Mehitable Cartright, whose primary function seems to be to provide comic relief from the elongated agony of the deathbed scenes. While Mary is consumed by an illness brought about by the sin of her father, Mehitable is a consumer of both cheap novels and eligible men. Sample Swichel, her chief suitor, aims to make a bonfire of "all her yaller novels" so "she'll talk as sensible as any of them decent gals" (16), and their courtship resembles a commercial exchange. Referring to Mehitable, Swichel comments, "I should like to have six yards more of that same piece of calico" (40).

Perhaps by century's end audiences had grown tired of the saccharine sweetness of a Mary Morgan and required the more worldly model of the American girl provided by Mehitable Cartright. It is easy to see Arthur's portrayals of American girlhood as throwbacks to another era, attempts to preserve in writing an earlier, more innocent time. Indeed, Gorham describes the image of the perfect daughter so popular in Victorian fictions as an attempt to reconcile a conflict between the morality of Christianity and the value of capitalism, an attempt "to satisfy the nostalgia for a simple, pastoral past amid the realities of the urban, industrial present" (37). But to the extent that Arthur's fictional daughters are embroiled in the consumer culture that plays so dominant a part in his stories, they are not so much sentimental vestiges of a domestic ideal, remembered or imagined, as harbingers of a new order in which girls have a role to play in a business world outside the home. While daughters in Arthur's tales sometimes serve as mere emotional barometers of their father's business dealings—as does Phebe in "The Wrecked Household," who suffers a physical spasm upon the arrival of bill collectors at her father's door—they as often respond more practically to financial setbacks, working in factories and paying back loans and, in general, meeting the demands of a commercial marketplace.[4]

Although Arthur's construction of a particular kind of girl character in his stories predates the death of his eldest and favorite daughter in 1862, this biographical fact likely served to increase his preoccupation with fictional girls. One account of Arthur's life claims, "In temperament and character she was more like him, perhaps, than any of his other children" (T. S. Arthur 12).[5] But what has perhaps more bearing on Arthur's fictional daughters than this discrete albeit traumatic fact is his dependence on a predominantly female literary establishment for his professional start and continued success. Susan Coultrap-McQuin, in her study of nineteenth-century popular woman writers, establishes the interesting fact that by mid-century women were the authors of almost half the published popular literary works, while by 1872 women wrote nearly three-quarters of all novels published (2). Arthur's personal encounters with representatives of the literary marketplace support this depiction of a predominantly female profession. He published his first story in *Godey's Lady's Book* through the intervention of the poet Lydia Sigourney, and one of his early editorial stints was as an assistant to Eliza Leslie in the formation of *Miss Leslie's Magazine* in 1843 (*T. S. Arthur* 16, Smyth 231). This periodical was eventually purchased by Arthur and transformed into *The Ladies' Magazine of Literature, Fashion and the Fine Arts,* a precursor to his most successful journal, the *Home Magazine.* But even when Arthur gained control over his own publishing enterprise, he was reliant on the contributions of women writers and assistants, most particularly Virginia Frances Townsend, who purportedly kept *Arthur's Home Magazine* alive singlehandedly during periods in which he suffered physical and emotional breakdowns (Koch xli).

Besides being dependent on woman writers and readers for his literary livelihood, Arthur seems to have constructed himself in feminized terms, most obviously in his use of female pseudonyms such as "Mrs. Mary Elmwood," but also in narratives of authorial development.[6] In a brief autobiography, he describes his literary development as a product of his failure to succeed in business, and focuses primarily on his sensitivity and weakness, attributes usually associated with the female. Claudia Nelson describes the Victorian evolution of an "androgyny of virtue" in which manliness becomes synonymous with womanliness, the best and defining attributes of the female appropriated for the male (44). Arthur's self-constructions suggest the possibility of an androgyny of authorship as he draws freely on qualities usually vouchsafed primarily to women. Arthur conjures up a "natural sensitiveness" inimical to the writing of autobiography and describes himself "faint[ing] by the way" on his path to literary success ("Brief Autobiography" 5, 8). Elsewhere he describes his writing progress as beginning in weakness: "I never feel as if I had any power of my pen" (*T. S. Arthur* 22).

In her study of consumer culture and the naturalist novel, Rachel Bowlby describes the predicament of the male novelist at century's end as follows: "If culture, as a space marked off from business or working concerns, was also associated with femininity, that meant that being an artist might not set well with a male identity" (11). Narrowing the field of culture to the particular genres in which Arthur achieved his greatest success—the domestic novel and story—only increases the accuracy of Bowlby's assertion. Arthur's success in female genres and publication venues won him only derisive attention from one of his contemporaries, Edgar Allan Poe, who referred to him as "uneducated, and too fond of mere vulgarities to please a refined taste," criticizing his autograph as that of "a commonplace clerk's hand" (*Works* 15:240–41).

I would suggest that in Arthur's employment of the figure of the girl, one sees a response to the criticism leveled against male participants in a female literary marketplace, a criticism inflected, as Poe's comments are, by both class and gender assumptions. In Arthur's fictional girls one witnesses the construction of a female subject position untainted by negative gender or class associations. He creates a feminized version of the self-made man or, more accurately, what Fisher has called the "half-made man," a self constructed of what one might, in the future, become (13). In his fictional daughters, who move impervious through barroom and factory, Arthur creates border figures able to engage in the vagaries of the marketplace without being tainted by systems of exchange. These girls are optimistic enactments of Arthur's own desire to balance his avuncular role as narrator of homely stories with his status as businessman publisher.

The sheer volume of Arthur's oeuvre renders any critical assertion precarious—for every generalization one makes about his treatment of a particular topic or type of character, one can find among his profusion of stories at least one exception to the rule. As a major writer of determinedly minor literature[7] and as a man operating in a literary market motivated by women writers and readers, Arthur necessarily embodied contradictions; it is as a compendium of incongruities that one can most accurately assess his work. One of these incongruities resides in stories that idealize the figure of the girl while censuring the female. Another lies in the irony of stories that insist on the girl in isolation, safe from an inevitably diminishing association with other females, but that are published in a woman's magazine in many regards progressive in its editorial stance on women's issues. Finally, there is the defining contradiction of Arthur's literary career, the fact that he both wrote tales that warned against frittering away one's money and earned a living by publishing them in that most ephemeral of consumer commodities, the woman's monthly magazine. Arthur's girl characters stride confidently into this welter of conflicting impulses, striving to make a place within the female publishing world of nineteenth-century America for a male popular author.

NOTES

1. Donald A. Koch's introduction to Arthur's *Ten Nights in a Bar-Room* is the most authoritative account of Arthur's life and work. Warren French provides a survey of Arthur's divorce fictions and of his treatment of the figure of the businessman. T. J. Matheson reads Poe in the context of Arthur's temperance fiction. "How Women Can Earn Money," a series by Mrs. Ella Rodman Church, began in *Arthur's Home Magazine* in January 1884 and continued throughout that year. All articles published in *Arthur's Home Magazine* that are identified as having been written by Arthur are included in the accompanying list of works cited under Arthur's name. All other articles published in the *Home Magazine* are listed by author (if known) or title. Pieces that cannot be authoritatively established as having been penned by Arthur are sometimes cited to demonstrate a representative Arthurian sensibility, since they were published under his editorial aegis.

2. Koch recalls seeing a performance of *Ten Nights* in the early 1920s and provides an account of the philanthropist Samuel Schoonover, whose 1952 will bequeathed twenty-five thousand dollars to the schools of Stroudsburg, Pennsylvania, on the condition that they always keep ten copies of Arthur's novel on school library shelves (vi, lxxx).

3. I wish to emphasize that men in Arthur's stories are equally consumed with desire for material objects; in fact, in "Window Curtains" Mrs. Melchor expresses discomfort with acquisitiveness far in advance of her husband. Still, in this story and others like it, women usually are first to articulate their desire for a particular object, and this articulation drives their husbands to try to satisfy what they represent to themselves as their wives' longings, even if they are equally caught up in this desire.

4. One example of this hardier type of daughter is the heroine of Arthur's 1867 story "The Factory Girl."

5. This anonymous pamphlet resides in the holdings of the New York Public Library and, along with a "Brief Autobiography" printed with Arthur's *Lights and Shadows of Real Life*, provides the main biographical source for the most thorough survey of Arthur's life and work, Koch's introduction to *Ten Nights in a Bar-Room*.

6. Arthur published *The Lady at Home* under this pseudonym.

7. See Louis Renza for a brilliant analysis of the dilemma posed by minor literature in his attempt to theorize a "minor criticism of minor literature" (41).

WORKS CITED

Arthur, T. S. "Agreeable Neighbors," "A Bad Habit Cured," "The House-Cleaning," "Saving at the Spigot," "Where the Money Goes." *Stories for Young Housekeepers*. Philadelphia: Lippincott, Grambo and Co., 1854. 75–88, 27–43, 107–17, 89–96, 7–26.

————. "Blossom's Baby Shower," "Brownie," "My First Summer in the Country." *The Prattler for Boys and Girls*. Philadelphia: J. B. Lippincott and Co., 1876. 347–49, 238–40, 42–44.

————. "Brief Autobiography," "The Factory Girl." *The Lights and Shadows of Real Life*. Philadelphia: John E. Potter and Co., 1867. 5–9, 13–36.

————. "Little Anna." *The Story Book*. Philadelphia: Godey and M'Michael, 1843. 9–15.

————. *Ten Nights in a Bar-Room*. 1852. Cambridge: Harvard UP, 1964.

————. *Window-Curtains*. *Arthur's Illustrated Home Magazine* 42 (1874): 30–36, 102–8, 170–75, 250–55, 299–304, 375–81, 444–50, 507–12, 564–69, 628–32, 692–96, 769–72.

Banta, Martha. *Imagining American Women*. New York: Columbia UP, 1987.

Bowlby, Rachel. *Just Looking: Consumer Culture in Dreiser, Gissing and Zola*. New York: Methuen, 1985.

Church, Mrs. Ella Rodman. "How Women Can Earn Money." *Arthur's Home Magazine* 52 (1884): 54–55.

Coultrap-McQuin, Susan. *Doing Literary Business*. Chapel Hill: U of North Carolina P, 1990.

Culver, Stuart. "What Manikins Want: *The Wonderful World of Oz* and *The Art of Decorating Dry Goods Windows*." *Representations* 21 (1988): 97–116.

Dare, Sydney. "Janet's Way." *Arthur's Home Magazine* 52 (1884): 394–96.

Elmwood, Mrs. Mary. *The Lady at Home*. New York: J. Allen, 1884.

"Filthy Paper Money." *Arthur's Illustrated Home Magazine* 42 (1874): 213–14.

Fisher, Philip. *Hard Facts*. New York: Oxford UP, 1985.

French, Warren. "Timothy Shay Arthur: Pioneer Business Novelist." *American Quarterly* 10.1 (1958): 55–65.

————. "Timothy Shay Arthur's Divorce Fiction." *Studies in English* 33 (1954): 90–96.

Geffen, Elizabeth M. "Industrial Development and Social Crisis." *Philadelphia: A 300-Year History*. Ed. Russell F. Weigley. New York: Norton, 1982. 307–62.

"Give the Boys a Chance." *Arthur's Home Magazine* 52 (1884): 208.

"Good for Nothings." *Arthur's Home Magazine* 6 (1855): 256–58.

Gorham, Deborah. *The Victorian Girl and the Feminine Ideal*. Bloomington: Indiana UP, 1982.

Harvey, Margaret B. "Getting Along." *Arthur's Home Magazine* 52 (1884): 470–72.

"Health of Women." *Arthur's Home Magazine* 52 (1884): 666.

"How to Keep From Drowning." *Arthur's Home Magazine* 52 (1884): 378.

Koch, Donald A. Introduction. *Ten Nights in a Bar-Room*. By Timothy Shay Arthur. Cambridge: Harvard UP, 1964. v–xxxiii.

Lears, T. J. Jackson. "From Salvation to Self-Realization: Advertising and the Therapeutic Roots of the Consumer Culture, 1880–1930." *The Culture of Con-*

sumption. Ed. Richard Wightman Fox and T. J. Jackson Lears. New York: Pantheon, 1983. 1–38.

Matheson, T. J. "Poe's 'The Black Cat' as a Critique of Temperance Literature." *Mosaic* 19.3 (1986): 69–81.

Nelson, Claudia. *Boys Will Be Girls: The Feminine Ethic and British Children's Fiction, 1857–1917.* New Brunswick: Rutgers UP, 1991.

Poe, Edgar Allan. "Autography." *The Complete Works of Edgar Allan Poe.* Ed. James A. Harrison. 17 vols. New York: AMS, 1965. 15.139–261.

Pratt, William W. *Ten Nights in a Bar-Room.* Chicago: Dramatic Publishing Co., n.d.

Renza, Louis A. *"A White Heron" and the Question of Minor Literature.* Madison: U of Wisconsin P, 1984.

Smyth, Albert H. *The Philadelphia Magazines and Their Contributors, 1741–1850.* Philadelphia: Robert M. Lindsay, 1892.

T. S. Arthur: His Life and Works. Boston: George Maclean, 1873.

MARTHA VICINUS

Models for Public Life: Biographies of "Noble Women" for Girls

Before the seventeenth century it would be difficult to imagine biographies of women that were not about either the religious or royalty; nondomestic roles were virtually nonexistent. But by the nineteenth century both boys and girls faced a vastly increased variety of public roles. Formulaic biographies mediated between young readers and the increasingly complex choices they might face by providing a series of clear-cut moral questions and solutions. As models for public action, they were an important alternative to the more familiar domestic girls' stories. Indeed, biographies served to validate adolescent dreams of doing good in a wider sphere than the home. The heroic plot both evoked a stereotyped emotional response and gave a vehicle for the reader's personal dreams. The factual narrative of a specific life history combined easily with personal fantasy; the reader did not so much identify with the heroine as with the heroic possibilities she represented. Popular biographies also raise interesting questions about the psychological underpinnings of formula literature, and in particular the importance of the father-daughter relation in shaping attitudes toward women's roles in the public realm. I have chosen examples from both sides of the Atlantic, as publishers made few distinctions between the English and North American markets in their subject matter, authors, and distribution.

After mid-century, when narrowly religious writings for children gave way to greater variety, works for girls can be divided into several loosely defined categories. The girls' equivalent of the boys' adventure story was the domestic tale. *Little Women* (1867) is the paradigmatic story: a tomboy leads her siblings into a variety of home-based adventures, and in the process is chastened by a sick or dying sister into behaving more thoughtfully "for her sake." In Susan Coolidge's *What Katy Did* (1872), the heroine is punished for her thoughtlessness and must do penance for several years as a cripple before being permitted to take up her rightful leadership role in the family. The most important figure in these stories is usually a single parent who benevolently watches over a large brood of children.

A favorite variant of this genre is the boarding-school story, popularized at the end of the century by L. T. Meade and slightly later by Angela Brazil. Here again a madcap, thoughtless girl learns the errors of her ways, but she is only lightly punished and even sometimes rewarded for her daring. The most significant changes are the shift from the family setting of earlier girls' stories to the school's enclosed peer group and the sanctioning of a limited form of disobedience and daring.[1] The spirited heroine, of course, is also a stereotype of the romance; her daring attracts the hero, and after a series of misunderstandings, they are united. Many adolescents were also reading *Jane Eyre* (1847) or Charlotte Yonge's *The Heir of Redclyffe* (1853) and other popular romances at the same time that they consumed school stories. Both of these genres shared with the domestic story an independent thinking heroine who must be chastened, either by circumstances or by marriage.[2]

Edward Salmon, in his 1886 survey of literature for boys and girls, lamented that "Girl-life does not lend itself to vigorous and stirring treatment in the manner that boy-life does" (516). He did recognize that if girls were bored with books written for them, they often borrowed their brothers'. But he strongly recommended the growing number of popular biographies as an ideal combination of moral teaching and adventure:

> Perhaps the best reading which girls can possibly have is biography, especially female biography, of which many excellent works have been published. One cannot help as one reads the biographies of great women—whether of Miss Florence Nightingale, Mrs. Fry, or Lady Russell—being struck by the purity of purpose and God-fearing zeal which moved most of their subjects. (527)

The most striking characteristic of these stories is their subordination of affectional ties to the heroine's public activities. Indeed, in many cases it was admitted that a girl could find her family life difficult and constraining.

Although written specifically for girls, these biographies are often paired with those for boys; for every *Noble Heroes* collection, there was bound to be *Noble Heroines*. The main figures share many of the same characteristics; courage, pluck, independence, initiative, and "a noble character" are admired, regardless of gender. The sturdy Protestant activism of these stories is revealed in the titles: *Heroines Every Child Should Know*, *Pioneer Women in Victoria's Reign*, *Twelve Notable Good Women of the Nineteenth Century*, *The World's Workers*, *Clever Girls of Our Time*, and *Women Who Win*. The emphasis is obviously upon hard work and success in this world. Girls are expected to be more home-loving and nurturing, but both sexes must overcome the same kinds of opposition, either from an uncomprehending family or from a ridiculing public. The battles are invariably those of an individual against cruel Nature, an indifferent society, or bureaucratic obstinacy.

These tales demonstrate how a boy or girl, grown to mature adulthood, could face adversity because of characteristics nurtured in childhood. The reader was clearly expected to emulate the virtues placed before her—and these were often, as befits a heroine, nontraditional. Once again we have an independent girl as the main character, but her childhood difficulties prefigure characteristics that will be vital to her later life. Elizabeth Fry's obstinate and questioning spirit was justified, for "out of this characteristic grew her independent thought and action respecting prison reform, twenty or thirty years later" (Thayer 400). Rather than being humbled by circumstances, the heroine learned to control and channel her assertiveness, and thereby to control her world. The biographer, however, must carefully define appropriate independence of thought and action. As Jennie Chappell explained at the beginning of her account of Agnes Weston, the founder of temperance hotels and refuges for sailors:

> Wherever power, which is strength in action, exists, it must inevitably make itself known. Wind, water, steam—every force of Nature, must have an outlet, and the strength of character with which some children are endowed from birth shows itself at an early age. . . . The eagerness must be curbed, the impetuosity restrained, the energies directed into right channels, and many are the conflicts which occur between the child and the parent, the pupil and the teacher, ay, and between the higher and lower nature of the subject himself, ere the victory for right alone is won. (55–56)

Each of the "four noble women" described by Chappell struggles with an ungovernable temper and personal religious doubts before she is ready to fight in the public world.

Child heroines precociously prefigure their adult life. Catherine Booth, the future wife of the founder of the Salvation Army, saw a crowd jeering at a drunken man being led to prison: "Instantly a sense of profound pity for the unfortunate culprit overmastered the horror which a gently nurtured little girl must naturally have felt, and springing to the man's side, Kate walked with him to the lock-up" (Chappell 126). One biographer of Florence Nightingale archly commented, "The truth is, Florence was born to be a nurse, and a sick doll was dearer to her than a strong and healthy one. So I fear her dolls would have been invalids most of the time if it had not been for Parthenope's little family, who often required their Aunt Florence's care" (McFee 7).

The most Victorian characteristic of heroines, like their brother heroes, is the progress they bring to some part of the public world. They act only for the greater glory of God and English-speaking peoples, and never for personal gain—but they are commemorated in a biography specifically because they had personally achieved public status. It is this character-istic, I believe, that makes such stories potentially radical encounters for girl readers. Indeed, Eva Hope, author of *Grace Darling: The Heroine of the Farne Islands; Her Life, and Its Lessons,* forthrightly declared, "A WOMAN'S WORK IS THAT WHICH SHE SEES NEEDS DOING":

> A woman should be so far free and independent as to do that which she feels to be right, no matter though the right seem to call her to heights which she had not occupied before. And if, in her ordinary avocations, she be allowed liberty of thought and action, there is the greater proba-bility that, when the occasion comes which demands from her strength of nerve and firm endurance, she will not be found wanting. (4–5)

Every biographer insisted upon the necessity of fulfilling home duties before venturing into new fields. But the disjunction between the overt message and the narrative was too great. Stories of real-life adventure, such as Grace Darling's, simply did not encourage quiescence. Even as biographies pur-ported to teach modesty and home duties, they awakened an imaginative affinity with active, public heroines.

Womanliness was always essential, yet—as with so many romantic hero-ines—the actions undertaken often contradicted the very characteristics praised. Heroines proved themselves in the male world but never lost their essential femininity. Grace Darling, the daughter of a Northumbrian light-house keeper, not only rows out in the storm to save nine shipwrecked people but also nurses them back to health. Mary Somerville was a brilliant mathematician, but she never neglected her home duties. Alternatively, a heroine achieved status by taking the feminine qualities of spiritual and physical nurturing into the public sphere; women could see neglected and needy people where men could not. Countless school-prize books com-memorated pioneering teachers, nurses, social workers, and missionaries.

The strong belief in religious faith and individual action that character-ized Victorian children's biographies grew from Evangelical roots. Biographies were part of the publishing artillery of the mid-century Evangelicals, who had broadened their literary base beyond discursive prose and biblical exegesis in order to continue to convert and hold the young.[3] Biographies of missionaries had long attracted many Evangelicals to a career in the church, as Joan Jacobs Brumberg has documented (68–78). Such figures continued to be extremely popular, as testified by the innumerable popular accounts of David Livingstone and Mary Slessor, two working-class Scots missionaries. Both had the added virtue of dying at their posts, adding the halo of martyrdom to their undoubted physical and spiritual triumphs.

But modern versions of John Bunyan's *Pilgrim's Progress* are only part of the popular biography's heritage. That other great narrative of nascent capitalism, *Robinson Crusoe,* was equally important, via contemporary boys' adventure stories.[4] In biographies, however, unlike adventure stories, Crusoe's individualism reigned supreme; boy and girl Fridays were reduced to nameless helpers. Nightingale's Crimean nurses were uniformly described as "gentle missionaries" or "a band of devoted women." Neither they nor the numerous friends who helped Nightingale were identified. Every hero or heroine was isolated, with few allies, although an admired figure from an earlier generation was sometimes mentioned. One biographer, for example, made much of Nightingale's brief encounter with Elizabeth Fry, the Quaker prisoner reformer: "What passed at that momentous interview we know not, but we may be sure that Florence Nightingale came away stimulated by the elder woman's example and enthusiasm, and encouraged to go steadily forward on the path she had determined to follow for herself" (Haydon 19–20). Sister Dora, the nurse of Walsall, was "fired with enthusiasm" by "the story of Florence Nightingale's heroism and self-sacrifice" (Chappell 95).

Faith alone was not sufficient for a hero or heroine; action in this world was essential. But for the Victorians, this had to be well-trained and controlled action. The concreteness of Crusoe's world was replicated in the matter-of-fact presentation of the necessary training, knowledge, and obstacles each hero and heroine faced before achieving his or her goal. Readers were warned that Nightingale

> devoted ten years to study and training before she undertook even the comparatively small responsibility of looking after Harley Street Nursing Home and Hospital for Governesses. But when she was called to higher duties she was fit for them, and she then performed her task in a way that won the admiration of the universe, and established a precedent for all time. (Pratt 121)

Exemplary actions successfully completed invariably win over the public to the heroine or hero, but he or she modestly steps aside, preferring
familial love and praise over all public accolades. Nightingale's exploits in
the Crimea had an especially satisfying end because of their conclusion:
"the English people" had planned "a public welcome of their heroine, but
with the modesty and calm judgment that always characterised her, she
slipped quietly into England by the carriage of a French steamer and so to
her country home" (Mabie and Stephens 277). Grace Darling, in spite of
being offered seven hundred pounds and the opportunity of more money if
she would travel with a stage company as an exhibit, refused to leave her
modest lighthouse home (Johnson 246).

By examining closely several biographies of Nightingale, we
can trace the various permutations the biographical formula took through
nearly a century of retelling. Nightingale was the supreme heroine of the
nineteenth century; myth-making about her exploits in the Crimea began
almost before she left England.[5] Nightingale deviated from the formula in a
few ways that were easily elided in popular accounts of her adventures. Unlike most heroines, she came from a wealthy family; this potential liability
was overcome by describing all that she gave up in order to become a nurse.
The author of *Women Who Win* commented, "There was every comfort in
her home that money could provide, and no one but a genuine philanthropist could have turned away from its attractions for the briefest season.
But Providence had other and larger plans for her" (Thayer 44). Since self-
sacrifice was a key feminine virtue, Nightingale's sacrifice of balls, London
nightlife, and country-house parties was seen as a great mark in her favor;
the fact that she had loathed these activities was ignored. Nightingale's cal-
culated decision to remain sick after returning from the Crimea in order to
be free from family obligations was transformed into the price she had paid
for her enormous labors on behalf of the English people. Her lobbying the
government to reform the army, public health, and India was suppressed
in favor of her efforts to turn nursing into a respectable female occupation.
Such alterations, of course, were common in all popular biographies. The
formula denied political manipulation, privileging stereotyped womanly
characteristics and work.

Consonant with other biographies, those about Nightingale begin by
describing the heroine's early signs of vocation. A favorite, never-to-be-
forgotten story was little Florence's successful nursing of the injured sheep-
dog Cap. She and the local minister, who had fortuitously trained in
medicine, make the rounds of the local villagers. They find Roger, the old

shepherd, unable to herd his sheep without Cap, who has been hurt by unruly boys; Roger must now kill Cap, because he cannot afford to feed him if the dog cannot work. Florence and the minister hasten to Roger's cottage, where they discover that Cap only has a bad bruise: "It was dreadfully swollen, and hurt very much to have it examined; but the dog knew it was meant kindly, and though he moaned and winced with pain, he licked the hands that were hurting him" (Mabie and Stephens 269). Under the eye of the minister, Florence heats water and applies hot compresses to bring the swelling down. Only when Cap is obviously better do they leave. On the way home, they meet the shepherd:

> "Oh, Roger," cried Florence, "you are not to hang poor old Cap; his leg is not broken at all."
> "No, he will serve you yet," said the vicar.
> "Well, I be main glad to hear it," said the shepherd, "and many thanks to you for going to see him." (Alldridge 14)

The next day, Florence returns to finish her task of caring for Cap, and Roger later says, "Do look at the dog, miss; he be so pleased to hear your voice. . . . I be greatly obliged to you, miss, and the vicar, for what you did. But for you I would have hanged the best dog I ever had in my life" (Alldridge 14).

The above incident is almost too obviously overdetermined. It is "mischievous schoolboys"—the enemies of all right-thinking girls—who have committed the thoughtless crime of harming a working farm animal. The young lady-bountiful prevents a sad mistake from being committed by the peasant-shepherd, who is driven by economic necessity to destroy an animal that cannot earn its living. Both the dog and the shepherd are suitably grateful. Cap, even when under great pain, does not nip those who do him good; when he later hears Florence's voice, he wags his tail in gratitude, but without taking his eye from the sheep he is guarding. Most accounts also add that Florence returned the next day to give two petticoats to the neighbor who had lent one to be torn up for compresses. Class privilege and class lines are maintained by everyone playing the appropriate role.[6]

Even more striking, however, is the audience for Florence's actions. She does not as a young girl travel alone around her father's property, but rather goes accompanied by the local Anglican clergyman, that figure of Christian wisdom and status. He teaches her, even as he instructs and counsels his parishioners. Moreover, his medical expertise, rather than the common sense of the experienced shepherd, leads him to "believe that the leg is

Fig. 1. Florence Nightingale and Cap, the shepherd's dog. From Maude E. Seymour, *Florence Nightingale as Seen in Her Portraits* (Boston: *Boston Medical and Surgical Journal*, 1916).

[not] really broken. It would take a big stone, and a hard blow, to break the leg of a great dog like Cap" (Alldridge 12). He correctly diagnoses and prescribes for Cap; Florence follows his orders in the time-consuming preparation and application of compresses. The girl Florence thus learns to strengthen her naturally feminine propensities to nurse under the aegis of a caring male. Her actions all take place, in Laura Mulvey's phrase, under the gaze of the male observer.

The device of a male observer approving the actions of the girl-heroine was repeatedly used in Victorian biographies. Often he was a sympathetic minister, teacher, or relative—desexualized, even feminized figures whom a girl was likely to know well. Suffering from her mother's disapproval of her eagerness to learn, Somerville confessed her love of Latin and mathematics to an encouraging uncle. Darling's father accompanied her to the half-submerged boat and presumably did much of the rowing, but Darling became the heroine of the hour. A minister, like a woman, was expected to care for and sympathize with the poor; an uncle could be concerned with a niece's future without worrying about discipline; even a father could bend to a child's needs in ways that a mother would not. These men, however, only guide the heroine; she herself takes the lead, following a natural, pre-existing bent—to nurse, to study, or to teach. Men introduced girls to the outside world, helped them to master necessary skills, and gave them moral approval; women, such as Fry, served as inspiration.

A major strategic difficulty faced by writers of girls' biographies was how to have the heroine overcome opposition without implying that she had a contentious spirit or that she was resistant to authority. Obviously no daughter could disobey her parents or a clergyman. William Thayer describes with relish the narrow, Puritan upbringing of Dorothea Dix by her "inflexibly conscientious" grandparents, culminating with the moral, "That such training was excellent for Dorothea there can be no doubt. . . . Miss Dix ever recognized her great obligations to her grandparents for their excellent, though severe, discipline" (62–63). Nightingale's complicated and tempestuous relationship with her mother and sister violated expected norms for both boys and girls; biographers focused on her close relationship with her father and ignored her mother (sister Parthenope appears only as a playmate). Heroines could suffer from bad tempers, temporary unbelief, or willfulness; in turn, parents could misunderstand or lack sympathy for them and their causes. But family love was inviolate.

Opposition was best characterized as an abstraction, such as unbelief, worldliness, general ignorance or prejudice, or even bureaucratic "muddle."

Specific persons or actions were never to blame, though sometimes a temporarily benighted figure, such as an African chieftain or a military officer, could be shown changing his mind about a missionary or a nurse. One author described Nightingale's life in the Crimea as

> a most difficult one. Everything was in disorder, and every official was extremely jealous of interference. Miss Nightingale, however, at once impressed upon her staff the duty of obeying the doctors' orders, as she did herself. . . . it would take far too much space to give all the details of that kind but strict administration which brought comparative comfort and a low death-rate into the Scutari hospitals. (Alldridge 25)

Another more bluntly blames the inefficiency of the "authorities" and "officials" without naming names:

> From the first the indomitable will of "the Lady-in-Chief," as she was called, made itself felt in every department, which gradually broke down all obstacles raised by the jealousy or bad tempers of the officials. . . . At the end of six months the hospital arrangements had been brought into order. (Carey 91)

A single description of the impact of the nurses—and not just of Nightingale—demonstrates the power that women were given, as well as what they might seize:

> The most hardened soldier could not be indifferent to such self-abnegation. The bare thought of such self-sacrifice by a woman to mitigate his trials would inspire him to appear at his best. The presence of women, as nurses, amidst the horrors of war, could not be otherwise than elevating and refining, begetting patience, contentment, and courage. For heroines to come to the aid of distressed soldiers must make heroes of them. They could not be weak, unmanly, and dispirited, with such examples of self-denial and Christian sympathy moving up and down the wards daily. (Thayer 52)

Women are placed in their traditional role of inspirer-of-men, but something more is added. They alone can change the hospital. Male space—the military hospital—has been successfully invaded and morally and physically revolutionized. Female morality is more powerful than male aggression. The women are first heroines, before the men can be reformed—they are the leaders of men who are "weak, unmanly, and dispirited." Heroines, not wars, create heroes.

Nightingale, with the help of her nurses, is the active agent who brings order out of military chaos, but the means by which she does so must be suppressed, lest it prove to be less than admirable. Like the tales of converting the natives, where the process of bringing hundreds to Christianity is silenced in favor of the end result, all heroines bring domestic order, religious belief, or physical safety out of public chaos by sheer force of will. In order to avoid such complications as ambition, cunning, manipulation, and possibly even dishonesty, the narrative slips over the tiresome details of Nightingale's actual daily behavior to the final accomplishment. A few examples of washing patients or insisting on medication for the dying speak for the whole. Or a specific event will mythologize the heroine. Nightingale's silent, nightly rounds through the miles of wards, where the waiting soldiers are said to kiss her passing shadow, transform her into the "Lady with the Lamp." Metonymy serves to cover the complexities of achieving social change.

But metonymy and narrative gaps also left room for the reader to insert herself. Too many uncomfortable details left little to the imagination. If formulaic biographies were to work successfully, they had to permit the reader imaginative escape into the life of the heroine. The reader, perhaps hopeful of a different, wider life, could interweave her inchoate dreams with the narrative. The simplified actions of the heroine made identification easy, regardless of how remote they might be from the reader's life. A shadowy Nightingale could be invested with desirable characteristics more easily than one encumbered with complex motivations. The creation of vivid symbolic behavior actually counteracted the tendency of the narrative to reify women. Even though the overt message was often womanly obedience, symbolic moments, such as Nightingale's nightly vigil, permitted an imaginative identification with independent action. Fiction—created by the reader and not just the author—was an essential part of the factual biography.

If we look to later biographies of Nightingale, a number of interesting alterations to the formula occur, all of them, however, confirming the importance of reading material to learning how to behave in the real world. Whatever modernizations were added to the biography, it remained a tale of upward mobility—upward in the sense of overcoming personal difficulties and social opprobrium in order to change public opinion. Nevertheless, the skills admired changed over time. In the early twentieth century the progress made since Nightingale's childhood was trumpeted. A. L. Haydon proudly wrote in 1909,

The wise old vicar was always at her elbow with talk about hygiene and practical suggestions for social improvements. Sixty years ago, it must be remembered, the condition of the lower classes was far different from what it is now. Local authorities were not generally pressing in their insistence on the observation of the ordinary laws of health, and the gospel of fresh air and cold water was one that was regarded as at least dangerous. (17)

During the 1910s and 1920s the story of Roger and Cap remained crucial, but Nightingale's disagreements with her parents were now discreetly described as her "gilded cage," for "she longed for some useful and definite work for which she might be trained so as to take an active part in a wider sphere of life" (Wakeford 16).

A major change in emphasis, however, was far more detail about the attractions of a wealthy life. What had been a subtheme, Nightingale's privileged social class, became a dominant characteristic to contrast with her desire to nurse. Self-sacrifice in and of itself was no longer attractive, so that it had to be redefined to become the sacrifice of material goods. Similarly, opposition is abstracted and then personified, rather than being characterized as unnamed but real people. For example, Society is caricatured as moralistic spinsterish women by Constance Wakeford in her 1917 biography: "The dear old Mid-Victorian ladies drew their shawls over their shoulders and held up their hands in horror at the very idea of a lady becoming such a low, unlady-like person as a nurse; and as for a woman going out to the battlefield, no such outrageous thing had ever been heard of!" (30). The material world and its attractions or constraints held center stage, rather than the spiritual strivings of an earlier generation of biographies.

In direct contrast to other twentieth-century biographies, all of which praised contemporary progress at the expense of the Victorians, was a pamphlet published by the Women's Freedom League at the height of the suffrage struggle. Marion Holmes, the militant author, indignantly indicts the current image of Nightingale:

Florence Nightingale, the strong, capable, "brainy" woman, the woman with force, the woman who exercised a bold authority, has been obscured by the persistent presentment of the Lady with the Lamp, gentle word here, a healing touch there. And even this one-sided and inadequate conception of her great work was accepted only after her mission proved an undeniable success. The most popular heroine in history had to pay the price that is exacted of all pioneers. Bitter, venomous attacks, misrepresentation, irredeemably vulgar slanders, signalled her departure for the Crimea. Before her name became for all time a name to conjure with, it was the butt for coarse wit and ridicule of the day. (2–3)

Militant feminism turned Nightingale into the greatest heroine of all time. The old clichés about the "Lady with the Lamp" no longer evoked fantasies of power, but rather constrained "a great administrator and sanitarian, a strong-minded, firm-handed genius" to the narrow role of nursing the sick and wounded. Biography must be rewritten to revivify the myth of "succour and service, tenderness and care . . . a beacon light for ages yet to come." The formula remains the same, but the tone has changed.

By the interwar years, Lytton Strachey's *Eminent Victorians* and Sir Edward Cook's definitive biography had diminished Nightingale's reputation. Her name less frequently appeared on the lists of famous women.[7] But in the 1950s, Nightingale reappears, suitably psychologized. She and Parthenope were no longer described as both interested in helping the poor; rather, "Parthe" was "entirely different" from Nightingale in her love of frivolity and easy living. Nightingale sounds like a typical idealistic adolescent in Yvonne ffrench's description:

> She had a precise, practical mind, and passionately intense feelings. She was morbid, she was self-willed, and a real problem to her parents who could not understand why she should not be as happy and contented as her sister.
>
> She became thoroughly out of sympathy with her family, her relations and their attitude to everything. Even before she was a fully grown woman she was conscious of being set apart. She felt that she had a mission to do good in the world; she felt in some way called to a dedicated life, but what that was to be she did not know. It worried her. (8)

To appeal to the modern girl reader, Nightingale's family troubles replaced Roger and Cap. The result was an attractive modernizing of an old story, but also the loss of the palpable lesson of public duty taught by nursing Cap. The twentieth-century focus upon the temptations of material wealth and family quarrels subtly undermined the arguments for individual initiative and responsibility taught by the earlier versions. Moreover, the unspoken space between initial efforts and final success that had characterized Victorian biographies now became an insurmountable gap. A girl heroine who was busy fighting with her parents and giving up balls for sick neighbors might have been more accessible than the austere heroines of the past, but she was also less capable of independent action. Indeed, ffrench credited Richard Monckton Milnes, the man Nightingale loved in her twenties, with influencing her to take an interest in the poor. Romance, rather than early childhood inclination, became the impetus for doing public good. The incorporation of sex, however muted, into the formula biography shifted the plot from a girl's negotiation between self and the public world into a triangle of self, romance, and public duty. Genres blurred, and biography joined the revised adventure story as yet another tale of choosing between personal happiness and public service.

The exact influence of these stories upon girl readers is impossible to recreate. Brumberg has discovered several examples of pious early-nineteenth-century American girls deciding to devote themselves to missionary work after reading about the lives of famous missionaries (68–70). But the numerous *Noble Heroines* series were consumed in such quantity that they appear to have left little direct impact upon readers. Perhaps one of the reasons why so few autobiographies include any "heroine" titles among the list of beloved and/or influential books may be their very commonplace familiarity. The lessons taught had been so well learned that they were not worthy of comment. Alternatively, once a woman had decided not to strike out on her own, to be a heroine, she forgot the idealism of a biography and remembered the emotional satisfactions of fiction. Whatever the reasons, biographies lack the nostalgia that clings so persistently to domestic and school stories.[8] Until more research is done, we are forced to speculate about the relative popularity and impact of biographies upon girl readers.

Biographies were probably most popular among girls during latency, when they were demarcating their public world, defining their nonemotional role in it, and gaining the skills necessary to negotiate within it. The plots encouraged girls to behave instrumentally rather than relationally. How well a heroine got along with her mother, sister, or friends was irrelevant; her self-control, knowledge, and determination, on the other hand, were crucial. These—unlike personal relations—might all appear to be within the control of a reader, at least imaginatively. To be a nurse under Nightingale, a social worker under Weston, or a prison visitor under Fry seemed both attractive and possible. In effect, the biographies provided vicarious practice in the unnatural role of public service at a time when girls usually had far too much practice in family duties.

But of even greater importance, I believe, was the subtext of the biographical plot. If we define school adventure stories as a means of coming to terms with homoerotic bonding, and romance as the journey toward heterosexual bonding, then the biographies are best seen as part of the process of individuation. Biographies, like the adventure story, ignore heterosexual conflict, but like the romance, they give male approval. They describe an individual girl's journey into the public world, with the assistance of a nonthreatening, nonsexual male. The father, representative of freedom and privilege, gives approval to the heroine at crucial early stages in her struggle. An active, instrumental role is rewarded with emotional support.[9]

Mother-daughter conflict is finessed in biographies by giving the mother a narrowly defined role. She teaches the young girl the proper moral behavior and then fades from the narrative. Occasionally the mother will reappear to criticize the heroine; although loving, she does not understand the nature of the girl. Somerville had to fight her mother's distrust of learned ladies, while Darling's mother opposed her rowing to the rescue of the shipwrecked. The father is absent during the child's initial training but present—either in himself or in a surrogate—when she first acts in the public domain; his support makes her action both attractive and possible. When the eighteen-year-old Frances Willard celebrated her coming-of-age by reading *Ivanhoe* in front of her father, he "was at first inclined to be indignant . . . but when his daughter gravely and respectfully asserted her newly attained right to do what seemed good in her eyes, he laughed and contested the point no more" (Chappell 24). After receiving her father's blessing, the girl moves decisively on to heroism by herself. A heroine doesn't seem to need her family as much as other people do; the domestic circle obligingly recedes from the narrative to await her triumphal return. All past difficulties disappear upon that happy event. What more attractive fantasy than this?

Biographies could keep their particular psychological hold over a youthful readership as long as they continued to create independent heroines who were guided but not led by asexual men. When they began to add romance, and especially the giving up of romance, they failed. Janice Radway has pointed out the failure of popular romances that create emotional triangles; her romance-readers overwhelmingly preferred plots that show the gradual removal of the barriers separating a woman and a man, rather than those that turn upon the winning of the beloved in competition with another person (171–72). Her insight, I believe, applies equally to girls' adventure stories and to biographies. Both of these, in different ways, also base their plots upon the opposition of two forces and not three. When the confrontation between the heroine and an uncomprehending society was changed to an interior struggle over choosing between a man and the reform of society, the biography was no longer the story of a successful public heroine but of a failed romantic heroine.

The helpful male guide cannot be sexualized without the dramatic loss of psychological independence for the girl. In her 1954 biography ffrench describes vividly the struggle Nightingale underwent before becoming a nurse:

> Gradually, very gradually a slow change in herself was being effected. A hardening process was beginning, and dedication to a cause replaced devotion to friendship. A deliberate renunciation of her friends gradually followed, and in her private notes she made the final act of self-denial: "Oh, God, no more love. No more marriage. Oh God." (17)

This account is truer to Nightingale's actual experience, but what young woman would want to choose public service after reading about Nightingale's painful sacrifice of the sympathetic and helpful Milnes? Who wants to struggle vicariously with Nightingale's dilemma? When personal love so conflicts with heroism, the preferred choice is obvious.

The mid-twentieth-century changes in the formulaic biography point to both feminist and literary contradictions. If an author added romance to the narrative, the heroine's identity became defined by her desire. Once romance was admitted, a woman could not be portrayed as a whole person if she had rejected a suitor. Literary conventions gave a man, but not a woman, heroic stature based solely upon his public life, regardless of his personal needs. The recognition of emotional conflict may have enriched the narrative of biography, but the price was a loss in the presentation of women's choices. Girls who sought affirmation outside the home learned that they could never escape their sexual identity—a lesson many feminists have been fighting their whole adult lives. Paradoxically, the single-minded two-dimensional heroines of the past provided more imaginative scope for the reader. Since these Victorian girls were not invested with sexual conflicts, they widened the definition of the possible. Noble heroines could have fulfilling public lives similar to those of noble heroes. As one biographer declaimed, "There is no sex among souls; hence there is none in success. One soul with the same talents, force, and opportunities as another soul will make as many and great things happen, whether found in man or woman" (Thayer iii). Asexual heroines could be admired for their intrinsic qualities, however stereotyped these may have been. The situating of famil-

68 MARTHA VICINUS

iar feminine characteristics in unfamiliar places was a potent appeal for social change. Is it too farfetched to speculate that formulaic biographies for girls may have engendered powerful fantasies that empowered the first feminist movement?

NOTES

1. I am indebted to Sally Mitchell for this insight.

2. For a discussion of the constraining gender roles of girls' fiction, see Elizabeth Segal, " 'As the Twig Is Bent. . . .' "

3. See Altick 99–128. Altick describes the reading of the Rev. Benjamin Gregory, editor of the *Wesleyan Methodist Magazine;* he had delighted especially in travel literature and biographies when he was growing up between the years 1825 and 1840.

4. Secondary works about boys' literature are legion. But see Turner, Green, and Arnold. Although no one has studied the borrowings of girls' fiction from boys' adventure stories, they are obvious.

5. Mary Poovey, in " 'A Housewifely Woman': The Social Construction of Florence Nightingale," discusses the relationship between the construction of Nightingale as a heroine and the social control of the working class and women.

6. The repetition of this story for over fifty years may have been due to its similarity to the immensely popular tales of innocent waifs and dainty girls saving irreligious parents, drunken outcasts, and other melodramatic figures. See Avery 112–20, 150–55.

7. I have found only two children's biographies of Nightingale dating from this period: Margaret E. Tabor's *Pioneer Women: Florence Nightingale* (1925) and I. B. O'Malley's *Great Englishwomen: Florence Nightingale* (1933). The latter was based on O'Malley's *Florence Nightingale, 1820–1910: A Study of Her Life Down to the End of the Crimean War* (1931). Rosalind Nash wrote *A Sketch of the Life of Florence Nightingale* (1937) for adults, following up her 1925 abridged and revised edition of Sir Edward Cook's *Life of Florence Nightingale* (1925).

8. Gill Frith has pointed out the continued importance of school stories among girls at a racially mixed comprehensive school. She argues that a recent theatrical spoof on the genre, *Daisy Pulls It Off,* was especially popular with women because it evoked "not a nostalgia for a lived event or an irrecoverable 'golden age,' but a nostalgia for a half-forgotten *reading experience*" (116; italics in original).

9. See Lamb, Tresch Owen, and Chase-Lansdale for a review of the literature and a discussion of the importance of the father in fostering instrumental behavior in daughters. I am indebted to Susan Contratto for this reference.

WORKS CITED

Alldridge, Lizzie. *Florence Nightingale, Frances Ridley Havergal, Catherine Marsh and Mrs. Ranyard*. London: Cassell, 1885.

Altick, Richard D. *The English Common Reader: A Social History of the Mass Reading Public, 1800–1900*. Chicago: U of Chicago P, 1957.

Arnold, Guy. *Held Fast for England: G. A. Henty, Imperialist Boys' Writer*. London: Hamilton, 1980.

Avery, Gillian. *Childhood's Pattern: A Study of the Heroes and Heroines of Children's Fiction, 1770–1950*. London: Hodder and Stoughton, 1975.

Brumberg, Joan Jacobs. *Mission for Life*. New York: Free, 1980.

Carey, Rosa Nouchette. *Twelve Notable Good Women of the Nineteenth Century*. London: Hutchinson, 1899.

Chappell, Jennie. *Four Noble Women and Their Work*. London: S. W. Partridge, 1898.

ffrench, Yvonne. *Florence Nightingale, 1820–1910*. London: Hamilton, 1954.

Frith, Gill. " 'The Time of Your Life': The Meaning of the School Story." *Language, Gender and Childhood*. Ed. Carolyn Steedman, Cathy Unwin, and Valerie Walkerdine. London: Routledge and Kegan Paul, 1985. 113–36.

Green, Martin. *Dreams of Adventure, Deeds of Empire*. London: Routledge and Kegan Paul, 1980.

Haydon, A. L. *Florence Nightingale, O.M.: A Heroine of Mercy*. 1909. London: Andrew Melrose, n.d.

Holmes, Marion. *Florence Nightingale: A Cameo Sketch*. 5th ed. 1913. London: Women's Freedom League, n.d.

Hope, Eva. *Grace Darling: The Heroine of the Farne Islands; Her Life, and Its Lessons*. London: Tyne Publishers, n.d.

Johnson, Joseph. *Brave Women Who Have Been Distinguished for Heroic Actions and Noble Virtues*. 1875. Edinburgh: Gall and Inglis, n.d.

Lamb, Michael E., Margaret Tresch Owen, and Lindsay Chase-Lansdale. "The Father-Daughter Relationship: Past, Present, and Future." *Becoming Female: Perspectives on Development*. Ed. Claire B. Kopp with Martah Kirkpatrick. New York: Plenum, 1979. 89–112.

Mabie, Hamilton Wright, and Kate Stephens. *Heroines Every Child Should Know*. New York: Grosset and Dunlap, 1908.

McFee, Inez N. *The Story of Florence Nightingale*. Dansville, NY: F. A. Owen, n.d.

Mulvey, Laura. "Visual Pleasure and Narrative Cinema." *Women and Cinema: A Critical Anthology*. Ed. Karyn Kay and Gerald Perry. New York: Dutton, 1977. 412–28.

Poovey, Mary. " 'A Housewifely Woman': The Social Construction of Florence Nightingale." *Uneven Developments: The Ideological Work of Gender in Mid-Victorian England*. Chicago: U of Chicago P, 1988. 164–98.

Pratt, Edwin A. *Pioneer Women in Victoria's Reign*. London: George Newnes, 1897.

Radway, Janice. *Reading the Romance: Women, Patriarchy, and Popular Romance*. Chapel Hill: U of North Carolina P, 1984.

Salmon, Edward. "What Girls Read." *Nineteenth Century* 20 (October 1886): 515–29.

Segal, Elizabeth. " 'As the Twig Is Bent . . . ': Gender and Childhood Reading." *Gender and Reading: Essays on Readers, Texts and Contexts*. Baltimore: Johns Hopkins UP, 1986. 165–86.

Thayer, William M. *Women Who Win or Making Things Happen*. London: T. Nelson and Sons, 1897.

Turner, E. S. *Boys Will Be Boys*. New rev. ed. London: Joseph, 1975.

Wakeford, Constance. *The Wounded Soldiers' Friends: The Story of Florence Nightingale, Clara Barton and Others*. 1917. London: Hadley Bros., n.d.

JULIA COURTNEY

The Barnacle: *A Manuscript Magazine of the 1860s*

Between 1859 and 1871 the English novelist Charlotte Mary Yonge (1823–1901) was "Mother Goose" to what her friend Mary Anderson Morshead called "a group of eager, merry schoolgirls, who almost lived on her works" (qtd. in Coleridge, *Yonge* 292). In traditional nursery mythology, Mother Goose is a teller of tales, a collector of rhymes—a figure at once homely and magical, slightly witchlike with her shawl and pointed hat. The spinster Yonge's adoption of the title "Mother Goose" can be seen partly as "playfulness," a favorite Yonge term indicating innocent light-heartedness, and perhaps partly as an unconscious symbol of her religious role as "a Mother in Israel"—"one, that is, from whom came the spiritual opening of the eyes, the spiritual formation and sustaining of character, of countless children in Christ," as the theologian Robert Campbell Moberly described her in his funeral sermon (1).

Throughout her long life Yonge consciously dedicated her talents to the furtherance and dissemination of "Church teaching," the tenets of the Oxford Movement as passed on to her by her spiritual mentor, John Keble. Keble's Tractarianism likened the divine scheme of God the Father working through Mother Church to instruct and guide the faithful to the earthly family consisting of authoritative father, whether priestly or familial; mother as teacher and exemplar; and loving, obedient children. This structure of belief, together with Keble's benevolent High Toryism and his injunction to seek out "the one thing needful" through a modest life of quiet usefulness directed by the twin beacons of scripture and tradition, informed both Yonge's fiction and her more overtly didactic writings. In *Womankind* (1874–77), her definitive statement of woman's status and responsibilities, she directed her female readers to accept their flawed and subordinate nature—but woman's inferiority should not prevent her striving for the highest plane of spiritual, moral, and intellectual improvement. As one who, in Morshead's judgment, "truthfully knew her own powers" (qtd. in Coleridge, *Yonge* 293), the author evidently achieved a satisfying lifestyle within the bounds of social and theological safety, a lifestyle she commended to her younger followers.

These admirers of "Mother Goose" were known as the Gosling Society. Again the name is significant, with its contemporary connotation of "silly geese"; in fact the Goslings labored to avoid silliness, so that the name may well be an example of what one of them later called "self-snubbing" (Rice 164). The members of the Gosling Society were in many ways typical of the readership for whom Yonge intended her work. According to Christabel Rose Coleridge, herself a Gosling and Yonge's first biographer,

> her relation to us precisely exemplified that in which she stood to num-
> berless other girls and young women who only knew her through her
> writings. The pleasure she took in all that pleased us, the guidance she
> gave without seeming to preach, the enthusiasm with which we re-
> garded her, also inspired her readers and made them all her life like a
> circle of friends. (*Yonge* 203)

Not only were the Goslings representative of the Yonge reading public; in many ways their backgrounds and expressed attitudes mirrored the high-minded, intellectual, self-educated figures of her fiction, such as Ethel May of *The Daisy Chain* (1856) or Sophie Kendal of *The Young Step-mother* (1861).

Coleridge adds that the Goslings flourished from 1859 to 1871 before being merged with "Arachne and Her Spiders" in the more public forum of the *Monthly Packet,* the magazine originally "For Younger Members of the English Church" that Yonge had founded in 1851 and that she was to edit for nearly forty years. The year 1871 is significant in that the 1870s and 1880s saw a move away from home education for middle-class girls. The Goslings of the 1860s thus represent the last generation of daughters from educated clerical or professional families to receive a largely home-based, parent-centered education—the generation that in turn provided the women teachers, college principals, and high school founders of the 1880s. In this context the contents of the Goslings' manuscript magazine, the *Barnacle,* take on added significance: What intellectual, religious, and social attitudes (inevitably, derived to some extent from the life and work of their "Mother Goose") did the contributors take with them into their subsequent careers as educators or writers?

The *Barnacle*'s name plays on the mythical connection between geese and barnacles; it also means "a companion not easily shaken off," accord-ing to *Chambers Dictionary.* During much of the life of the Gosling Society, the magazine was produced by the members and circulated among their families and friends. It was, said Coleridge, "modelled on *The Hursley Magazine* of [Yonge's] own youth. . . . [It] lasted for several years and died a natural death as some of the chief contributors found their way into *The Monthly Packet* and its Christmas Numbers" (*Yonge* 202).[1]

The *Barnacle* is best described as something between a family magazine and an in-house version of the *Monthly Packet*. Most of the contributors remained anonymous or used a pen name; the following list indicates all those featured on the circulation list or as actual contributors, some represented by a single article, others by substantial contributions: Chelsea China, Ladyfern, Ladybird, Glowworm, Humble Bee, Irene, Gurgoyle, Cobweb, Magpie, Firefly, Kittiwake, Rowan Tree, Turkscap, Cricket, Heather, Hedgerose, Shamrock, Mignonette, Fernseed, Potato, Ugly Duckling, Bog Oak, Thistle, Hoopoe, Sparrowhawk, Iceberg. Toward the end of the series Coleridge appended a key to the pen names; but as by then (1867) some of the most prolific early contributors had dropped out, some mysteries remain, and it is not possible to identify everyone. Fortunately each issue contains a list indicating the circulation order, often with full names and addresses—but editorial references suggest that the circulation was far wider than the bare address list, with contributions from a much wider circle sought and accepted.

One serial, for example, which Yonge described as "most promising" (vol. 7), appeared above the name of "the Firefly's Friend," of whom one can deduce only that she was involved in infant school teaching and that she lived in Firefly's home town of Brighton, since Firefly was directed to show her friend the *Barnacle* before sending it to the next accredited Gosling.[2] Similarly, a charming *jeu d'esprit* showing intimate knowledge of several Goslings and written from the viewpoint of an interested outsider is signed only "E.C."—just possibly Coleridge's younger brother Ernest Hartley Coleridge (vol. 9, Christmas 1865). Under these circumstances it is hardly surprising that in volume after volume "Goslings are entreated to keep *The Barnacle* as short a time as is possible,—putting it to their conscience what *is* a reasonable time—for being read, not for lying forgotten upon tables" (vol. 4, June 1864), and "wandering" issues are sought.

Despite some unavoidable gaps in the material, however, various inferences about *Barnacle* readers and contributors can be drawn. First, the names and addresses alone suggest a social range spanning the middle and upper-middle classes, from Elinor Champernoune, Dartington Hall, Totnes, to the less distinguished but scarcely humble Miss Younghusband

of Twenty-three Maryon Road, Woolwich, a military neighborhood close
to the Arsenal and Academy. Possibly as it grew larger toward the end of
the run of extant volumes, the group became less socially exclusive. But
perhaps the most noticeable feature—apart from the high concentration of
members of the Coleridge family—is the predominance of clerical/educa-
tional households, many of whose surnames read like a list of distinguished
second-rankers of the later Oxford Movement. The Coleridges of Hanwell
and Hurstpierpoint, the Helmores, Hullahs, Johnses, Lonsdales, Fursdons,
Mitchells, and Moberlys were all concerned with teaching or the church,
and frequently both. Among apparent lay people, there is substantial representation from such strongholds of "advanced" High Church religious
views as Torquay and Brighton.

Closer investigation reveals that most of the more active contributors
were related to each other and often to Yonge herself. Coleridge pre-
pares the way by indicating that the Goslings were largely composed of
"the cousinhood," as she rather despairingly called it (Coleridge, *Yonge*
202), and there were certainly ties of blood or marriage among Coleridges, Yonges, Martyns, Morsheads, Pridhams, Helmores, and possibly
Fursdons. Originally, as Christabel Coleridge explains, the Goslings were
instituted at the suggestion of Yonge's childhood friend Mary E. Coleridge
for the benefit of her niece Mildred, daughter of John Duke Coleridge, a
lawyer/politician who later became Lord Chief Justice:

> Mildred was then [1859] an exceptionally brilliant and clever child, in
> her early teens, and there were several girl cousins growing up, cousins'
> cousins also and young friends. Most of these girls had time on their
> hands. Education was often desultory and High Schools had not been
> thought of. Magazine competitions were not invented, and it occurred
> to Miss Coleridge that the young ones needed a spur to their energies.
> She proposed that they should form a society among themselves, setting
> four questions a month in turn, and sending in the answers, the best set
> to be chosen and travel round the circle. She very soon, if not at once,
> proposed that "Cousin Charlotte" should be the critic and referee. I
> think Charlotte was asked to be Minerva to a set of young owls. She
> chose to be Mother Goose to a brood of Goslings. (*Yonge* 201)

Born in 1847, Mildred would have been twelve in 1859 and sixteen when
the first *Barnacle* appeared.[3]

But although Mildred, as Ladybird, and her aunt Mary Coleridge (The
Old Secretary) continued to head the *Barnacle* circulation list through-

out the early issues, by far the most dominant contributor was Christabel Coleridge, as Chelsea China. Clearly the *Barnacle* fulfilled a tremendous need for her. From the beginning lengthy historical serials in her sprawling handwriting constituted a major part of each issue; by volume 13 (Christmas 1866) she was subeditor, handling the circulation and chivvying contributors. As Coleridge was born in 1843, she was already twenty when she began contributing to the *Barnacle,* which proved to be a jumping-off point for her subsequent career as novelist, children's writer, essayist, and second editor of the *Monthly Packet.*[4]

In an interview published in the *Torbay Directory* of 8 January 1896, Coleridge explained that she had been writing since the age of twelve. A holiday with relatives in Rugby, when she was fifteen, brought her into contact with Archbishop Benson's future wife, Mary (Minnie), who inspired her to try writing a novel; a little later she joined "an essay club started among her friends by Miss Charlotte Yonge . . . the Gosling Society." This led directly to her contributions to the *Monthly Packet* and subsequent career as a successful novelist.

Christabel's branch of the Coleridge family was closely associated with the Helmores, represented in the *Barnacle* address list by Katie Helmore (possibly Cobweb), Christabel's first cousin. Katie's father, Thomas Helmore, came to Saint Mark's College, Chelsea, as vice-principal in 1842, later becoming its precentor and enjoying a long and distinguished musical career as director of the Choir of the Chapel Royal.[5] He came from an Evangelical background, being the son of a celebrated "lady preacher" (Helmore 3), but was ordained as an Anglican priest. (His political stance may be deduced from the story that he horsewhipped a young former chorister whom he found attending a Chartist meeting.) Katie, his eldest child, was born in 1845, two years before Mildred Coleridge and two years after Christabel Coleridge.

In later life Katie Helmore was destined to be a devoted home daughter, without Christabel's additional interest of a successful literary career.[6] When her mother died in 1886, the older woman's "chair was filled by a thoughtful and affectionate daughter . . . surrounded by familiar objects, hiding, as far as love could hide, her father's loss" (Helmore 122) and nursing Thomas through his four remaining years. As Helmore evidently shared her family's musical talents—in 1890 she was a member of the Bach Choir and of Barnaby's Royal Choral Society—it is tempting to see her as the author of an anonymous series on the early musicians Guido Aretino, Josquin des Pres, Christopher Tye, and Thomas Tallis that ran in the early issues of the *Barnacle*. Her name disappears from the circulation list in the summer of 1865 (vol. 8), although she may well have seen subsequent issues since her relative M. Pridham (Hedgerose) makes her appearance at about this time.

Helmore would have known Miss Hullah, whose name appears once only (summer 1865). The nomenclature implies that she was the eldest daughter of the "rather numerous family" resulting from the first marriage of John Hullah, an inventor of the tonic sol-fa notation that opened choral singing to the Victorian masses.[7] John Hullah too had taught at Saint Mark's, and was a strong advocate of women's rights in general and education in particular while simultaneously belonging to the Tractarian circle of Keble, William Butterfield, George Richmond, and John Henry Newman, who influenced his religious views. He encouraged his eldest daughter, Caroline (born c. 1840), presumably the Miss Hullah of the 1865 *Barnacle*, to develop her artistic talents; for a time she studied under Holman Hunt and by 1865 was becoming a successful, independent professional painter and illustrator. At twenty-six Caroline Hullah was older than the other *Barnacle* contributors, however, and by reason of her age, her established professional status, and her single mention in the magazine, she stands rather on the fringes of the group.

From this nucleus of London contributors, the *Barnacle* circle reached out to the Martyns of Torquay; the Fursdons of The Vicarage, Dawlish, and later of Tiverton (they probably used the pen names Irene and Glowworm); and the Anderson Morsheads of Plympton. A. E. M. (Mary) Anderson Morshead, writing as Bog Oak, came relatively late to the *Barnacle* scene. Her first contribution dates from summer 1866, and by 1868 she was off to South Africa to work as a missionary under Bishop Grey. Bog Oak made a tremendous impact on the *Barnacle* with her vivid sketches and cartoons, quite unlike the carefully detailed productions of the other illustrators, and her poems and articles, jokes and satires. More than any other contributor, Morshead displayed the "playfulness" that so appealed to Yonge. Unlike several of the other Goslings, Bog Oak never became a professional writer; she was probably one of those gifted individuals who, without ever reaching a wider public, produce end-of-term shows and school magazine verses enshrining the in-jokes of a like-minded group. She and Yonge remained lifelong friends and correspondents, and years later Morshead helped her mentor with the church history essay society attached to the *Monthly Packet*. Writing to Christabel Coleridge after the novelist's death, Bog Oak commented, "It is a great pleasure to be able to say something of her to whom I owe almost more than to anyone of the highest, best and loveliest influences of my life!" (qtd. in *Yonge* 293–94).

As prolific as Bog Oak, and perhaps as talented, was Gurgoyle, who had been a contributor from the first issue. She designed all the covers and was both a skillful illustrator and the author of fiction, verse, articles, translations, and riddles. Christabel Coleridge's list shows that Gurgoyle was Alice Mary Coleridge, a young cousin of Mildred Coleridge's father. Her address was "The College, Hurstpierpoint"; Saint John's College had been founded in 1853 as the first of the "public schools for the middle classes" organized by Nathaniel Woodard to further the social and educational ideals of the Oxford Movement. Alice was being brought up by an elder sister and her husband, Dr. Lowe, the headmaster of the college. This educational background, which led Christabel Coleridge to say that "she had a boy's education" (Rice 155), eventually enabled her appointment in 1873 as lady warden of Saint Anne's, Abbots Bromley, the first Woodard school for girls. So thoroughly was Alice Coleridge imbued with High Church ideals that

> contact with Miss Coleridge meant such direct contact with the Tractarians that it was comparable to being brought up at the feet of Mr. Keble. . . . Miss Coleridge was brought up upon Miss Yonge's novels, and no doubt they helped to mould her character and to call forth her sense of vocation; indeed she was wont to say that *The Pillars of the House* had a very great influence upon her life. (Rice 70, 3)

Like Christabel Coleridge, and indeed like such Yonge heroines as Ethel May, in later life Alice Coleridge was to experience conflict between "home duties" and a desire for independent action. Her biographer, Marcia Rice, recorded that

> for some reason she was required to absent herself from Abbots Bromley for a considerable period, and for reasons she evidently thought inadequate. She was greatly tried and wrote thus to a friend, "it is impossible to say how hard it is to keep away when one's whole heart is set upon being at St. Anne's. One feels like being in prison, and every hour is a struggle to be patient and reasonably amiable. I have been told to look upon it as a preparation for death, and a cutting myself off from the things one longs for, and I must try to do so, but oh! it is so hard. Sometimes one thinks that at thirty seven one might choose one's own way of life." (165)

Perhaps not surprisingly, several of the nonfamily Goslings were concentrated in or around Winchester, the cathedral city near Yonge's home
village of Otterbourne. During the 1860s the author enjoyed an intimate
friendship with the family of Dr. George Moberly, headmaster of Winchester College. Often likened to the Mays of *The Daisy Chain*, the fifteen
Moberly children included eight daughters, all of whom visited and corresponded with Yonge. Five of these sisters married, four of them to Anglican
clergymen. Of the three unmarried Moberlys, only Yonge's goddaughter
Annie broke away from the role of "home daughter"; like Alice Coleridge,
Annie found that her upbringing in a boys' public school qualified her
for leadership in women's education, and she became the first principal of
Saint Hugh's College, Oxford.[8] The representative Moberly on the *Barnacle* circulation list is Miss E. Moberly, probably Humble Bee. Although
the initial could signify Edith, it is more likely to stand for Emily Frances,
the sister who was always closest to Yonge. Nineteen when the first *Barnacle* appeared, she married William Awdry in 1868 and published several
books both for children and general readers, one of them (*The Miz Maze*,
1883) in collaboration with Yonge, Christabel Coleridge, and others.

Other Winchester Goslings were members of the Johns family, again a
well-known clerical and educational household. Dr. C. A. Johns, the head
of the family (although not necessarily the father of the two Johns Goslings), had been a colleague of Derwent Coleridge before the latter's move
to Chelsea. Johns was a celebrated naturalist, as was his son Dr. E. F. Johns,
and both were headmasters of Winton House, the preparatory school
founded by the elder Johns on the outskirts of Winchester. Interestingly,
C. A. Johns was known locally for his Broad Church views; he cannot be
counted as a Tractarian. Nevertheless, the Johnses were on visiting terms
with Yonge. The two Johns girls on the *Barnacle* circulation list are Katie,
who helped with the compilation of the magazine, and A. D. Johns (Kittiwake), the most talented of the *Barnacle* artists.

A final member of the Winchester circle was Turkscap, Florence Wilford.
Like the Devonian Frances Peard (Fernseed), this Gosling was recruited
after Mildred Coleridge's defection to set a high standard of contributions
for younger members. Both Wilford and Peard were established writers of
fiction for the young when, in the late 1860s, Yonge wrote to Peard,

> You must know that Goosedom has had a shock and a revolution,
> chiefly induced by Mildred Coleridge having no time for it, and her
> aunt therefore losing her interest in it. So after having very nearly bro-

ken up, we are beginning again in a more brilliant manner, and the thing is, would you condescend to be a Gosling? (Harris 51)

Christabel and Alice Coleridge had "kept on," and the group was "very glad to catch Florence Wilford" (Harris 51).

The remaining Goslings were based mainly in the south and west of England, again usually emanating from clerical families. Almost the only Midlander was Margaret Lonsdale, daughter of the Bishop of Lichfield; the latter was an Eton contemporary of Mildred's father. By the end of the extant series of the *Barnacle,* solitary contributors hailed from Lancashire and Scotland, while two Anglo-Irish girls, Miss Synge and Miss E. Maconchy (appropriately dubbed Shamrock and Potatoe [sic]), wrote from Chelsea and Torquay respectively.

Before leaving the subject of the contributors, it is important to acknowledge the large part Yonge herself played in the production of the magazine. Just as she was editor of the *Monthly Packet,* as Mother Goose she kept a firm hand on the running of the manuscript magazine. In such historical stories as *The Caged Lion* (1870), Yonge covers even more pages and gets more words to the line than Christabel Coleridge. She also contributed verses—some quite ingenious, such as "A Literary Squabble on the Pronunciation of Monckton Milnes' Title" (which, being Lord Houghton, lent itself to considerable punning on the vagaries of English spelling)—plus puzzles, articles, and at times editorials. All this came at a period when she was occupied by the *Monthly Packet* and by the production of about fifteen books, including two major works of fiction. Given Coleridge's observation that "at this time her health was less good than it had been or than it afterwards became," presumably because Yonge was experiencing menopause, one can only admire her industry and stamina (*Yonge* 227).

This overview should serve to clarify the social strata represented by the *Barnacle* contributors. Despite some differences of status, possible professional disagreements, and variation in the shades of religious opinion within the established Anglican community, the evidence suggests a tightly knit group, often interrelated, with whom Yonge shared cultural assumptions, social beliefs, and artistic standards. Given the large size of her reading public, this unity of background could not hold good for numbers of her actual readers; but certainly the *Barnacle* contributors and their families were of the solid Anglican groups from whom Yonge drew the experiences that helped to fashion her fictive world—an assumption fully borne out by an examination of the contents of the twelve surviving volumes of the

Barnacle. One might also argue the converse: that in their experiences as home daughters, novelists, Church stalwarts, or educators, many former Goslings found themselves leading lives already imaged by those of Yonge and her heroines.

Yonge's editorial in the September 1863 issue of the *Barnacle* suggested that

> we know that our own immediate public, though it will criticize its own Gosling's productions most severely[,] will in its secret soul prefer them to all the rest, or if their imperfection be palpable, at least think them "next best" to the acknowledged superior.

This first editorial also established the principle on which the circulation order was based: "The principal contributors have the first turn, on the acknowledged principle that nothing is so interesting as what one knows before and has written oneself," a scheme that has helped in identifying contributors. Yonge also operated a system of selection (in March 1865 [vol. 7] "a couple of drawings have been left out as rather too commonplace"), commendation ("The story by Firefly's friend is very promising"), and criticism ("We own ourselves to be less than satisfied with the lament over the Alabama"). Further, she was a strong literary influence on the contributors, who were apparently avid readers of her work: the cover for Christmas 1864 shows delighted Goslings receiving gifts of books, all by Yonge, from a splendid Christmas tree. *A Book of Golden Deeds* (1864) would seem to be a favorite, with *Heartsease* (1854) and bound volumes of the *Monthly Packet* also visible.

In content, the *Barnacle* resembled contemporaneous issues of the *Monthly Packet.* Both magazines contained a significant minority of items that were not original, being translations (mostly from German or Italian) or quotations from printed sources considered worthy of a wider public. The rest of the contents were in both cases a mixture of fiction, usually serialized; nonfiction; and verses and anecdotes. There are some differences; for example, the *Monthly Packet* carried book reviews and more directly religious material than the *Barnacle,* which substituted puzzles and material of interest to Goslings only. A major advantage the *Barnacle* enjoyed was the ability to display original illustrations and decorations, often in color and sometimes of high quality; it looked much more attractive than the *Monthly Packet.*

Serialized fiction constituted a major part of every issue of the *Barnacle.* Besides Yonge's contributions, Christabel Coleridge almost always had a story in progress, and one of the other Goslings was usually represented. Coleridge was the most prolific author, however, and her fiction, like that of the majority of contributors, was historical. In fact the contents of the *Barnacle* overall suggest that the Goslings shared with Yonge an interest amounting almost to an obsession with the past. Here gender explains much. The restricted lives of Yonge and most of the Goslings—and they were restricted, if only by an internalized conception of women as subordinate or even inferior—could be extended by an imaginative examination of history, an area both acceptable as serious study and liberating when fantasy and imagination shared in the re-creation of events. In reconstructing the past, novelist and student alike would find an area of power and control within the framework of accepted "facts," just as the female writer of didactic contemporary fiction would find a means of fulfillment sanctioned by social and theological acceptance of woman's role as teacher. The historical novel might also provide a space in which to act out personal fantasies freed from the bonds of typical nineteenth-century existence.

An example of the liberating function of historical fiction is Christabel Coleridge's *Giftie the Changeling* (vol. 17, 1867). Set in "the early years of Henry VIII," the story features an elfin heroine ("a not ungraceful figure, yet weird and strange, with her fair shaggy hair and her deep set eyes") whose failure to conform to the female stereotype of any period known to the author gives rise to the belief, shared by Giftie and those around her, that she is under the influence of evil powers. Rehabilitation comes in the shape of a noble youth whose ministrations enable her to take her rightful place as the beloved daughter of the household that had formerly rejected her. Hugh sees her simply as an uncouth, shy child whom he teaches to read and encourages to conduct herself in a "maidenlike" manner. Significantly, it is only when Giftie decides to "do her hair and to practice sewing and demean herself silently and quietly" that she is accepted into society as a "real" woman rather than a malevolent changeling. Later, hints the story (sadly, it is incomplete), Giftie will repay Hugh's kindness by acts of bravery that will make her an achiever in both male and female spheres.[9] Coleridge's story is redolent with the pressures of growing up in a clerical household dominated by an elderly, eminent father and by the Coleridge tradition of worldly and moral achievement.

Giftie is set in the early sixteenth century and Coleridge's first extant published work, *Lady Betty* (1870; *Barnacle* 1867), in the eighteenth. Other periods particularly favored by the Goslings were the later Middle Ages, the Civil War, and the Elizabethan—or rather the Armada—epoch. Generally the standard of historical knowledge seems high. Cricket (Elizabeth Yonge) does introduce some unlikely details into *Shirley Hall* (vol. 9, Christmas 1865), where lack of money for modern improvements has caused rush-strewn floors and a center-floor hearth to linger on into the 1640s, but overall the young women have done their background reading—as might be expected, given the emphasis placed on education by the families to which many of them belonged. As will become clear later in this essay, a preoccupation with history, whose moral and patriotic implications are also highlighted in Yonge's own historical works, likewise informs much of the nonfictional *Barnacle* material.

Leaving aside the fiction contributed by Mother Goose herself and by the already established novelists Fernseed (Peard) and Turkscap (Wilford), five examples of fiction set in the mid-nineteenth century remain, although unfortunately not all of these are complete. For instance, *Nell Abercrombie's Tale* (vol. 13, Christmas 1866) is a gripping Scottish ghost story, attractively illustrated.[10] It is frustrating to read in its surviving form, however, as the last page is missing, taking with it both the conclusion of the story and the author's name. Perhaps it came from Thistle, the Edinburgh Gosling. Of the four remaining novels, *The Painter's Child, What Is Really Noble?, A Story of Four Months,* and *Dean Pollock's Granddaughters,* all but the first show strong signs of influence from Yonge's novels—and all four reveal talent and intelligence.

The Painter's Child, which began in volume 2 (Christmas 1863), is both delightful and psychologically revealing. It was written by Ladyfern, a major contributor to the early issues, whose last contribution appeared in volume 11 (summer 1866); she was a prolific collector of games, puzzles, and verses, but *The Painter's Child* was her only attempt at fiction. William Leicester, the painter of the title, is far from rich—"It was a bad time of year now for selling pictures"—and his home is humble "yet the home of a gentleman." A widower, he lives with his daughter, Aurora, aged five at the opening of the tale, and their faithful and humble servant, Deborah. The late Mrs. Leicester, whose likeness is preserved in a large allegorical painting, came, as Aurora learns, from a noble house Mr. Leicester had visited in order to copy some pictures. Short of inspiration for a work of his own, the young painter prayed for a glimpse of a suitably angelic model, at which point his future wife happened to pass along the corridor: "The painter, transfixed, could only mutter to himself, 'The answer—so soon!'" Love and marriage followed, but the gently nurtured bride did not long survive the hardships of the artist's lodgings, leaving Aurora "at an age when most children are in the nursery or at best but newly introduced into the schoolroom . . . [to be] looked to by her father for sympathy as well as rational companionship."

As the story progresses, Aurora grows older but very little taller; her hairstyle is almost the only attribute that changes between the ages of seven and twelve. Meanwhile, her father is assailed by "the slow creeping hand of chill poverty" (vol. 5), especially after being robbed on his way home from the savings bank whence he has just withdrawn his last one hundred pounds. (The unlikelihood of his handling this relatively large sum indicates that Ladyfern herself had little experience of "chill poverty.") To add insult to injury, Mr. Leicester wanders into an art auction to find a picture, commissioned from him for a small sum by an unscrupulous dealer, being "knocked down as a genuine Rubens" for one hundred and fifty guineas. Losing heart, the artist sinks into weakness and despair despite Aurora's efforts to rouse him in "the little womanly tone she sometimes used when doing him good against his will." Going without food for several hours, he finally collapses: " 'My little one,' he murmured faintly, 'I think I am going to die.' " At the beginning of his illness, Mr. Leicester had been working on a painting that was to bring in a reasonable amount of money, and as he lies helpless the date set for its completion and delivery draws closer. Approaching the canvas, Aurora completes it with "rapid masterly strokes," at last "exclaiming below her breath, 'I can do it!' " Rising from his sickbed, her admiring father surveys her work. " 'My child,' he said in a low voice, 'do you know what is this spirit which is within you—it is not mere cleverness—it is more than talent—it is genius, a great holy gift of the soul' " (vol. 5; this religious reference indicates the author's serious motives).

The Painter's Child is a splendid piece of wish-fulfillment. Aurora is the only daughter of a widowed father, his only companion—at once child and woman, protected and protecting, at last saving the beloved object by the exercise of a gift that brings forth his homage and admiration. The writer of this story was perhaps rather younger than some of the Goslings and certainly less sophisticated; her heroine, with whom she clearly identifies, is a child rather than a young lady, and there is obvious naïveté in her description of a lifestyle so different from her own. But the story is effective because it is a retelling of the almost universal fantasy of saving a beloved person from danger or distress. Moreover, Aurora's beloved is her father, a significant relationship in view of the general Gosling membership of households headed by eminent or dominant fathers.

The other three contemporary stories are more polished if slightly less
memorable productions. The first to appear was *What Is Really Noble?*, by
Firefly's friend (vols. 7–8, spring 1865–Christmas 1866). Although the end
is unfortunately missing, enough of the novel exists to suggest why Yonge
considered it "promising." Once again a widowed father takes center stage:
Mr. Davidson

> was a man by no means without feeling, but circumstances had not
> been such as to soften a character naturally rough and hard, and he was
> more feared than loved by his children—with the exception of little
> Nellie who was his pet and plaything. He was not an unkind father—
> he worked hard for his children and was fond of them in his own way,
> but though a man of ability he had not much education, or refinement
> of feeling and he had a temper of his own as well, so that his good
> qualities (and he had some very solid ones) were not much appreciated
> by his children. (vol. 7)

As this introduction suggests, *What Is Really Noble?* is concerned less
with external happenings than with the protagonists' reactions to them.
Mr. Davidson is (just) a gentleman, and although his family lives in near-
squalor with "greasy cushions" and "a cracked mirror," this is due to poor
management rather than real poverty. He is too busy to spend much time
with his family, headed by two girls reminiscent of Kate and Emmeline in
Yonge's *The Castle Builders* (1854). The elder Davidson girl, Sybil, is the
real heroine of the novel as she struggles to abandon her habits of day-
dreaming and romancing in order to take her place as a valuable, helpful
member of the family, attending to the home duties that are more "Really
Noble" than reading poetry and imagining great deeds. Her main ally
within the family is "Emma, a clumsy looking, thickset girl of twelve,
slightly lame, and an ugly likeness of Sybil, only with a larger face, and a
cross, heavy, fretful expression," who hides deep feelings beneath an apparent reserve. She is clearly a reworking of Sophie in Yonge's *The Young
Stepmother*. Another ally is the new vicar. Before his arrival Redpond is a
spiritual desert:

> the Sunday service was generally performed once in the day . . . by
> some stranger clergyman who drove in in time to put on his surplice
> before the bells stopped, and despatched as soon as the congregation
> were safe out of church, so the poor of Redpond had consequently had

but little to do with gentry, or educated people, and were, for the most part, a rough, blunt, unmannerly set. (vol. 7)

To cure this general spiritual malaise, the vicar brings with him new, presumably Tractarian ideas—he institutes a daily service, strongly suggestive of Oxford Movement influence.

Sybil's moral struggles are focused on her father's decision to marry again. Mrs. Mercer, his second wife, is a good-natured, plump, vulgar caricature of a woman who is ignorant of grammar, uses malapropisms, and seduces the younger Davidsons with generous slices of plum cake. Sybil can remember their "own Mamma," who came from an entirely different class, being "the daughter of a clergyman who was pretty and good, but not clever and quite unfitted for the struggling life her marriage doomed her to." In Sybil's eyes, "better we had none of us been born—better to be in one's grave before that dreadful woman comes here to make my life a misery to me, and to insult our Mother's memory." Sybil's initially unsuccessful attempts to adjust to her father's remarriage take up the first four (lengthy) chapters; chapter 4 appeared in volume 13 (Christmas 1866); there is no episode in volume 14, and presumably the tale was completed in the now missing volumes 15 and 16. As it stands, the story ends with an announcement familiar to readers of Victorian fiction: "Nellie's so ill, so very, very ill, and Nurse says she is sure it is the scarlet fever!" One is left wondering how the Davidson family will cope with the epidemic that is clearly about to break out.

A remarriage is also at the heart of another incomplete novel, *Dean Pollock's Granddaughters* (vol. 17, 1867). This time it is the girls' mother who remarries, taking as her second husband a bluff old general who has been captivated by her "clear, cold, proud kind of beauty—brilliant and hard as a diamond—scarcely thirty nine years old, her ten years of widowhood had failed to produce any blemish on her smooth, broad brow, and her hair was just as bright and brown as ever." Lilly and her virtuous elder sister, Alethea, like the pairs of contrasted sisters in Yonge's *The Castle Builders* and the previously quoted *Barnacle* serial *What Is Really Noble?*, have to adjust to a changed life with a remarried parent and his or her new partner. Reluctant to leave the Deanery, "the two sisters . . . worked themselves up into a state of indignant grief, and dislike to everything they were to meet at Felsham," their new home. Lilly's exaggerated response, however, is not fully shared by Alethea, who is gifted with "humility, patience and

unselfishness." She is also perceptive, saying of her cousin Heathcote, "It
is so provoking in him when we know how much good sense and good
nature he really has, to see him behaving himself like a conceited shallow-
brained goose," a comment that makes him a close relative of Yonge's own
favorite, Louis FitzJocelyn of *Dynevor Terrace* (1857). Once at Felsham,
where they meet the general's neglected son Harry and wonder about the
former occupant of their room with its "photographs of sacred subjects"
and its "white marble cross," Alethea "could not feel the behaviour she
and Lilian had previously agreed upon, to be either dutiful or maidenly."
Much to Lilly's disgust, her sister's "right and ladylike feeling" prompts
her to be at least civil to their stepfather.

Unfortunately, the surviving version of the story ends at this early stage,
with characters and situations sketched in and ready to develop. The identity of the author, who signed her work only with a monogram combined
apparently of Y, I, J, and M, remains a mystery, and an especially provoking one as she was clearly familiar with Winchester ("an old mulberry tree
in the Deanery garden, and the lamp over the Close archway") and the
Yonge circle (apparent from her use of the current names "Alethea" and
"Heathcote").

Dean Pollock's Granddaughters begins on the same folded sheet of paper
as the conclusion of this Gosling's previous novel, *A Tale of Four Months*
(vol. 17). This has the distinction of being the most nearly complete of the
three longer contemporary serials, with only one episode (describing a skating party) missing. In one sense *A Tale of Four Months* is of the same genre
as Yonge's *Abbeychurch* (1844), with very little happening outwardly and
a great deal going on within—a validation, perhaps, of typical middle-
class female experience as meaningful and even absorbing. Nevertheless,
it moves away from obsessive observation of parent/child relationships to
present a love story dependent on the agonies of teenage passion: " 'I must
see him, I must, I must,' she repeated over and over again in tremulous excitement." "Alas for Matty" (adds the author quickly), "the last fortnight
had done irreparable mischief" (vol. 17).

In *A Tale of Four Months* the contrasted girls are the cousins Emily and
Matty. Emily, like Lilly neither irredeemably fast nor eminently virtuous,[11]
is a witty rattle, aware of her own idleness and halfheartedly striving after
better things:

> I sleep away the mornings till past eight o'clock, I come down and frit-
> ter away an hour or two over breakfast and little nonsensical things,

talk and letters and so on. Then if I feel inclined I practice a little, or
loiter about in the garden, and do a little worsted work till luncheon.
And then I spend the afternoon in riding or paying visits, and after dinner employ myself with bagatelle or a novel . . . I suppose if I were to
marry or die you would miss me a little,

she concludes (vol. 11). Interestingly, serials in the *Monthly Packet* often
equate death and marriage as provoking equal grief in the families of young
females.

Matty, on the other hand, is the universally useful eldest child of a large
clerical family. She looks after the younger children, teaches Sunday school,
sews for the poor, and cuts out shirts for her six brothers, about whom
she worries constantly: "No one guessed at half the love and thought that
Matty gave to her brothers." Significantly, she tells Emily, "I don't believe
one person has more duties than another: we *must* all have enough to
do to fill our life-time if only we find it out" (vol. 11). "Finding it out"
must have been one of the preoccupations of Gosling home daughters.
Matty's development over the four months of the title into the "clear-
headed, tender-hearted woman" of the author's ideal is a major theme of
the story.

Before the novel opens, Matty has spent a year away at school, but "her
eyes now trained for two years in her sober parsonage home saw things
in another light than when in continual contact with the schoolroom fri-
volities"; the author shares Yonge's low opinion of the moral tone of girls'
schools. Matty at seventeen now enjoys "books she had once thought dry"
and is both refined and dutiful.

Her status as the moral daughter is defined via her relationships with
her brothers and her father: "The boys little imagined how their sister's
tender conscience shrank at the thoughtless speeches and slight irrever-
ences which other people would scarcely have noticed" (vol. 14). When
she is provoked into mild retaliation by her favorite brother's thoughtlessness, her conscience is tortured until she can seek him out and apologize.
As for Papa, "Papa knows best. It is indeed a happy home where this is
the family motto." Ever considerate, Matty "has regard for the servants'
evening hours of rest" and sweeps up the mess resulting from putting up
the family Christmas decorations, meanwhile cross-examining herself as
to whether she has transgressed the rules of etiquette on an afternoon visit.
Alone in her bedroom, she continues to brood: "I have nothing to make me
unhappy—but myself. And I am not unhappy either, I don't think I under-

stand myself—can it be right to fix one's thoughts so much on oneself? I wonder if any one else does it" (vol. 14). In this connection, the author is able to quote the official Keble line on introspection:

> Telling oneself on every possible occasion that one is vain is not the most successful mode of conquering the fault. Perhaps the best way would be to think as little as possible of either our merits or our faults, and give ourselves rather to practice love and faith and prayer. (vol. 14)

A Tale of Four Months also shows an awareness, similar to that taught by the *Monthly Packet*, of class differences and responsibilities. Discussing that typically Tractarian activity, church Christmas decorating, Matty and Emily decry the evils of "talking and laughing" inside the church; but, says Emily, such unseemly behavior can be avoided if the gentry take the lead: "most of your workers are the tradespeople's daughters, and they would not talk if we did not, and you have Aunt Mary and Lady Helen St. Leger for a head" (vol. 11). Again, when Seaford Wye arrives on the scene, Matty frequently describes him as "gentlemanly"; her meaning is indicated when Emily teases her for using the word "respectable," saying, "The baker is respectable." "You know I don't mean that sort of respectable [—I mean] . . . a gentleman," responds Matty (vol. 11).

It is the gentlemanly Seaford who provides the romantic interest. An undergraduate of Magdalen College, Oxford, Seaford means to give up dancing when he is ordained, but meanwhile he can enjoy the Christmas ball, taking Matty first to supper and then to gaze at the stars before inviting her to inspect some photographs of Oxford in his room—where "Alas! Open within the work of study lay a well-worn Waverley novel." Seaford has read *Framley Parsonage* as well as Scott and enjoys intellectual conversations with Matty's father:

> These conversations Matty delighted in. She never took part in them herself but would sit in the background with her work, watching and listening, generally agreeing with Seaford when he spoke, but often disappointed by bearing her father differ—and then would try to reconcile the two opinions in her own mind, a thing not always easy to do. For she had learned to like her new acquaintance very much, and wished to believe him right in all things, beginning for the first time to break through the long-established creed that everyone who did not think the same as Papa must be in the wrong. (vol. 14)

Seaford's opinions include his preferences in women: "Women were intended to have soft hearts—and if they harden them and despise little
weaknesses they only grow coarse and loud-voiced. I do think a strong-
minded independent woman is the most intensely detestable thing in the
world" (vol. 17). Emily, who is at least one degree nearer independence than
Matty, discovers that Seaford (evidently a devotee of the new art of photography) treasures the photo of a lovely girl he has met in Oxford. Matty's
reception of this news coincides with Seaford's departure for Oxford and
the outbreak of whooping cough in the parsonage. Having reproached herself for being "as bad as any silly girl in a novel," Matty applies herself
to her home duties, while still thinking "gravely" of Seaford. Her "hope
deferred" makes her "more and more womanly," until at last she passes

> out of a merry childhood into a real thoughtful life. . . [. S]he never
> forgot his name in her prayers, and never failed to add a petition, in un-
> feigned love, for her who should one day be his wife. She did not know
> for many years that she had been praying for herself. (vol. 17)

Matty's patience is rewarded in the novel's closing sentence.

Yonge is known to have disapproved of stories focused on romantic attachments, but presumably she passed *A Tale of Four Months* because of
its highly moral treatment of the subject. The Tractarian tone is marked
throughout, for Matty does and says almost all the right things; yet personal experience seems to gleam through her attempts to understand herself, to determine her mission in life, and to cope with her "tremulous" love
for the wooden Seaford. Furthermore, as well as adopting Yonge's social
and religious values, the author of *A Tale of Four Months* also shared her
interest in clothes, giving ribbon-by-ribbon accounts of the costumes made
"on Lady Bentley's sewing machine," some of which are reproduced in the
illustrations.

Although fiction formed a large part of the *Barnacle,* there was room
for a variety of other material. Like the *Monthly Packet,* the manuscript
magazine relied heavily on accounts of travels and visits to places of interest both at home and abroad. These came in various forms, such as letters,
journals, or straight descriptions, usually illustrated and always enlivened
by a personal touch sometimes lacking in the *Monthly Packet.* Both the
places visited and the reporters' reactions to them merit a brief summary.

Volume 1 includes illustrated excerpts from Indian letters received by the
contributor; an account of a visit to the United Service Museum in Lon-

don, with a commentary full of admiration for the "valour" of the armed
services; and an open letter from Glowworm about a recent visit to London, where she stayed with her uncle's family near Hyde Park. This last
paints a vivid picture of fashionable London in the early 1860s, from the
early morning "London cries . . . in full force [with] a hurdy gurdy in the
distance," to sightseeing at "St. Paul's Cathedral, which I think is out and
out the ugliest place I ever saw," to cultural visits to the Royal Academy
("*The Wolf's Den* by Millais is delightful, as also *My First Sermon* by the
same painter, only I think 'my' stockings are rather too red") and performances of *Il Trovatore* and *Figlia del Reggimento*. The highlight of the trip,
however, was an Italian recital by the "tragedienne" Kristori: "as Kristori was on her way to her carriage, we met her in a narrow passage and
thanked her in her native tongue, and she shook hands with us each in a
most enchanting manner, saying 'Grazie, Grazie.' "

Glowworm was the *Barnacle*'s chief travel writer; her account of London is followed by descriptions of Corfu (vol. 2), Rutland (the Old House
at Market Overton appears in vol. 5), H.M.S. *Achilles* (vol. 6), and New
Quay (vol. 7). The penultimate report on "one of the new ironclads" reveals
both a taste for romance and a conscientious desire to give contemporary technological advances their due. Like Yonge, Glowworm was not a
wholehearted admirer of modern technology; having begun by praising the
traditional wooden ships, she remarks that "we look and look, at the huge
mass of iron, for some redeeming point." The latter was evidently not to
be found in "a massive, black, iron bas-relief of Achilles with a very thick
nose, surrounded with enormous wreaths, and devices of laurel," although
a sketch of this is included as the most picturesque detail available. Factual
information is also provided. Glowworm notes that the *Achilles* is "a four
masted ship. The masts even of iron, hollowed however, so as to admit of
a sailor climbing up inside. It is a 24 gun ship, on the upper deck there
were four great Armstrong guns, with piles of the new shaped missiles, at
the sides." She then offers an account of the newest gadgets: "various, and
charming, were the little contrivances in different parts of the ship," among
them "Electric Telegraphs which shut and opened little doors, showing different messages to the man at the wheel." The visit ended with a descent
to the "Domdaniel caverns" of the engine room (a reference to Robert
Southey's *Thalaba*), which "made some of the party feel faint." The *Barnacle*'s occasional male contributors were also represented in this volume
by "Christmas Day in Ithaca," by W. Bingham Wright, an army officer.

The *Barnacle*'s travel writing tended to appeal either to patriotism or to piety. Georgina Battiscombe, for instance, notes the idiosyncratic nature of Rowan Tree's "My Oxford Journal" (vol. 7; Battiscombe, *Life* 107), in which, significantly, the highlight was a visit to Littlemore, where she mused on "the first incumbent," Newman:

> Surely at times amidst the din of the Great City where he now lives and amidst the gaudy splendour of Churches of his own Communion he must look back with affectionate remembrances of this peaceful English house and of the exquisite taste and beauty of the Church in which he once ministered.

Likewise, Kittiwake reported from Cannes in volume 8 (Christmas 1865) that she filled her days not only with reading, practicing her music, walking, and sketching,[12] but also with attending "the daily service in our home-like little English Church." Although she had gone to Cannes for her health, Kittiwake was quite energetic; after a stiff climb

> we sat down on the rocks and sang some of Mendelssohn's part songs with a tuning fork, but there was a tremendous wind blowing so that not one of the performers could hear the rest and the effect, to windward, must have been fine. But we enjoyed the fun of clinging to our dangerous positions (for the rocks overhung a deep gorge) and one of the girls lost her hat. To make use of an expression used by one of the young ladies, the mountains were "quite past description"! Seriously, I should have liked to be quiet a little, to have a look at the glorious snowy Alps with the pink of the "afterglow" on their beautifully shaped peaks and the shadows resting lightly in their clefts and ravines in a lovely blending of delicate blues and greens—and the soft colour of the valleys of olives at our feet, too, formed a beautiful background for a handsome bronzed mountaineer who passed down the path, his rich colour and dark, long Vandyke-like hair contrasting well with his blue clothes and the usual scarlet sash, and the scarlet tassels on his mule's harness. Perhaps I had better not describe too closely, or I shall come to the garlic, which always makes one think how exceedingly picturesque and delightful these people are *at a distance!*

I have quoted this letter at length because it illustrates so clearly the spirit of much of the *Barnacle* travel writing, with its personal tone, its romantic love of beauty, and its touch of unsophisticated xenophobia.

Volume 8 also contained part 1 of an anonymous series, *A Few Notes on a Tour Abroad,* which presumably continued in the missing issues. The existing section deals mostly with the Rhineland and is illustrated with photographs, evidently commercially produced and purchased on the spot. (One shows the "new tubular bridge" across the Rhine from Deutz to Cologne.) Writing in 1865, the traveler noted

> signs of the gradual decay of national ideas and prejudices, the consequence of the increasing numbers of mixed travellers enticed from home by the easier means of communication—But, along with its improvements, one cannot but regret to see the decrease of pleasant national peculiarities, such as those of costume and pastoral song.

In practice, however, the same writer complained of her hotel in Cologne that "the company was none of the best—they seemed to be all Germans." A group of Prussian officers came in for particular censure owing to their "noisy" conversation and over-dinner cigars. Even worse, on another occasion she was forced to stay in a "secondrate" hotel where "we were received with much bowing and scraping into its unclean apartments." But there was a touch of home:

> The English Service on Sundays is held in a room in the English Consul's house, and as this was not until eleven am we first went to the Cathedral to witness the ceremony of High Mass, which is performed here with more than ordinary magnificence—the ritual was imposing and the music most exquisite, but we were glad to have our own quiet service to go to in a foreign country.

Like Rowan Tree's remarks on Newman's old home and Kittiwake's depiction of the daily service in Cannes, A Few Notes stresses that the best religion is inseparable from domesticity.

The remaining articles are a mixed collection. They show awareness of current affairs; for instance, an account of "The Marriage of Queen Hedwiga" (of Poland) appeared in 1863, the year of the Polish revolt against Russia, and suggests that

> rumours of European politics must from time to time reach [the Goslings'] ears—And just now, surely, the gallant struggle which the Poles are making, to throw off the yoke of Russia, which they look on as not only barbarous, but heretic, cannot fail to be known to the Goslings, and to claim their sympathies. (vol. 2)

"Queen Hedwiga" is also a good example of the regular articles on famous women of the past who presented "a very safe example for Goslings to follow, in self-denial, and quick discharge of duty, in the state of life to which God had called" them—a point illustrating why history should have been considered a suitable subject for girls' interest. Other informative articles covered music; painting, with a series on medieval illumination providing dazzlingly professional illustrations; literature; and natural history. Conspicuously rare were items on mathematical subjects (there is only one on arithmetical puzzles, by E. C. Dundas in vol. 2) and unadulterated religious teaching (again limited to one by Dundas, who had "lately learnt many useful lessons [on duty in common things] from my sewing machine" [vol. 2]). Perhaps, as the author of *A Tale of Four Months* put it, the Goslings "shrank from bringing holy words into common conversation." It was fully accordant with Yonge's principles that the girls should not set themselves up as doctrinal instructors.

The articles were seldom intentionally humorous; wit was generally reserved for verse, although one topical item, Turkscap's essay "The Men and Women of Books" (vol. 17), poked caustic fun at contemporary romantic conventions. Bog Oak, too, produced some splendid pieces of spurious literary criticism, attributing "Cock Robin" plausibly to Shakespeare and "The Great Panjandrum" to George III, while the nursery rhyme "The Old Man of Thessaly" was revealed as "the Prologue of one of the forty three lost comedies of Aristophanes." These *Nursery Classics* (vols. 11, 13, 14, and 17) were all illustrated with spirited cartoons by their author.

As I have suggested, there was a great deal of verse, both serious and amusing, in the *Barnacle*. The best light verse was that of Bog Oak. Mostly it was full of personal allusions aimed at the Goslings, but at times it was more general, as in "The Distressed Damsel" (vol. 17), whose head was turned by reading romantic novels about knights, squires, and damsels while more solid reading "lay upon the shelf,"

> With Goldsmith, Clarendon and Hume,
> Macaulay and Miss Strickland's *Queens*,
> With Bacon's *Essays*, Johnstone's [sic] *Lives*,
> Good little books of village scenes,
> Theology in ponderous tomes
> Written by bishops and by deans.

The serious verse consists mainly of historical epics of interminable length and spidery appearance. One of the more accessible efforts is the anonymous "Thoughts of a Cavalier mortally wounded on the field of Preston" (vol. 4, June 1864), complete with a soulful illustration that owes much

to the contemporary Tory iconography of Charles I (see Meisel 239ff).
Generally the cavalier's sentiments are predictable:

> The toil is over now, and I am dying—
> To worlds unknown my soul its flight must wing,
> Among the fallen steeds and warriors lying,
> Gladly I yield my life-blood for my King!

But the eighth stanza has some sympathy for the other side:

> Brave English hearts, a cruel creed believing,
> I dare not judge them, now that death is nigh.
> God will draw the tangled web they're weaving
> Forgive them, maybe, when they come to die.

More topical subjects for verse included the *Alabama* incident and, looking back a few years to 1857, the Indian Mutiny. On the whole, the verses
are more competent than inspired, but the writers had clearly read enough
poetry to give them a practical sense of composition.[13]

A substantial amount of verse was translation work, proof of the emphasis placed on languages in the education of upper-middle-class girls.
German and Italian are more popular than French, with Friedrich Schiller,
F. H. K. de la Motte-Fouqué, and Dante, all Tractarian favorites, well represented. Ladybird also set to music the German original of the "Pilgrim's
Song" from *Sintram*. Classical learning was displayed only by Ladybird
(who is said to be "remarkable" for her knowledge) and Bog Oak. Finally,
a special class of item, including both prose and verse, carried specific
allusions to the Brood, relying for its often ponderous humor on puns and
references to "cackle." Here Bog Oak excelled:

> Ho, Goslings of Old England! Ho, fellow-Goslings! hear
> The deeds of your great ancestors, and cackle loud and clear! . . .
> Wherever unfledged Goslings through Goosedom's bounds run loose,
> Shall be great glee to all who see the form of Mother Goose.

Battiscombe has done less than justice to the *Barnacle,* especially in
her scathing dismissal of the artwork. Visually, the magazine is a delight,
as the contributors often reached a high standard of artistic execution;
"sketching" should not always be dismissed as a "ladylike accomplishment" designed to fritter away leisure hours. Further, the illustrations provide useful evidence of the artists' preoccupations for those who study
nineteenth-century iconography as an expression of cultural assumptions

and images. The *Barnacle* artists' vision of the medieval past is symbolized by the handsome, fully armored knight who stands in a graceful pose gazing meditatively from his battlements (vol. 2). Although Bog Oak dared to laugh at this obsession with the past, it went deep, producing not only historical novels and verse epics, quasi-medieval drawings and watercolor sketches of Elizabethan maidens, but also a more serious study of illumination, literature, and architecture. Like the two upper-class girls of Yonge's *Conversations on the Catechism* (1859) and the protagonists of many of her novels, the Goslings were extremely well read, although in a rather limited range of subjects. Clearly, as was expected of readers of the *Monthly Packet,* they were "educating themselves at home." Girls' schools are stigmatized as frivolous or second rate; home life, so long as one avoids idleness, is a healthier setting for the acquisition of a solid knowledge of languages, history, literature, music, and art.

Reading Yonge's novels would form part of this lifestyle, with its common culture and literary experience based on Scott, Southey, Dante, de la Motte-Fouqué, Schiller, Shakespeare, Edmund Spenser, T. B. Macaulay, and others. The budding novelists of the *Barnacle* were creating worlds based on materials known to Yonge, at the same time incorporating forms and values they had imbibed from her own writing. The culture of girlhood, in other words, was not inevitably dependent on the institution of girls' schools. The Goslings are a perfect example of a group within which ideas and ideals were exchanged through a fiction derived from and embracing experiences already made common by an articulate and self-conscious society—as these girls were, even within a larger and more amorphous group of upper-middle-class Tractarians. Later in the century young women like Alice Coleridge, Mary Morshead, and Christabel Coleridge would have been found within the expanding institutions of women's education. With the disbanding of the Goslings in 1871, Yonge had presided over the training of the last generation of home-educated professional-class and clergy daughters, several of whom went on to become teachers and writers themselves. Their subsequent careers illustrate the common dilemmas of late-nineteenth-century middle-class women: the plight of the home daughter, the struggles of those who sought autonomous lives, the need to adjust to spinsterhood. The *Barnacle* provides a direct and vivid experience of the texture of life for a group of this key generation in their late teens and early twenties.

NOTES

1. The first issue of the *Barnacle* (vol. 1) dates from September 1863 and, thanks to Georgina Battiscombe, who presented her collection to Lady Margaret Hall Library in 1978, is still available for study, together with volumes 2, 4–9, 11, 13–14, and 17. No trace has been found of the other issues, at least two of which (volumes 12 and 15) would seem to have been missing since 1866 and 1867 respectively, causing, as Coleridge complained at the time, "great inconvenience to The Brood" (vol. 13).

2. Material from the *Barnacle* is reproduced by kind permission of the Principal and Fellows of Lady Margaret Hall, Oxford.

3. After her mother's death in 1878, Mildred ran her father's wealthy household and involved herself in various worthy causes including the Anti-Vivisection Society; here she met an able but unreliable adventurer, Charles Warren Adams. Their relationship and eventual marriage in 1885 sparked off a spectacular family quarrel culminating in a series of widely publicized libel actions and a lifelong rift between Mildred and the rest of her family.

4. Christabel Coleridge was the daughter of Samuel Taylor Coleridge's second son, Derwent, who until becoming rector of Hanwell in 1864 was principal of Saint Mark's College, Chelsea, a training college for teachers at National Schools. The district was renowned for its china—hence Christabel's pen name.

5. Derwent Coleridge was likewise an expert on sacred music, and Saint Mark's became the center for a revival of Gregorian plainchant.

6. Another difference between the two was that according to Coleridge's collection of essays *The Daughters Who Have Not Revolted* (1894), she apparently experienced some conflicts in adjusting to her role as a home daughter or "Middle Aged Maid."

7. All information on this family is taken from Frances Hullah's *Life of John Hullah*.

8. For further information on this family, see C. A. E. Moberly's *Dulce Domum*.

9. Although according to a publisher's advertisement *Giftie* was issued by Frederick Warne in 1868, I have been unable to trace a copy, so the ending and even the length of the story remain a mystery. Coleridge may have produced here a tale as long as her first *Barnacle* effort, *Melicent Wardour, or, A Tale of Old Chelsea*, which ran to a total of twenty-six chapters, although the Goslings' historical stories were generally rather shorter.

10. Glowworm and Irene's *An Illustrated Christmas Ghost Story: The Phantom Horses of Devonshire* (vol. 6) furnishes another example of the supernatural, in this instance using a historical rather than contemporary setting.

11. Lilly's frivolity in *Dean Pollock's Granddaughters* is established in the first chapter through her bantering conversation with Heathcote. Such dialogues between young persons of opposite sexes (significantly, usually related to each other),

in which the girls give as good as they get, also appear in Yonge's novels, where they are probably based on the exchanges between the Yonge and Coleridge cousinhood that she is known to have recorded. Both Yonge's and the Goslings' depictions of these scenes illustrate the free verbal interplay possible to even the most proper mid-Victorians within a controlled family setting.

12. Kittiwake's skill as an illustrator surpassed that of any other contributor; her miniature watercolors reach a professional standard. Their deep, rich coloring is particularly striking. There are also pen-and-ink sketches, including one of "the young artist" herself at work, the only contemporary portrait of an individual Gosling. She is wearing a flat hat, snood, and full-skirted dress ending just above the ankle, and she looks about sixteen (or eighteen at most).

13. Inevitably, the less successful efforts raise the occasional unintended smile. In "The Mill Stream," contributed by the sixteen-year-old Gurgoyle in 1864, a disobedient boy plays by the river, heedless of warnings that the Miller's activities are about to make the stream dangerous: "But the wheel is still no longer,— / The pleasant dream has gone; / The Miller has begun his work / And turned the water on."

WORKS CITED

Barnacle. 1863–67.

Battiscombe, Georgina. *Charlotte Mary Yonge: The Story of an Uneventful Life.* London: Constable, 1943.

——— . *John Keble: A Study in Limitations.* London: Constable, 1963.

Coleridge, Christabel Rose. *Charlotte Mary Yonge.* London: Macmillan, 1903.

——— . *The Daughters Who Have Not Revolted.* London: Wells Gardner Darton, 1894.

Harris, Mary J. *Memoir of Frances Mary Peard.* Torquay: W. H. Smith, 1930.

Helmore, Frederick. *Life of the Rev. T. Helmore.* London: Masters, 1891.

Hullah, Frances. *The Life of John Hullah.* London: Longmans, 1880.

Meisel, Martin. *Realizations: Narrative, Pictorial, and Theatrical Arts in Nineteenth-Century England.* Princeton: Princeton UP, 1983.

Moberly, C. A. E. *Dulce Domum.* London: Murray, 1911.

Moberly, Robert Campbell. *Funeral Sermon for Charlotte Mary Yonge.* Eastleigh: Eastleigh Printing Works, 1901.

Monthly Packet. 1851–92.

Rice, Marcia. *The Story of St. Anne's, Abbots Bromley.* Shrewsbury: Wilding and Son, 1947.

Torbay Directory. Jan. 1896.

Yonge, Charlotte. *Womankind.* Serialized in the *Monthly Packet*, 1874–77. London: Macmillan, 1881.

CHRISTINA BOUFIS

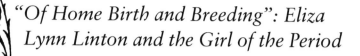

"Of Home Birth and Breeding": Eliza Lynn Linton and the Girl of the Period

Eliza Lynn Linton's essay "The Girl of the Period," published anonymously in 1868 in the *Saturday Review,* both provided a catchphrase and fueled a debate over the representation of women. Linton, the first full-time paid female newspaper writer, had earlier been a champion of women's rights both in her views and in her personal accomplishments. But in "The Girl of the Period" and in other essays that followed it—such as "Foolish Virgins," "Modern Mothers," and "La Femme Passée"—Linton turned "turncoat," attacking modern womanhood in all its phases and advocating instead a return to motherhood and housekeeping as "women's first social duty" (Layard 139; Van Thal 79). Yet none of these essays made as tremendous an impact as "The Girl of the Period." Not only did the essay sell more than forty thousand copies in pamphlet form, it also provoked a cultural sensation, permitting the merchandising of myriad forms of Girl of the Period "offspring" (Helsinger et al. 1:114). There were Girl of the Period almanacs, comedies, waltzes, cartoons, parasols, bonnets, valentines, and a miscellany in the form of a thirty-two-page monthly with articles on French and Irish Girls of the Period (Bevington 112; Colby 17). One journal, *Echoes from the Club,* even changed its name to the *Period* to capitalize on the excitement (Crow 202).

This textual and commercial proliferation suggests a need to codify and contain "representative" woman; it also points to a general concern about England's self-definition. Poised on the brink of empire and social transformation, the nation engaged in a public debate on the role of young women in national life. Linton's essay strikes a keynote for a decade anxious over the increasing democratization initiated by the Second Reform Bill of 1867, the expansion of Britain's international influence, the growth of industrial capitalism, and the Woman Question.[1] In addition, the Girl of the Period may be seen as a focal point for fears of class dissolution and societal changes, particularly those involving women's roles, which gained momentum in the latter half of the nineteenth century.

Linton's attack on the Girl of the Period, the "pert modern miss of the sixties" (Colby 17), while certainly one of the decade's most vituperative attacks on women, is not the first of its kind. Rather, it comes at the end of much heated criticism of the manners and morals of the upper-middle-class girl, which also included attacks on the heroines of women's sensational novels. Using Linton's article as a starting point, this essay will discuss the increasingly contentious depiction of the middle-class girl in the 1860s, and then turn by way of example to the sensational fiction of Rhoda Broughton, whose heroines were a possible target for Linton.[2] I suggest that the reactions to Linton's essay demonstrate that regulating the modern girl and controlling her presentation and representation is part of a larger struggle in England for national self-definition. Conflating girlhood with "distinctive national character," in the 1860s the representation of women became a nationalistic—and perhaps jingoistic—enterprise.

Though antifeminist feeling was strong throughout the 1860s, it was young women, as future mothers, who received heightened scrutiny. In 1864, the novelist Dinah Mulock (later Craik) warned that "the rise and fall of nations is mainly dependent on the condition of their women—the mothers, sisters, daughters, wives—who . . . mould . . . the natures, habits, and lives of the men to whom they belong." This being so, Mulock asks, "Does it not behoove us . . . to look a little more closely after our 'girls'?" ("Teens" 219). In this essay, ostensibly a review of a volume of poetry entitled *Thoughts from a Girl's Life*, Mulock acknowledges the "strange conflicts" that occur as a result of living in a transitional age, but when she metonymically identifies teenage girls as symptomatic of all that is most "artificial" in society, she prefigures Linton's conflation of the girl with the period, though in a much less hostile way.

Four years later Linton makes a similar charge and bemoans the fact that Britain can no longer take pride in her women. For according to her, the "modern miss" is no better than the prostitute she seems to model herself after. The Girl of the Period, as Linton portrays her,

> is a creature who dyes her hair and paints her face, as the first articles
> of her personal religion; whose sole idea of life is plenty of fun and luxury; and whose dress is the object of such thought and intellect as she
> possesses. . . . Nothing is too extraordinary and nothing too exaggerated for her vitiated taste. . . . If a sensible fashion lifts the gown out of
> the mud, she raises hers midway to the knee. (340)

Although attacking the way women dress is nothing new, Linton's caustic remarks cap a decade of journalistic debates over extravagant clothing as "one of the prevailing vices of the age" (qtd. in Crow 119). The crinoline, which required extra material to clothe its circumference, was only one of the most obvious signs of increased wealth and display (Crow 119).[3] Many reviewers, including Linton, were fond of linking women's sartorial excess with moral turpitude, and some worried that such lavishness was a sign that the Empire was in decline (Van Thal 83; Oliphant 275).

In addition to the degeneration assumed to result from extravagance in dress, the clothes controversy reveals a breakdown in the symbolic hierarchy that distinguishes the classes. In another anonymous essay in the *Saturday Review,* "Costume and Its Morals," Linton writes that "dress should . . . be individual and symbolic, so as to indicate clearly the position and character which we desire to obtain and hold" (44). Arguing against the "sham" and indecency of modern women's dress, she expresses concern that

> in its symbolism . . . [such artifice] is in the highest degree objectionable, for it not only aims at what is unreal and false, but it simulates that which is positively hateful and meretricious, so that it is difficult now for even a practised eye to distinguish the high-born maiden or matron of Belgravia from the Anonymas who haunt the drive and fill our streets. (44)

The false representation that results from "pinchbeck" in women's clothing threatens not only class distinctions but also the Victorian belief in the moral and aesthetic value of realism: modern clothing "lacks that truthfulness which is, and should be, the base of all that is attractive and beautiful" (44).

At issue here is Linton's concern that the "real value" of women is no longer clearly determined by their presentation. "It comes to be a grave matter of doubt, when a man marries, how much is real of the woman who has become his wife," Linton writes, "or how much of her is her own only in the sense that she has bought . . . it" (45). Women not only "paint and powder," but they delight in display. Linton states that "the female bosom is less the subject of a revelation than the feature of an exhibition" (44). She is further alarmed at the booming trade in false parts, including "hair, teeth, complexion, ears, bosom, [and] figure" (45).

One may see in this stridency a concern with both artifice and the possibility that women's outward display will be misconstrued as "reality." Linton points to a troubling aspect of the growth of such novel cosmetics— namely that they will alter the "real value" of womanhood itself. In many ways this concern with consumerism invites comparison with the growth of the commodity under industrial capitalism. Britain in the 1860s witnessed increased consumption, monetary expansion, and the evolution of the term "capitalism" into common currency (Weeks 21). But while there were many credit booms fostered by overspeculation in the cotton industry, there were also credit busts (particularly in the last few years of the decade), which were triggered by overinflated values (Harcourt 89). It is tempting to speculate that anxiety over women's conspicuous consumption was a displaced expression of serious economic concern.

Cultural critic Thomas Richards dates the Victorian obsession with the "new commodity culture" even earlier—starting from the 1851 Great Exhibition—and claims that it was then that such feats of production first became "autonomous icons" that "spoke for themselves" (4). In detailing this history, Richards charts the rise of the spectacle and advertising as particularly capitalistic modes of representation. Linton's concern with the sham commodification in women's costume also underlines a fear that such representation will indeed become a (false) system of signification in itself. She appears to be fighting against the degradation of womanhood in general, as if commercialism were endangering women's "real" value. Yet ironically, her diatribe against misrepresentation in women's costumes was apparently based more on beauty advertisements than on life (Bevington 113).

In "The Girl of the Period" Linton also asserts that by imitating the demimonde in dress, young women are turning themselves into commodities. By modeling herself upon her less respectable sisters, the girl of the period approaches them in "manner and feeling," which "leads to slang, bold talk, and fastness; to the love of pleasure and indifference to duty . . . to uselessness at home, dissatisfaction with the monotony of ordinary life . . . in a word, to the worst forms of luxury and selfishness" (340). Linton's tone throughout this essay is harsh; she condemns young women for imitating men in their speech and prostitutes in their dress, and generally for succumbing to a "national madness" (340). The essayist's ostensible target is the upper-middle-class girl, who thinks only of herself and of snaring a wealthy husband for "his house, his carriage, his balance at the banker's, [and] his title" (340).

But Linton is not original in her attack on the (fast) Girl of the Period. In an article of July 1860, the *Saturday Review* had noted that while the tone of society had improved over the last hundred years, it had "generated its own peculiar indecency—the fast girl," whose modesty is a little "off" as she participates in "male" vices—drinking, smoking, and betting (Bevington 109). As an index of civilized society, the modern girl became a scapegoat by which to judge the nation's ills. Furthermore, her "fast" character (a term of opprobrium that until the 1860s was more widely and harshly applied to men) was seen as distinctly a sign of the times. By the 1860s, according to the *Victoria Magazine,* "speed and high pressure every-where [were] the order of the day" ("Latest Crusade" 194). The steam engine, transatlantic telegraph cables, and revolution in printing technology had "transformed society"—but this transformation, the *Victoria* found, was having an adverse effect on both "individual and ultimately national character," permitting little time for "self-examination" (194).

In its response to Linton's "Girl of the Period" essay, the *Victoria* (which was operated by the feminist Emily Faithfull) pleaded for female education as one of the ways of curing the afflictions of modern society. Furthermore, it recognized that Linton's attack targeted girls in "scarecrow" fashion to answer for "all that is most debased and intolerable" in British society (193).[4] Though the magazine claimed that such an assault was unwarranted, women were frequently cast as an index of national morality and rectitude.

The *Victoria* cites a want of "earnestness" as the defining mood of the time, a result of increased material prosperity and the Pax Victoriana. Redirecting national attention away from the behavior and dress of young girls (which it saw as only a distraction from a more imminent social "revolution"), the journal further states that "history plainly shows no country can afford to stand still, dry rot or foreign conquest must inevitably supervene" (197). Historians and critics have only recently begun exploring the years 1866–68 as an important turning point in British social and imperial history.[5] Freda Harcourt locates a "new phase of imperialism" beginning with Benjamin Disraeli's 1867 Abyssinian Expedition and urges scholars to look less toward the "official mind" and more toward periodicals for a "panoramic view" of imperialist and social preoccupations (88, 87). According to Harcourt, "it is inconceivable" that for the Victorians the connections among reform, class dissolution, and British economic and international standing were "anything but obvious" (87). It seems clear from the *Victoria*'s response to Linton that many of these concerns were indeed uppermost in the public mind; and the Girl of the Period controversy highlights these connections. While Nancy Fix Anderson finds it difficult in some ways to understand why Linton's essay created such a stir (given that her accusations were hardly original [120]), I would suggest that it was the timing of the piece, its coincidence with the national anxiety about the socio-political issues Harcourt outlines, that helped create the furor.

When Linton compared the modern girl to a prostitute, the analogy brought with it to the mind of mid-Victorian England a variety of class and social meanings. As Judith Walkowitz indicates, the prostitute was a storm center—a figure who was both sentimentalized and feared, a target for class guilt, and "a powerful symbol of sexual and economic exploitation under industrial capitalism." Both literally and metaphorically, the prostitute was seen as the "conduit of infection" between the classes (4). Regulating her activities and controlling her sexuality became the subject of legal, medical, and journalistic discourses that culminated in the Contagious Diseases Acts of the 1860s. But while the Acts "reinforced existing patterns of class and gender domination," they also generated discussions that served to deflect attention away from these class issues (Walkowitz 4, 41).[6]

Furthermore, according to Lynda Nead, prostitution "represented a nexus of anxieties relating to class, nation and empire" (94). Using the Greek and Roman civilizations as models, the Victorians were haunted by "the spectre of imperial decline," believing that such decline results from the "moral degeneration" of a people (93). As Nead states: "Morality was a central component within the ideology of empire. International leadership and the domination of foreign competition were believed to depend directly on the existence of a stable domestic base, and social stability, it was claimed, was a consequence of moral purity" (91).

When Linton compared the Girl of the Period to the demimonde, she played on class fears.[7] By modeling herself after "certain savages in Africa" or Madge Wildfire, the modern girl loses her "purity of taste," for she "thinks herself all the more beautiful the nearer she approaches in look to a maniac or a negress" (340). In her alliance with such marginalized figures, Linton's Girl threatens class distinctions. She not only is seen as decidedly "other," but she also loses her "distinctive national character" (340). The modern girl who brushes too closely against the demimonde thus bears the brunt of class contamination and the fear of class dissolution. Keeping her pure becomes an act of great national importance.

The concern with young women's innocence is part of the dichotomized Victorian view of women as either asexual angels in the house or fallen creatures. But it is also, as Leonore Davidoff asserts, "directly related to the power structures of gender and class" (23). Davidoff states that in rescue work young women "carried the burden of purity and pollution and indeed of projected male sexuality" (22).[8] This fascination with young girls was part of an attempt to control not only the perceived sexuality of the lower classes but also that of middle-class males. In addition, such containment of sexuality was also believed to quell class guilt, disorder, and, in economic terms, "the immoral forces of the market" (Davidoff 20). Anthropologist Mary Douglas asserts that in primitive societies, ideas of pollution act as powerful enforcers of social boundaries and that "wherever [such] lines are precarious we find pollution ideas come to their support" (qtd. in Delamont and Duffin 23). Her findings apply to the mid-Victorian climate surrounding the passage of the Reform Act of 1867, which opened the franchise to some members of the working class and most of the middle class, and the campaign for women's suffrage (brought before Parliament by John Stuart Mill in 1866). Focusing on young women's purity may thus serve to deflect attention from more serious class politics.

When Linton compared the modern girl to her fallen sisters, she was also responding to a relatively recent cultural phenomenon—the high visibility of the "queens" of the Victorian demimonde, who first appeared publicly in Hyde Park in the early 1860s (Mitchell 75). These "Anonymas" of the marketplace, successful prostitutes, also complicated visible class markers by imitating upper-class women in their dress and their lifestyles. Extravagantly clothed, they were seen riding in their carriages in the park, where one of them, Catherine Walters (a.k.a. Skittles), is said to have caused traffic jams by the attention she excited (Crow 216).[9] In their dress and manners, as they frequented the opera or luxuriated in their suburban villas, such hetairas were imitating the life of the upper-middle-class woman (Crow 213). Even lower-class prostitutes, the painted women on the street, imitated in their showy dress "the conspicuous display of Victorian ladies" (Walkowitz 26).[10]

The irony of the Girl of the Period imitating the demimonde imitating the upper class may have been lost on Linton. But what this imitation of dress reveals is that the visible signs of class consciousness were becoming increasingly unstable. In her emulation of the forms of female deviance— namely the indulgence in "pleasure" and "display"—the Girl complicates the tropes of respectability the Victorians used to categorize women. As Linton's harsh tone makes clear, there was "a sense of urgency in this appeal for absolute categories" separating the respectable from the non-respectable woman (Nead 180). At issue is that the "real" woman and her presentation are at variance, which complicated Victorian notions of decorum and further confused the predominant belief in mimesis as an aesthetic and morally viable category.

While Linton accuses the Girl of the Period of modeling herself after the demimonde, she asserts that such imitation is fruitless. Not only do men fear this modern girl "with her false red hair and painted skin," but they also do not take her seriously: "she is only a poor copy of the real thing; and the real thing is far more amusing than the copy, because it is real" (340). Linton's concern with mimesis is reminiscent of Luce Irigaray's theory about the self-consciousness involved when women attempt to write themselves into a discourse. Irigaray states:

> To play with mimesis is thus, for a woman, to try to recover the place of her exploitation by discourse, without allowing herself simply to be reduced to it. It means to resubmit herself . . . to "ideas," in particular to ideas about herself, that are elaborated in/by masculine logic, but so as to make "visible," by an effect of playful repetition, what was supposed to remain invisible: the cover-up of a possible operation of the feminine in language. (qtd. in Russo 223)

One may see the Girl of the Period controversy as reenacting this process. The modern girl, playing with the tropes of female representation, self-consciously attempts to reclaim a space for (self) representation. Though Linton asserts that young women misread these tropes, one may see also in this emulation a more complex awareness of the "male" codes that govern female display. In the more balanced responses to Linton's "Girl of the Period," most notably those by Henry James and Mary Elizabeth Braddon, it is indeed apparent that the source of this playing with female dress is inexorably tied to the young man of the period, whose desires are responsible for shaping the Girl's imitation. In her article "Whose Fault Is It?" Braddon points to the degenerate young man whose scorn for "everything domestic as 'slow' " encouraged the Girl to model herself after the fast: "Who taught the girls of England this hateful slang? who showed them—nay, obtruded upon and paraded before them—these odious women?" (214). Claiming that "when men cease to admire vicious women, good women will cease to imitate them. . . . When the apotheosis of the courtesan is over, modesty will come into fashion again," Braddon defends the "weaker" sex by again positing male desire as the shaping force behind young women's symbolic fall (215).

Similarly, in his review of the American edition of Linton's collected articles from the *Saturday Review, Modern Women and What Is Said of*

Them, James finds the improprieties of young women understandable only as part of the follies of young men. He writes that women "reflect with great clearness the state of the heart and imagination of men," for it is men who "give the *ton*—they pitch the key" of society. Unlike Braddon, however, James does not see the "follies of modern civilization" as part of a general degeneration, but rather as one of the "blunders" that occur as a result of progress ("Women" 334).

While James encourages the new freedom of women, Linton condemns the Girl of the Period as a "loud and rampant modernization" ("Girl" 340). She posits instead the "genuine girl of the past" who embodies the ideal of British womanhood. By this she means "the ideal of womanhood . . . of home birth and breeding," an advantage English girls presumably have over their European or American counterparts. Indeed, Linton states, "a fair young English girl [is] something franker than a Frenchwoman, more to be trusted than an Italian, as brave as an American but more refined, as domestic as a German and more graceful" (339).

Significantly, this girl, "with her tender little ways and pretty bashful modesties," is distinctly a fiction, a product of a rural past in which "love in a cottage" was the romantic ideal (Linton, "Girl" 340). This myth of an idyllic rural England was perpetuated in both literature and painting and, according to Nead, was important because it helped form a "national identity" based on the "ideological continuity between the past and the present" (40). When Linton compared the Girl of the Period to the demimondaine, she invoked a decidedly urban figure, as the Girl's alliance with the prostitute—a figure of urban and modern life—makes clear. But Linton's ideal English girl is indeed a "girl of the past." Not only was the image of love in a cottage irrelevant to a world where many "redundant" women had to work and many more to forgo marriage, such representation was also anachronistic in the changing socio-political climate of mid-Victorian England. By the 1860s, though its ideal of itself remained rural, England was a thoroughly "urban and industrial" country (Howkins 62). Thus the romantic girl of the past (an increasingly impossible vision) and the modern girl of the period become mythical figures in an ideological debate over English self-representation.

Paradoxically, it was Linton herself who was accused of treason for her attack on the "representation of English womanhood." One particularly enraged reader suggested she receive a sound thrashing for her lack of patriotism (Layard 145). Even the satirical journals, most notably *Punch* and *Judy,* defended British womanhood from what the latter publication dubbed the "Saturday Sneerer." Outraged at this attack on upper-class girls, "the pride and flower of England," *Judy,* using Linton's own words, accuses her of creating a "new race of women utterly unlike the old insular ideal" ("Sneerer" 297). The anonymous Linton, whom *Judy* also labeled a "miss-creant" (Layard 144), thus serves as a lightning rod, drawing to herself the heated debate about the publicity surrounding the nation's girls. An April 1868 cartoon sketch of a "Prurient Prude" drawn by Matthew Morgan for the *Tomahawk* further illustrates the censure heaped on the Saturday Reviewer. It shows an old woman deliberately misrepresenting a young girl whose portrait she paints with demonic features. The legs of her easel are covered in true modest style, but the painter's brush is dipped in venom and gall.

When Linton posited a "genuine girl of the past" who was "*romanesque*" as the antithesis of the modern girl, she invited an excursion into narrative, her diction invoking both the adjectival and the literary meaning. According to Mulock, there is something "decidedly adjective" about young women; they appear unformed, a collection of qualities until they become women or "noun substantive(s)" (*Thoughts* 96). Linton always considered herself a defender of "true womanhood," and by this she meant women who embodied adjective qualities—"sweet and dainty and delectable" (qtd. in Layard 149). The "brown-haired girls at home" who are Linton's English ideal are fictional characters of the dovecote stamp (Linton, "Girl" 339–40). Retiring and domestic, they do not assert themselves or make spectacles like the modern girl. Rather, this "genuine" girl's role is to chronicle her life in her person: "the title-page of which you may read in her quiet countenance; her manner . . . her unfailing interest in all things and people" (Mulock, *Thoughts* 16).

That the girl of the past forms the grammar of other's narratives but does not write her own, we can see in the responses to Linton's essay. In the *Tomahawk,* the modern girl is not only an aspect of punctuation, "a girl who is too fast to mind her proper *stops,*" but also a verb to be declined: "The Future of Woman—This, otherwise irregular verb forms its future regularly, 'I will, or shall, woo-man.' Its optative mood takes the form of an *infinitive heir-ist*" ("Girl" 153). *Punch* also takes advantage of the potential for grammatical punning: "If the Girl of the Period is as she is represented, the sooner a *stop* is put to her the better" (qtd. in Layard 144). The replies to Linton's essay—songs, almanacs, miscellanies, plays, and parodies—represent a flurry of textual proliferation that not only capitalized on a unique marketing opportunity but also became an exercise in linguistic dueling.

The anonymous Linton was believed to have started all the fuss. In the original essay, in which satire and caricature predominate, Linton claims that it is only when things have come to a terrible state that censure of women manifests itself. This "fall" into writing is part of a tradition, as Helena Michie reminds us in *The Flesh Made Word*, about "the assumed purity, innocence, and relative iconicity of spoken language" (103). Linton blames the debasement on the Girls of the Period: "It is only when [women] have placed themselves beyond the pale of masculine respect that such things could be written as are written now" (340). The invocation of the "fall metaphor," Michie notes, "in turn throws into relief the figure of the fallen woman who comes to stand for rhetoric, ornament, manipulation, and insinuation—for all the seductions of language" (103). But it is the essayist herself who comes under attack for being a fallen creature. One reviewer of Linton's *Modern Women* collection writes of this link between writing and prostitution:

> The general impression received from these varying and very unequal essays is that the Girl of the Period is entirely worthy of the Critic of the Period. In him the fine elements of satire are as degenerate as those of dressing and pleasing in her; extravagance, coarseness, and commonness characterize both; and if the girl has taken her costume and manners from Anonyma, it appears that the critic has formed his ideas and opinions upon the same authority. ("Modern Women" 639)

Though mistakenly identifying the critic as a "he," the reviewer later admits the work of several (probably female) hands (640). Linton's literary excesses, her manipulation and distortion, were seen as a fall from the usually high standards of the *Saturday Review*.

Like this *Atlantic Monthly* reviewer, James accuses Linton of the same charges she herself leveled against the Girl of the Period; he condemns the essays as "all equally trivial, commonplace, and vulgar" ("Women" 332). James also points out that the critic bears the brunt of the scorn: "As we read the volume, modern women—heaven save the mark!—passed quite out of our thoughts, and our attention transferred itself to modern scribblers" (333). Linton's Girl of the Period, with her "slang, bold talk, and fastness," is more appropriately seen as the Girl's critic.

It is not surprising that the essayist herself was perceived to be fallen. A public woman such as Linton, one who supported herself and who left the safe enclosure of the domestic realm, was often seen to have transgressed decorum. One school of Victorian thought lumped all "work outside the home with prostitution" (Michie 33); this stance is evident in the responses to "The Girl of the Period." As Linton claims in that essay, to become public is to risk censure.

While the responses to Linton's article alleged that the essayist herself was a sister of Anonyma, they also repeatedly asked where her fictional Girl of the Period was to be found. Most journals were certain that the essayist borrowed from the sensationalism that was in the air. James thought the comparison of this girl with the demimondaine "a wanton exaggeration [done] in the interest of sensationalism" ("Women" 334). Furthermore, he faults the reviewer for a complete lack of style and grace as well as for her "colloquial slanginess," calling the entire publishing history "an almost inconceivable spectacle" (332–33). In "Mrs. Punch's Letters to Her Daughter," the satirical magazine ridicules both women's suffrage and the Girl of the Period, who casts her vote based on the candidate's ability to defend her from "those horribly critical creatures who find fault . . . and want us to leave off chignons and Sensational novels" (143). Most responses to Linton's article link the general decline of manners and morals with the increase in sensational novels. In the words of the *Victoria Magazine,* that "overwhelming swamp of books and papers which [is] hasty and ill-digested, it is a sacrilege to call literature" ("Latest Crusade" 194–95). Sensational fiction, particularly that written by women writers, was perceived to be the staple food for the Girl of the Period.

In her review of novels for *Blackwood's Magazine* in 1867, a year before Linton's notorious essay, Margaret Oliphant had identified the "young woman of the period" as the fast heroine of sensational fiction, particularly in the works of Braddon and Broughton (265). The phrase did not become a catchword, as did Linton's, but the debate over these novelists' heroines was a source of controversy throughout the 1860s. Responding in part to a review in the *Revue des Deux Mondes* that praised Annie Thomas and Edmund Yates as "representative novelists of England," Oliphant writes that such praise is an injury to "our national pride" (260–61). As a "test of [a country's] moral standard" (Dicey 557), sensational literature, particularly that written by women, was perceived as a threat to national integrity.

Indeed, women sensation writers were often faulted for their "pernicious and disgusting lucubrations," and according to the *Victoria* these works contributed to the demoralization of the country ("Latest Crusade" 200). Similarly, Oliphant writes that the "wickedness of man is less ruinous, less disastrous to the world in general, than the wickedness of woman" (275). After scolding women for writing shamefully and claiming that "women's rights and women's duties have had enough discussion," Oliphant insists that "a woman has one duty of invaluable importance to her country and her race which cannot be over-estimated—that is the duty of being pure. There is perhaps nothing of such vital consequence to a nation" (275). Consistent with the Victorian rhetoric that subsumed women's rights under women's duties, Oliphant also aligns such duties with patriotic responsibilities. Like Linton, she links the depiction of young women with the race and the nation.[11] Moreover, according to these beliefs, it is important for any representation of women to stress chastity and purity. Women sensation novelists not only violate the canons of respectability when they portray women as other than innocent, but they also commit a form of treason.

In her other essays on women, Linton, too, describes the importance of their duties to the nation. In "Modern Mothers," which also appeared in the *Saturday Review* in 1868, she bemoans the fact that "society has put maternity out of fashion" (268). Her rhetoric suggests the plots of the sensation novels Oliphant and her ilk were condemning; for instance, she claims that "this wild revolt against nature, and specially this abhorrence of maternity, is carried to a still greater extent by American women, with grave national consequences resulting" (268). Betraying a class consciousness, Linton castigates mothers who selfishly leave the care of their children to working-class nursemaids: "A great deal of other evil . . . is taught in the nursery; a great deal of vulgar thought, of superstitious fear, of class coarseness" (269).[12] Similarly, in a heated letter to the editors of the *Daily Graphic* condemning their illustration of "Lady Footballers at Play," she states that "the woman who violates the canons of modesty of her own times is as reprehensible as if those canons were as essential as the elementary crimes and obligations of organized society" (qtd. in Van Thal 89).[13] As we can see in these debates over women's representation, the only acceptable image of public woman was as modest and maternal. Sensation novels—and criticism drawing upon their mode of expression—invoked this image's opposite.

Oliphant likewise uses the tropes of prostitution to describe the productions of these public women, the sensation novelists such as Braddon and

Broughton. Furthermore, her metaphors apply to the young women readers who no longer crave the wholesome fare of novelists like Walter Scott, but require more stimulating "mental food." Arguing that sensational novels come from the "lower strata" of fiction, Oliphant links such works with a literary demimonde.[14] In a word reminiscent of this transaction, she urges Braddon to be true to her "*clientelle*" by following her own imagination and not borrowing plots from other authors, most notably Charles Reade (265). These works from the "lower regions of book-making," which "circulate everywhere," are a threat to young women readers, who—she claims in a touch reminiscent of Linton's evocation of a mythic rural idyll—were formerly free from such corruption.

In addition, the "female monopoly" that women sensation novelists had over the literary marketplace in the 1860s was viewed unfavorably as an inappropriately commercial enterprise. Challenging the single notion of the father/author figure for women writers, Catherine Gallagher proposes another ancient literary metaphor—that of "the author as whore" (40). Gallagher distinguishes between a procreative father/author who "generates real things in the world through language" and the sterile whore in whom "language proliferates itself in a process of exchange through the author" (41). This metaphor is particularly apt for women sensation novelists, who were seen as answering only to the demands of the marketplace: they too had lost their "modest, maternal" qualities in moving into the commercial literary demimonde.

The client of sensational fiction is the (upper) middle-class girl, the patron of Mudie's and the fast young lady in Linton's essay.[15] Elaine Showalter describes the "covert solidarity" between the predominantly female readers and the women sensation novelists who "articulated [their] fantasies" (159).[16] But the interaction between these novelists and their young women readers was also thought to be dangerous in an overtly sexual way. Oliphant's metaphors of depraved appetite are reiterated more dramatically in the *Victoria Magazine*, which describes a seduction scene in which "the slave of Sensationalism," an almost vampiric reader "breathless with morbid excitement . . . closes the latest admired effusion, and turns with undiminished craving to his [sic] library for fresh food" ("Sensational Novels" 460). While bigamy, murder, and intrigue were the rule in women's sensational fiction, the journal saw a greater charge in "their sensuality—with many amounting to, in nearly all inculcating immorality" (458). The threat was particularly acute to the young woman reader, whose critical faculties were believed to be "weak."

Though Oliphant criticizes Yates for the representation of his bigamist heroine, she severely castigates women novelists, particularly Broughton (whose work she mistakenly attributes to Thomas) and Braddon:

> It is a shame to women so to write; and it is a shame to the women who read and accept as a true representation of themselves and their ways the equivocal talk and fleshly inclinations herein attributed to them. There [sic] patronage of such books is in reality an adoption and acceptance of them. (275)

Writing of Braddon and the Aurora Floyds of fiction, Oliphant asks, "Is, then, the picture true?" Reluctantly, she answers "yes." For while Oliphant claims that others are crying out against such misrepresentation, the young women readers of Mudie's Circulating Library accept it "as something like the truth" (260). Not only do such girls "not disown the picture" presented of themselves in such novels, but they also hang "it up in the boudoir and drawing-room [where] . . . the books which contain it circulate everywhere and are read everywhere, and are not contradicted" (259). As in Linton's "Girl of the Period" essay, it is women who are responsible for undermining the difference between "reality" and their (self) representation.

It is this practice of sensationalism—a public representation of the morally unrepresentable—for which Oliphant condemns women writers. Yet while she accuses them of misrepresentation, she also recognizes the novelty that such vision entails. In particular, she cites Broughton's *Cometh Up as a Flower*, stating: "The wonderful thing in it is the portrait of the modern young woman as presented from her own point of view" (265).[17] Broughton, according to Oliphant a "disciple" of Braddon, was at first considered a "fast" novelist for the outspoken tendencies of her heroines. Though largely unknown today, for Victorians the name Rhoda Broughton on a title page was "almost a national institution" (Sadleir 84). Broughton's first two novels, *Cometh Up as a Flower* and *Not Wisely, But Too Well*, both published in 1867, established the author as "wicked" and scandalous, and were considered unfit reading for girls. Though *Cometh Up* sold more than ten thousand copies in seven years, Broughton's works were thought to be too "fast" for the Mrs. Grundy of circulating libraries and were not available at Mudie's until the latter 1870s (Fryckstedt, *Jewsbury* 85–86).

What was so "wicked" about Broughton's work? As Oliphant writes, the problem lay in the modern girl's viewpoint, which Broughton tied to women's passion and sexuality. When *Cometh Up* was first published, it was an immediate success despite its perceived wickedness and within a year went into a second edition. The nineteen-year-old heroine, Nell Lestrange, with her "redundant crop of curly [red] hair" (7), comments candidly throughout her "autobiography" about her passion for a soldier, Richard McGregor. Oliphant's simultaneous attraction and repulsion toward Broughton's heroine reveal a tension between her moralizing role as a reviewer and her recognition of the novelty of Nell's position as she attempts to write the truth about her own body.

The story begins with Nell in a graveyard contemplating the tombstones and her eventual burial among her ancestors. Here Nell meets her future lover. It is an appropriate meeting place: not only is the romance doomed from the start, but it also becomes apparent early in the narrative that Nell is writing her story from her deathbed and that her lover is already dead. Nell's vision of heaven is a decidedly sexual one, and significantly, her only hope for romantic satisfaction lies in the next world: "Oh, my Dick, my bonny, bonny sweetheart! . . . I wonder in that distant *Somewhere* where you are; or when we meet next, shall we two be bodiless spirits, sexless, passionless essences. . . . God forbid that it should be so!" (44). Oliphant notes that Nell's description of her body is "curious language . . . for a girl," and she condemns this passage as "disgusting in the fullest sense of the word" (267). This novel, like many of Broughton's works, has much to say about the disposal of women's bodies both before and after death. Nell continually comments on the position of her body—imagining herself on the sofa, on her deathbed, or in a coffin—thus demonstrating the way women's bodies are framed for display in both narrative and convention.

The critique of heaven and Nell's longing for sexual fulfillment, a union not to be granted in this world, establish a conflict between the patriarchal rules governing the sexes and Nell's more female-centered romance. In her article "Dialogic Plots and Chameleon Narrators," Elizabeth Langland uses Mikhail Bakhtin's dialogism to outline this multivoiced aspect in Charlotte Brontë's *Shirley* as representative of nineteenth-century women's novels in general. Langland states that a dialogue occurs between the "authoritatively persuasive (or patriarchal imprimatur) and the internally persuasive (the female or feminist sensibility) [which] are often in marked conflict" (24). Though she does not discuss Broughton, Langland's paradigm applies to Broughton's work and her version of the sensational novel, for sensation fiction is generally thought to be a hybrid form in which "romance" and "realism" are violently joined (Hughes 16). I would argue further that in Broughton's case, these forms are drawn in specifically gendered terms.

We see this doubleness at work throughout the novel, most notably when

Nell and Dick first meet. Nell remarks, "There was nothing impudent in his gaze, none of the fervent admiration with which, at a first introduction, the hero in a novel regards the young lady who, at a later period of the story, is to make a great fool of, or be made a great fool of by him" (5). Despite this claim, Dick asks Nell when they next meet, "Have you never heard of a sort of inexplicable sympathy and attraction between two people at first sight?" (15). The answer is obviously yes, and Nell responds by kissing her lover in the garden. Broughton was known for evoking in her readers what Alfred Austin called a "disposition to be made one with all pleasurable states of emotion" (202). Though the reviewer was referring to the vivid portrayal of nature in her work, for which Braddon labeled Broughton "a genius and a prose poet" (qtd. in Black 44), it is also apparent in the sensuous description of Nell's first kiss:

> The rain dripped from his hat, and from his curly yellow hair, and Heaven's tears washed his bronzed cheeks; I looked up at him with shy rapture . . . looked into his passionate eyes, and forgot the rain, and the long tangled grass, and my own mortifying silly behavior, forgot every thing in my new-found wonderful bliss. . . . He kisses me softly, and I forget to be scandalized. (45)

Such passages, in which the heroine willingly engages in passionate embraces and comments on them, occur frequently in Broughton's work. What shocked her Victorian audience was that Broughton's modern young girl had sexual feelings.

When the penniless Dick goes to Ireland and Nell's letters to him remain unanswered, she marries wealthy landowner Hugh Lancaster to save her ailing father from financial ruin and declining health. Breaking the Victorian code of silence that governed the physical relations between men and women, Broughton writes openly about the sexual repulsion Nell feels for Lancaster: she "shudders" whenever he is near. Thoughts of her future marriage cause Nell to exclaim, "Merciful Heavens! If the prologue is so terrible, *what will the play be?*" (135). Broughton's work is full of this kind of epigrammatic wit, which, as Langland states, serves to undermine the patriarchal "reality" in favor of the romance (27). The analogy also reveals that such dominant conventions inescapably frame women in narratives that are not of their making.

When Hugh and Nell are married, Broughton underscores that sexual relations between husband and wife are often a form of prostitution:

His arm is around my waist, and he is brushing my eyes and cheeks and brow with his somewhat bristly mustache as often as he feels inclined—for am I not his property? Has he not every right to kiss my face off if he chooses, to clasp me and hold me, and drag me about in whatever manner he wills, for has he not bought me? For a pair of first-class blue eyes warranted fast color, for ditto superfine red lips, for so many pounds of prime white flesh, he has paid down a handsome price on the nail, without any haggling, and now if he may not test the worth of his purchases, poor man, he *is* hardly used! (135)

What is sensational about this passage is what Oliphant calls "shameful language," an avowal that women's bodies are part of a market economy. To represent them in this way is to call into question what Victorian ideology holds most dear—the basis of marriage. As Broughton makes clear, matrimony is often a patriarchal contract, governed by the laws of exchange, and operating much to the disadvantage of women.

In a final dramatic scene, the married Nell meets Dick for the last time and finds that her evil sister, Dolly, has been responsible for preventing the lovers from corresponding. Nell tries to convince Dick to let her run away with him. She exclaims melodramatically, "Oh, don't go . . . don't you know how I love you? For *my* sake stay. I cannot live without you!" and continues, "He strained me to his desolate heart, and we kissed each other wildly, vehemently; none came between us then" (153). Oliphant calls this passage "objectionable" but not "disgusting," as the feelings of the lovers on discovering the source of treachery that has kept them apart are understandable (268). But Geraldine Jewsbury, reviewing Broughton's novel for the *Athenaeum,* condemned it as the work of a man [sic] "destitute of refinement or thought and feeling, and ignorant of all that women are or ought to be" (qtd. in Fryckstedt 87). Jewsbury's heated response echoes the predominant view of women's sexuality—namely that women are passionless. In the words of William Acton, "the majority of women (happily for them), are not much troubled with sexual feelings of any kind" (qtd. in Marcus 31).[18]

Broughton's first two novels, which both end unhappily for the heroine and her lover, provoked one reviewer in the *Spectator* to label her "the novelist of revolt . . . [for the] feeling . . . that there is some mistake, some misarrangement, some failure in the grand scheme" (Review of *Not Wisely* 1173). And although her heroines were thought to be realistic "flesh and blood" creations—in part due to her characteristic style, as "Life, *verve,* elasticity pervade her pages" (Austin 202)—such characters, though perhaps "growing more common every day" (205), were still exceptional types. "The world would be a pandemonium if they were not, and will be a pandemonium if they ever become a clear majority," Austin noted (205). If such heroines did exist, Austin feared, these fast girls, by taking "their hearts and lives into their own hands," were distinctly signs of the times, pursuing one of the newfound paths to emancipation open to young women—"the direction of love and sentiment" (205).[19]

Interestingly, Linton praised Broughton's work in an 1887 review. The article complimented Broughton on "the sparkle, the *verve,* the epigrammatic 'go'" of her prose ("Novels" 196). Furthermore, Linton admired *Cometh Up* for the appropriateness of its form and subject matter: "The whole thing is, as it should be, a story of life and love told by a girl from a girl's point of view" (198).[20]

But in general the early critical reception of Broughton's works and the controversy over her outspoken heroines mirror the response to Linton's essay. Repeatedly the realism and the whereabouts of such representative modern girls are questioned. In addition, Broughton's heroines were considered dangerous role models for young women readers.[21] Initially criticized in the journals, lambasted as a fast writer, Broughton was considered "one of the novelists who owe[d] all their success to themselves and the public, and nothing, or comparatively nothing to the press" (Linton, "Novels" 196). The relationship that Broughton shared with her readers was ridiculed by James, who wrote that her novels were "devoured by the young ladies of England, among whom the appearance of a new work by Miss Broughton is a literary event of high importance" ("Jackson" 514). Condemning the style as coarse and crude, James nonetheless saw Broughton's novels as a sign of the times, "in which young girls must be supplied with a strongly-seasoned literary article for their own especial consumption" (515). The young woman reader, as James recognized, was a new target audience. One may see in Oliphant's scolding and James's scorn a fear that the "author as whore" was catering to the "reader as whore"—that through the medium of sensation fiction, the ideal "girl of the past" would transmogrify into the corrupt Girl of the Period. In the new alliance of commercial author and commercial (girl) reader, fiction, whose responsibility it was to inculcate morals, would instead erode them by giving the real-life Girl a sensation heroine after her own heart.

Such fears were by no means unfounded. While throughout the 1860s the behavior of girls was an area for both commentary and regulation, discourses such as Linton's—for all their treatment of the Girl as a scape-goat—may paradoxically have helped to advance her cause. What Ray Strachey refers to as the "discover[y]" of girlhood in the 1870s education debates (187–88) is prefigured in the 1860s "discovery" of the Girl as consumer. Subsequent literature aimed at this market—such as the *Girl's Own Paper* (founded in 1880)—had perforce, as Jane Mackay and Pat Thane observe, "to grapple with the question of how to reconcile domestic ideology with the new aspirations of women" (194). In voicing the aspirations of the Girl toward a lifestyle characterized by elements not formerly contained in the Victorian ideal of feminine domesticity, such as sexual desire and a place in the market economy, both Linton and Broughton played a part in making the "sensational" dream a reality.

NOTES

1. See Helsinger et al. for an excellent discussion and parodies of the Girl of the Period controversy. The authors acknowledge Linton's anachronistic idealization of True Womanhood, which largely ignores many of the issues in the Woman Question. Duncan Crow sees the essay as part of an attack on Emily Davies and her "strong-minded friends" (195). See also Nancy F. Anderson's biography of Linton, *Woman Against Women in Victorian England,* for an analysis of Linton's diatribes as expressing "projected self-hatred" (133) and "self-revolt" (135).

2. Elaine Showalter notes that in her "Girl of the Period" series Linton attacked the sensationalist writers and their heroines, but she does not develop the point (177). To Vineta Colby, the Girl of the Period is "a sister of the high-spirited 'anti-heroines' who figure in a good deal of minor Victorian fiction from Mrs. Oliphant to Rhoda Broughton and M. E. Braddon" (17). Patricia Thomson also links Linton's Girl with Broughton's outspoken heroines, asserting that they share "familiar attributes" (156).

3. The crinoline was widely discussed in the journals. One periodical, *Town Talk,* thought it ridiculous for the "public self-exhibition which it exacts" of its wearers. On a more serious note, the journal found it a "sign, or symbol, of the general extravagance and inflation of existing manners and customs; the emblem of a style of living out of all measure and compass" ("Crinoline" 5).

4. The *Victoria*'s astute observation may be seen as an instance of what Stan Cohen, discussing the youth crisis of the 1950s and 1960s, labels a "folk devil." According to Cohen, societies at various times (usually preceding social or legal transformation) identify "a condition, episode, person or group of persons . . . as a threat to societal values and interests." Once targeted, this group is taken up by the mass media and produces a "moral panic [that] crystallises wide-spread fears

and anxieties, and often deals with them by not seeking the real causes of the problems . . . but by displacing them on to 'Folk Devils' . . . (often the 'immoral' or 'degenerate')" (qtd. in Weeks 14). The *Victoria*'s response to the Girl of the Period controversy makes clear that Linton's Girl is indeed such a folk devil.

5. See John M. Mackenzie's *Imperialism and Popular Culture* for a valuable collection of essays discussing the ways in which imperialist ideology was at work in forms of popular culture. Jacqueline Bratton's contribution to this anthology, "Of England, Home and Duty: The Image of England in Victorian and Edwardian Juvenile Fiction," examines how "Englishness . . . as a moral and ethical baseline, and therefore a starting point for the justification of Empire," works in boys' fiction (78). For girls, Bratton claims that "Englishness as a personal ideal" was emphasized later in the century (91). See also Robert Colls and Philip Dodd's *Englishness, Politics and Culture 1880–1920* for the preoccupation with the formation of Englishness and national identity in the culture during this period.

6. While in the 1850s and 1860s there was no longer a fear that societal inequities would lead to revolution, according to Walkowitz, increased proliferation of discourses served as "diversions" from more heated class issues. It was in the 1850s that "prostitution was enshrined as the 'great social evil' " (41–42).

7. Though the Girl of the Period, like the prostitute, is a scapegoat for class issues, Linton's attack was again not original. Since 1860 the *Saturday Review* had been calling for a more realistic approach to the "Great Social Evil." Tired of what it considered a soft approach to prostitution, where every "fallen sister" became a "heroine of a sentimental tale," the journal articulated a need for increased police regulation (qtd. in Bevington 109). In addition, it saw the real "social evil" in the increased contact between the modern girl and her shameful sisters, in which not only were "the manners of the courtezans . . . creeping into the verge of the court," but such courtesans had become "the goddesses of modern fashion . . . the extant models, in manners and conversation, of the British fast young lady" (qtd. in Bevington 109).

8. Davidoff adds that this preoccupation with young girls was "reinforced by the legal system" and is apparent in the age differences of many marriages. Often an older man would raise a ward to be his future wife (23). Furthermore, this concern contributed to the paradoxical belief in both young girls' innocence and their inherent corruption (23).

9. Skittles was also the subject of a scandal when in 1861 her portrait by Edwin Landseer hung in the Royal Academy with the title *The Shrew Tamed* (Nead 61). According to Nead, this painting was remarkable in that it did not show a fallen woman suffering "the wages of sin" and because it subverted the class codes of moral respectability usually associated with portraiture (62). The Victorians relied on such visible codes. That a portrait of a courtesan "hung on the walls of the Royal Academy signified a breakdown in the distinction which separated the pure from the fallen" (61).

10. According to Walkowitz, however, this aping of class costume was mostly lost on "self-righteous middle-class observers." She further states that for most prostitutes, as opposed to the queens of the demimonde, a closer examination proved this affluence of dress to be "illusory" (26).

11. Jane Mackay and Pat Thane assert that a "clearly defined, uncontested, image of the Englishwoman is surprisingly elusive in this period [1880–1920]" (190), but that her superiority was apparently measured by the extent to which her domestic and maternal qualities exceeded those of other women. They further claim that women were identified more with the race than the nation, though the term "race" was "slippery" throughout this period (192). One may see the Girl of the Period controversy as a prelude to the preoccupation with Englishness and imperialism that was to occupy the latter half of the nineteenth century.

12. Linton's fears of "class coarseness" perhaps also carry sexual overtones. Davidoff contends that class and gender divisions were formed in the nursery and that it was often nursemaids "who first awakened sexual as well as other feelings" in children (23, 24).

13. Linton was neither entirely consistent nor entirely misogynist in her views on women. In 1885 she wrote that "women should have an education as good in its own way as, but not identical with, that of men; that they ought to hold their own property free from their husbands' control . . . [and] that motherhood should be made legally equal with paternity" (qtd. in Van Thal 74). Colby writes that such inconsistency "is not mere waywardness, nor the reflection of an irrational, hysterical nature," but rather mirrors Linton's own times (22).

14. See Nead for an astute analysis of the debates surrounding "low" and "high" culture in painting and the way in which class and national identities were shaped around these issues. In many ways Nead's conclusions invite interesting comparisons with the mid-century debate over literature and "light literature" mirrored in Oliphant's essay.

15. The sixteen-year-old girl was the standard for determining the acceptability of fiction at Mudie's library, and throughout the latter half of the nineteenth century this standard was the subject of heated criticism on the censorship involved in reconciling "literature and young girls" (Griest 138). Interestingly, in 1890 Linton wrote against the restrictive approach that dictated that all literature should be fit for girls to read; she proposed "locked bookcases" as an alternative (qtd. in Griest 139).

16. Linton herself wrote sensational novels in which "murder, madness, and melancholia were basic ingredients" (Colby 37). She often portrayed matronly "bloodhound" figures who would reveal the dark truths lurking behind deceptive appearances (Van Thal 83–84).

17. In his *Theory of the Novel in England 1850–1870*, Richard Stang notes that the earliest modern usage of the term "point of view" occurs in a July 1866 essay on Mulock's 1856 novel *John Halifax, Gentleman* (107). What is interesting about

Oliphant's comments on Broughton and those outlined by Stang is the concern with "point of view and its relation to verisimilitude" (Stang 109). In the case of many sensation writers, particularly women, this notion was complicated by Victorian notions of decorum and morality.

18. Leaving aside the falsity of such assertions, Steven Marcus observes that this remark reflects an inherently class-conscious belief; the "majority of women" does not include the lower classes (32).

19. While Austin praises Broughton in this review, he first complains that the domestic novel has helped to increase the insularity of England, "the only truly imperial people" since the Romans (198–99). The British have narrowed their focus to the novel instead of epic or tragedy. Austin writes, "The world is one big circulating library, and the circulating library is the novel" (200).

20. Linton states that Broughton's *Joan* (1876) "is perhaps the prettiest of all Miss Broughton's novels" ("Novels" 203). Her choice is revealing, as *Joan* is Broughton's most class-conscious work. It chronicles the story of Joan Dering, who, after losing her wealth upon her grandfather's death, is forced to live with her lower-class cousins. Joan's response upon meeting them is one of horror: "First cousins! with such hats! such jackets! such ear-rings! such beads! and with such a trolloping length of uncurled curls down their backs!" (20). Linton praises the influence of Joan's "good-breeding" in bringing order to this household and writes of the novel, "It coincides with an old idea of our own, touching the connection of vulgarity and disorder—want of delicacy and want of care" (204).

21. Fryckstedt asserts that "the impact of popular novels [on their female audience] was undeniable" (*Brink* 39). According to the *Saturday Review,* young women, who were perceived as consuming nothing but such fiction, modeled themselves after their reading. In condemning this pervasive influence, the journal states that "from these [the girl] draws her ideas; by these, to a great extent, she regulates her conduct" (qtd. in Fryckstedt, *Brink* 39).

WORKS CITED

Anderson, Nancy Fix. *Woman Against Women in Victorian England: The Life of Eliza Lynn Linton.* Bloomington: Indiana UP, 1987.
Austin, Alfred. "The Novels of Miss Broughton." *Temple Bar* 41 (May 1874): 197–209.
Bevington, Merle Mowbray. *The Saturday Review 1855–1868.* New York: Columbia UP, 1941.
Black, Helen. *Notable Women Authors of the Day.* 1893. Freeport: Books for Libraries, 1972.
Braddon, Mary Elizabeth. "Whose Fault Is It?" *Belgravia* 9 (August 1869): 214–16.

Bratton, J. S. "Of England, Home and Duty: The Image of England in Victorian and Edwardian Juvenile Fiction." Mackenzie. 73–93.

Broughton, Rhoda. *Cometh Up as a Flower: An Autobiography*. 1867. New York: D. Appleton, 1870.

———. *Joan*. 1876. New York: D. Appleton, 1882.

Colby, Vineta. *The Singular Anomaly: Women Novelists of the Nineteenth Century*. New York: New York UP, 1970.

Colls, Robert, and Philip Dodd, eds. *Englishness, Politics and Culture 1880–1920*. London: Croom Helm, 1986.

"Crinoline and Its Relation to Marriage." *Town Talk* 2 (16 May 1859): 5.

Crow, Duncan. *The Victorian Woman*. London: Allen and Unwin, 1971.

Davidoff, Leonore. "Class and Gender in Victorian England." *Sex and Class in Women's History*. Ed. Judith L. Newton, Mary P. Ryan, and Judith R. Walkowitz. London: Routledge and Kegan Paul, 1983. 17–71.

Delamont, Sara, and Lorna Duffin. *The Nineteenth-Century Woman: Her Cultural and Physical World*. New York: Barnes and Noble, 1978.

Dicey, Edward. "The Women of the Day." *St. Paul's Magazine* 2 (June 1868): 302–14. Rpt. in *Victoria Magazine* 11 (October 1868): 551–64.

Fryckstedt, Monica Correa. *Geraldine Jewsbury's "Athenaeum" Reviews: A Mirror of Victorian Attitudes to Fiction*. Uppsala: Almqvist and Wiksell, 1986.

———. *On the Brink: English Novels of 1866*. Uppsala: Almqvist and Wiksell, 1989.

Gallagher, Catherine. "George Eliot and *Daniel Deronda:* The Prostitute and the Jewish Question." *Sex, Politics, and Science in the Nineteenth-Century Novel*. Ed. Ruth Bernard Yeazell. Baltimore: The Johns Hopkins UP, 1986. 39–62.

"The Girl of the Period." *Tomahawk* 2 (18 April 1868): 153.

Griest, Guinevere L. *Mudie's Circulating Library and the Victorian Novel*. Bloomington: Indiana UP, 1970.

Harcourt, Freda. "Disraeli's Imperialism, 1866–68: A Question of Timing." *Historical Journal* 23 (March 1980): 87–109.

Helsinger, Elizabeth K., Robin Lauterbach Sheets, and William Veeder. *The Woman Question: Defining Voices, 1837–1883*. 3 vols. New York: Garland, 1983.

Howkins, Alun. "The Discovery of Rural England." Colls and Dodd. 62–88.

Hughes, Winifred. *The Maniac in the Cellar: Sensation Novels of the 1860s*. Princeton: Princeton UP, 1980.

James, Henry. "Helen Hunt Jackson and Rhoda Broughton." 1876. *Henry James Literary Criticism: Essays on Literature, American Writers, English Writers*. Ed. Leon Edel. 2 vols. New York: Library of America, 1984. 511–15.

———. "Modern Women." *The Nation* 7 (22 October 1868): 332–34.

Langland, Elizabeth. "Dialogic Plots and Chameleon Narrators in the Novels of Victorian Women Writers: The Example of Charlotte Brontë's *Shirley*." *Nar-*

rative Poetics: Innovations, Limits, Challenges. Ed. James Phelan. Columbus: Center for Comparative Studies in the Humanities, Ohio State U, 1987. 23–37.

"The Latest Crusade." *Victoria Magazine* 11 (July 1868): 193–201.

Layard, George Somes. *Mrs. Lynn Linton.* London: Methuen and Co., 1901.

[Linton, Eliza Lynn]. "Costume and Its Morals." *Saturday Review* 24 (13 July 1867): 44–45.

———. "The Girl of the Period." *Saturday Review* 25 (14 March 1868): 339–40.

———. "Miss Broughton's Novels." *Temple Bar* 80 (June 1887): 196–209.

———. "Modern Mothers." *Saturday Review* 25 (29 February 1868): 268–69.

Mackay, Jane, and Pat Thane. "The Englishwoman." Colls and Dodd. 191–229.

Mackenzie, John M., ed. *Imperialism and Popular Culture.* Manchester: Manchester UP, 1986.

Marcus, Steven. *The Other Victorians.* 1974. New York: Norton, 1985.

Michie, Helena. *The Flesh Made Word.* New York: Oxford UP, 1987.

Mitchell, Sally. *The Fallen Angel: Chastity, Class and Women's Reading 1835–1880.* Bowling Green: Bowling Green UP, 1981.

"Modern Women and What Is Said of Them." *Atlantic Monthly* 22 (November 1868): 639–40.

"Mrs. Punch's Letters to Her Daughter." *Punch, or The London Charivari* 55 (3 October 1868): 143.

Mulock, Dinah. "In Her Teens." *Macmillan's Magazine* 10 (1864): 219–23.

———. *A Woman's Thoughts About Women.* 1858. Leipzig: Bernard Tauchnitz, 1860.

Nead, Lynda. *Myths of Sexuality: Representations of Women in Victorian Britain.* Oxford: Blackwell, 1988.

Rev. of *Not Wisely, But Too Well. Spectator* 40 (19 October 1867): 1172–74.

[Oliphant, Margaret]. "Novels." *Blackwood's Magazine* 102 (September 1867): 257–80.

Richards, Thomas. *The Commodity Culture of Victorian England.* Stanford: Stanford UP, 1990.

Russo, Mary. "Female Grotesques: Carnival and Theory." *Feminist Studies/Critical Studies.* Ed. Teresa deLauretis. Bloomington: Indiana UP, 1986. 213–29.

Sadleir, Michael. *Things Past.* London: Constable, 1944.

"The 'Saturday Sneerer's' Views of English Girls." *Judy* 2 (1 April 1868): 297.

"Sensational Novels." *Victoria Magazine* 10 (March 1868): 455–65.

Showalter, Elaine. *A Literature of Their Own: British Women Novelists from Brontë to Lessing.* Princeton: Princeton UP, 1977.

Strachey, Ray. *The Cause: A Short History of the Women's Movement in Great Britain.* 1928. Bath: Chivers, 1974.

Thomson, Patricia. *The Victorian Heroine: A Changing Ideal 1837–73.* 1956. Westport: Greenwood, 1978.

Van Thal, Herbert. *Eliza Lynn Linton: The Girl of the Period*. London: Allen and
　Unwin, 1979.
Walkowitz, Judith. *Prostitution and Victorian Society: Women, Class and the State*.
　Cambridge: Cambridge UP, 1980.
Weeks, Jeffrey. *Sex, Politics and Society: The Regulation of Sexuality since 1800*.
　2nd ed. London: Longman, 1989.

LESLIE WILLIAMS

The Look of Little Girls: John Everett Millais and the Victorian Art Market

The Victorian taste for reductive single-figure paintings of pretty girls seems to strip girlhood of all but its marketable visual value, couched in terms of a masculine ideal that the male painter projects. In Britain these diminutive figures are first seen in portraits by Sir Joshua Reynolds and Sir Thomas Lawrence, but their most representative type is found in the later work of Sir John Everett Millais. His subjects, in such canvases as *Cherry Ripe* (1879; see p. 164) or *For the Squire* (1882; fig. 1), look up at an unseen authority, their gaze suggesting the superior position of the viewer.[1] While Millais made his fortune painting portraits, from the 1860s onward these sentimental pictures of little girls were his signature pieces in the fashionable annual springtime exhibition of the Royal Academy. What induced a man whose early reputation rested on his revolutionary stance as a member of the Pre-Raphaelite Brotherhood to close his career in this way? What did these icons of girlhood signify to Millais and the Victorian art market? I will argue that what drew Millais—and many of his contemporaries— to the representation of girlhood was its complicated symbolic value as a meeting-point for subordinance and control, marketability and priceless- ness, eroticism and innocence. In discovering how to produce the images of girlhood that his audience craved, Millais simultaneously put aside his ideals of artistic truth and arrived at new insights into the artist's position (strangely akin to the Girl's) in Victorian society.

Millais made his early reputation by painstakingly illustrating literary texts. By 1849, he had adopted a superbly finished style with which to outshine his fellow Pre-Raphaelite James Collinson's Wilkiesque render- ings. Collinson's highly finished genre paintings *The Charity Boy's Debut* and *The Rivals* had been accepted for the Royal Academy exhibition of 1848, while Millais's *Cymon and Iphigenia* had been refused. The terms of the competition between the two men during this period merit a closer examination, as they shed light on some of Millais's subsequent artistic decisions.

The duality of the Millais piece—classical nubile maidens contrasted

Fig. 1. John Everett Millais, *For the Squire*, 1882. 33½ × 25 in. The Forbes
Magazine Collection, New York.

with a rustic Cymon as country bumpkin—did not conform to the taste of the hanging committee. The painting sends a mixed message, comic and classic, possibly meant as a parody of the older Academicians' Olympian style. Collinson's work, on the other hand, was much more in keeping with the genre types that Sir David Wilkie had created and Thomas Webster continued. Collinson's first painting shows a cottage interior with a poor family admiring their scholar, who is dressing in his charity school uniform for the first time. His sisters are awestruck. The eldest girl tests his bath water with her elbow to see whether it is still warm enough for the next child. Collinson's contrast between the aspiring, schoolbound boy and the nurturing, homebound girl is typical of the value-laden normative domestic scenes that characterize British genre painting for most of the nineteenth century. His other painting, *The Rivals,* shows a little boy offering an apple to a little girl, evoking the jealousy of a second young boy seated with them on the same school bench. The offering of the fruit is, of course, a sexual symbol. That the *Art Journal* praised Collinson's work as "a small picture, very faithful in its reading of childish character" (1848, 167) makes clear that childhood attachments and rivalries were recognized social norms. Finally, in both Collinson paintings, the girls are clearly subordinate to the boys.

Furious at the rejection of his classical piece, Millais countered with the hyperreality of *Christ in the House of His Parents,* which was accepted for the Royal Academy exhibition in 1849. He chose to use a local carpenter as the model for Joseph, to show curls of wood shavings on the floor, to normalize a biblical story as a kind of genre painting.[2] Again his efforts did not achieve the desired result. The combination of sacred text with the factual reportage of ordinary people in a carpenter's shop led some critics, especially Charles Dickens in *Household Words,* to savage the piece.

Recovering from this onslaught, Millais submitted two works for the exhibition of 1851 that focused on the sexuality of young girls. He refused to give up his project of normalizing scenes from the Bible. However, in *The Return of the Dove to the Ark,* he reduced the narration to two girls, the dove, and the straw beneath their feet. It is a deliberately derivative piece, with the girls in robes rather like those of the Lutheran painter Albrecht Dürer's four apostles at Munich. Since the Pre-Raphaelites were being accused of Tractarianism, and since Collinson was on the verge of reverting to Roman Catholicism, that Millais's subjects were not saints but Old Testament figures done in a "protestant" style was politically important at the time. The two girls, scarcely mentioned in the biblical text, are the wives of Shem and Japheth. They seem to be just above the age of consent, about thirteen or fourteen. Millais made a full-sized nude study for the work (it is in the collection of the Royal Academy), presumably to document the figure beneath the drapery and the exact angle at which the cascade of hair would break over the breast. He must have considered their youth historically accurate, and certainly indicates here his own awareness of women's early sexual maturation. While their heavy robes make it impossible to divine whether they are yet pregnant, these girls will bear the children who will repopulate the earth. It is to them and to Ham's wife that God's command to be fruitful and multiply is directed.

The *Art Journal* dismissed the piece with a minimal review: "Two girls, one in green, the other in white, drapery caressing a dove. These figures are relieved by a perfectly black background, and the whole affects the medieval manner" (1851, 160). Nevertheless, the painting's treatment of girlhood as a time of commanded sexuality—mandated at once by God, the artist, and ultimately the spectator—makes it an important foreshadowing of the direction of Millais's later career. This combination of sexuality and control was to appear again and again; its salability suggests much not only about Millais's own ideas of girlhood but also about the Victorian art market's willingness to perceive girlhood as a commodity at once to be admired and to be devoured.

Similarly, the second piece, *The Woodman's Daughter* (fig. 2), recalls both Millais's rival Collinson's early success with genre paintings featuring children, and the art market's readiness to consume pictures of children, especially poor children, in large numbers. The work suggests that its creator had embarked on a compromise. He would combine Pre-Raphaelite finish with a contemporary literary text on children, but one with a high moral message. Millais's immense admiration for Coventry Patmore led him to illustrate a scene from the latter's poem "The Woodman's Daughter" in which the squire's son first offers fruit to the poor little girl:

And sometimes, in a sullen tone,
    He offer'd fruits, and she
Received them always with an air
    So unreserved and free,
That shame-faced distance soon became
    Familiarity.

(412)

The scene is a variant on Collinson's young sweethearts, with the same sexually symbolic exchange of fruit. But Millais chooses to enrich the tale by stressing the chasm of social class separating his protagonists. Again the girl's sexuality is at the command of the male, who is her social superior. At the same time, however, her age and innocence mark her, in Patmore's lines, as "free" from the "sullen," "shame-faced," guilty sexuality that characterizes the squire's son. If she is an object for control in one sense, in another his power has yet to affect her. This tension between class and purity extends beyond Millais's painting, illustrating the dilemma of a culture that valued girlish chastity but left it at the mercy of male sexual and social dominance.

The Victorians were certainly aware of the sexuality of children, both boys and girls. But while sexuality is evident in the discourse on all girls during the Victorian period, it is most apparent in reference to the poor. The 1842 Report of the Commission on the Employment of Children left no doubt as to the sexual exploitation of young girls working in the mines (Report no. 231). Similarly, the "physical and moral injury" to girls in agricultural gangs was both widespread and deplored (Pinchbeck and Hewitt 393). The sense of suppressed and frustrated desire in Frederick Smallfield's *Early Lovers* (1858) is a sanitized record of rural practice. According to later investigations of agricultural gangs, girls who worked as gang members were subject to sexual as well as economic exploitation—a concern that led to the Gangs Act of 1867, although the problem was more effectively addressed by the Education Act of 1876. The poignant anonymous photograph of a pregnant London ten-year-old, "Mrs. Barry," in Graham Ovenden and Robert Melville's *Victorian Children* is an index of early sexual intercourse as an urban working-class phenomenon. Thus the comparative absence of discourse, visual and verbal, on the sexuality of middle- and upper-class children marks a significant class distinction. Adult males of the comfortable classes imposed/permitted sexuality for those beneath them but not for their class equals. The girls of their own class were counted as treasures to be protected and retained as a form of wealth; more valuable than the evanescent purity of working-class girls, their erotic innocence was to be hoarded, not spent.

The works of Collinson and his contemporaries played to middle-class patrons' expectations by focusing on courtship more than on sexuality in their depictions of bourgeois childhood. Collinson's little round-headed girl is the passive pivotal figure in *The Rivals*, while the boys are the active elements of the narration—a normative view of sexuality for the period.

Fig. 2. John Everett Millais, *The Woodman's Daughter*, 1851. 88.9 × 64.8 cm.
Guildhall Art Gallery, London.

William Maw Egley's boy and girl enacting *Pyramus and Thisbe* in their own backyard (c. 1860), and later, Arthur Boyd Houghton's nose-to-nose, almost kissing toddlers in *Interior with Children Playing* (c. 1863), are humorous acknowledgments of childhood affection and experimentation in courtship behavior. There is nothing here to disturb the spectator; love is a game at which even infants may safely play.

But in illustrating *The Woodman's Daughter,* Millais insisted on a higher level of meaning, not simply the socialization of sexuality but death and damnation. Young Maud's acceptance of the proffered strawberries is the moment that brings about her ruin and the eventual drowning of her bastard child. It was meant as a moral drama, part of the Pre-Raphaelite campaign to add moral tone as well as craftsmanship to art. Here was a chance to show Collinson, briefly and haplessly cast as Millais's rival in the Brotherhood, how great art by great artists should aspire to higher morals and deeper meaning.

Additionally, in the tragedy of the little girl as a victim of love, Millais seems to be dealing with an issue central to his own young manhood. In "Style and Content in Pre-Raphaelite Drawings 1848–50," Alastair Grieve remarks that "the subject [of] young love ending in disaster and death . . . [a] subject involving physical and psychological violence, seems to have particularly attracted Millais" (26). Grieve points out that love mixes with death as an inevitable outcome for one of the partners in *Isabella* (1848–49), *The Woodman's Daughter, Ophelia* (1852), and *A Huguenot on St. Bartholomew's Day* (1851–52). In *Isabella,* the heroine's lover will be killed by her brothers; the woodman's daughter will drown her love child; Ophelia is a suicide; the Huguenot dies for the honor of Protestantism. The mixture of thanatos and eros that Freud found so fundamental to the life of the organism in *Beyond the Pleasure Principle* (50–51) reveals itself almost obsessively in these works done for high art. Moreover, in this set of paintings, it is the feminine role to carry the emotional element and the masculine role to refuse emotional ties. The commitment of the heart, it would seem, is what places these girls and young women at men's mercy; but it is also the source of the female's superior virtue. Feeling and powerlessness are intertwined.

The inevitability of tragedy is the basis of the appeal in these works. The demonstration of that inevitability was part of Millais's dilemma. Millais had been secure in the viewer's literary knowledge of Ophelia's fate. He predicted the viciousness of Isabella's brothers by painting a furious kick at the family greyhound. But he was unable to achieve a suitable embodiment of the "unreserved and free" nature of the woodman's daughter. He seems to have overdramatized the idea in some unacceptable way. Something in the girl's expression offended the public, and the painting remained unsold until his half-brother Henry Hodgkinson took it. Over thirty years later, Hodgkinson asked Millais to repaint the girl's face. Millais complied. He had wanted, perhaps, to imply the madness that causes Maud to kill the child sired by the squire's son. Patmore himself felt that it was "a charming picture in all save the principal point. The girl looked like a vulgar little slut" (Tate 86). Whether in foreshadowing sensuality or madness, Millais had offended by violating the conventional codes for depicting poor innocence.

Millais was a student at the Royal Academy by age eleven. He was a child prodigy of the visual but not the verbal. His repeated efforts at text-based painting usually ended in failure from the critics' viewpoint. Immersed in a society that relied on texts for religion, law, literature, Millais floundered in his attempts to connect image and word. Unlike the product of writers, which permits a linear output capable of endless editing and subsequently of endless revisionary and equally linear criticism, painting as a product is nonlinear. A painting is the map of its subject; it acts as the instantaneous conveyor of two sets of information. One set converts to descriptive language, forming a linear text to be read. The other is nonverbal, nonlinear, and designed to be visually experienced. This duality has a physiological basis.[3] A painting is comprehended by both hemispheres of the brain simultaneously, and two sets of information are created from it, one language-based and the other nonverbal. That Patmore felt the child was vulgar, a prostituted figure, is a verbal reaction to a visual input. Since the painting did not sell outside the family, we may see here an early indication of Millais's inability to satisfy both the aesthetic (visual) and narrative (textual) demands of Victorian taste.

In the "map" of *The Woodman's Daughter,* Millais had already made stylistic compromises in his preferred spatial organization of close-up or bas-relief. The setting in the wood shows depth, almost like a stage set, unlike the flattened condensation of space of *Isabella* or the cavernous blackness of *The Return of the Dove.* Millais had normalized space and action, but this return to naturalistic perspective was a useless sop to convention because he could not produce an acceptable signifying expression in the child's face.

Thus in depicting girlhood, Millais found it easiest to forsake textual sources such as Patmore's poem. In 1854 he set out to portray two almost expressionless working-class females in *The Blind Girl* (fig. 3), which recorded a contemporary pair of young beggars. It was a typical post–Irish Famine roadside scene. Two impoverished children, one blind, one sighted, are seated on the verge of a road below the town of Winchelsea. The blind girl is a traditional musician figure; she holds a concertina in her lap and is accompanied by her guide-apprentice. Such pairs have occurred in landscapes since the sixteenth century. John Ruskin, at the time a friend and supporter of Millais, reviewed the work very favorably:

> The freshly wet grass is all radiant through and through with sunshine; the weeds at the girl's side as bright as a Byzantine enamel and inlaid with blue veronica; her up-turned face all aglow with the light which seeks its way through her wet eyelashes. Very quiet she is, so quiet that a radiant butterfly has settled on her shoulder, and basks there in the warm sun. Against her knee, on which her poor instrument of beggary rests, leans another child, half her age—her guide. Indifferent this one to sun or rain, only a little tired of waiting. (14:241–42)

The inspiration for this painting may have come from Millais's young friend Walter Howell Deverell, who had died in February 1854, just six months before Millais began the background for *The Blind Girl*. Deverell had left unfinished a painting of *The Irish Vagrants* (1853–54) that showed Irish children begging. William Holman Hunt recalled that Deverell

> was an eager reader, and had contracted the prevailing taste among the young of that day, which Carlyle had inaugurated and Charles Kingsley had accentuated, of dwelling on the miseries of the poor, the friendless and the fallen, and with this special interest he had, perhaps all the more, a general sympathy for all social and human concerns. (1:137)

Because Deverell had been reared as an atheist, Millais was in the house trying to have his friend send for a clergyman when the young artist died. Presumably Millais had seen *The Irish Vagrants* during their friendship and chose to repeat its basic subject matter of begging while varying it with the addition of the girl's blindness, which has made her the innocent object of charity.

Deverell treated poverty as an accusation against the English attitude toward the influx of Irish immigrants. But Millais approaches it as a personal tragedy, and perhaps as a challenge to his critics. The calm assurance of the seated figure resists our visual invasion of her space. We have no

Fig. 3. John Everett Millais, *The Blind Girl*, 1856. 32½ × 24 in. By permission of the Birmingham Museum and Art Gallery.

impact on her. She transcends our gaze. She is a figure with whom Millais could happily identify, not in her sightlessness but in her spiritual independence. To make absolutely evident the meaning of the painting, Millais adds a placard to the girl's chest that reads "Pity the Blind." Yet in her solidity, grounded to the earth, sensing the life around her, the girl is not in the least pitiable. We may read it as an ironic comment by Millais: pity the blind critics whose text-biased linear mentality failed to appreciate Millais's genius, his stunning visual accomplishments. In its historical context, the sign might also have been an oblique reference to Deverell and his disbelief. The little girl companion peering through the dark plaid her sister wears is faintly reminiscent of the Bible verse "Now we see darkly, but then face to face." If Deverell has been cast as the blind child, then Millais in his Anglican faith may have identified with the younger sister. But whether there are religious overtones or not, certainly there is abundant evidence that sight is a splendid blessing. The girl's closed and sightless eyes cannot perceive the doubled rainbow, the butterfly, her amber skirt, or the flowers she strokes. And the brilliance of Millais's rendering of these natural objects shouts how wonderful it is to be able to see, and especially to see this painting. The girl's blindness confirms to the viewer the supremacy of the visual over text.

Though Millais had tried to portray his wife, Euphemia Chalmers Gray, as the sightless beggar, the results were unsatisfactory. He had previously used Effie as the model for the powerful woman who unlocks the prison door for her incarcerated husband in *The Order of Release* (1853). She was the wife of Ruskin at the time, although the marriage had not been consummated. It could be said that it was her sexuality that released Millais, for a time, from the confusion of eros with thanatos, of sexuality with death. While in Scotland with the Ruskins, Millais had drawn Effie handing him a small saucer of tea (the liquid of life) as he crawls out of a ditch. In the sketch, incidentally, his lips are on a level with her genitals. In *Accepted* (c. 1853), he also sketched a young man falling to his knees before his intended in passionate surrender and gratitude. Having waited for a year after the annulment of her marriage, Millais married Effie and removed himself for a time from the London art scene to paint in Scotland.

Effie sat for *The Blind Girl* in August of 1855, almost a year after Millais had done the landscape at Winchelsea. She found the effort an arduous task:

It was dreadful suffering, the sun poured in through the window of the study. I had a cloth over my forehead and this was a little relief but several times I was as sick as possible, and nearly argued. [Another] two days I sat in the open air, and when the face was done Everett was not pleased with it and later in the year scratched it out entirely. Then he put in Matilda. (Tate 134)

Matilda Proudfoot came from the local School of Industry to take over the "dreadful suffering" of sitting outdoors. As a member of the lower classes, she might have been expected to be inured to such hardships. The second figure in the painting was modeled by Isabella Nicol, the daughter of a local woman who lived in Low Bridgend and cleaned house for an invalid in exchange for Isabella's reading lessons. Both children were clearly from impoverished backgrounds. Effie Millais described Isabella as "a great amusement to us [as] she was so old fashioned and thoughtful." The child is spoken of here in nostalgic terms, as though being poor and being a child, she is from another time. She and Matilda, children from deprived backgrounds, were both

quiet, good models. When they were not wanted they sat in the kitchen, helped peel the Potatoes or watched the door or sat still looking into the fire for hours in perfect Idleness quite happy. Matilda the ladies tell me who teach her is a clever intelligent girl but it was not possible to get a word out of her either to us or the Servants. She was perfectly silent and had come from a miserable home. (Tate 141)

Finding a model for a begging child at the School of Industry shows, first of all, Millais's effort to make his pictures authentic. It parallels his use of a real carpenter for the figure of Saint Joseph in *Christ in the House of His Parents*. But it is also a distancing technique. As Millais's rescuer from the thanatos/eros cycle, Effie could not be the proper model for a blind beggar. Blindness symbolizes castration in the oedipal tradition. It was mythically much safer for the artist to use children from the lower class, the authentically poor, upon whom Millais could impose his visual will more easily. These were girls to be controlled, not girls as figures of salvation. Poverty also lent a distancing factor to Millais's identification with death—both the death of his friend Deverell and the death of the soul through lack of faith. The barrier of class separated self from other for all these issues.

While painting *The Blind Girl*, Millais began *Autumn Leaves* (1854–56) as a conscious attempt to produce an asemiotic picture, one "full of beauty and without subject," according to Effie Millais. He was convinced that a child's face was more nearly the Platonic ideal of human beauty than any adult's could be. Millais's conviction about the perfection he was attempting to achieve is expressed in a letter to his friend Charles Collins:

> The only head you could paint to be considered beautiful by everybody would be the face of a little girl about eight years old. . . . A child represents beauty more in the abstract. . . . I believe that perfect beauty and tender expression alone are compatible and there is undoubtedly the greatest achievement if successful. (Warner 137)

With this belief as an aesthetic starting point, he painted four girls raking and burning autumn leaves. The gleaming last light falls behind the girls. Backlit, their hair glows in an aura about them, and the brightest touch of color in this subdued palette is Matilda's red hair. There is a class division inherent in the painting: the girls on the left in the dark green linsey-woolsey dresses are Effie's younger sisters, Sophie and Alice Gray. They look directly at the viewer, returning the gaze directed at them. The red-haired girl on the right and the small girl clutching a red apple at the far right are Matilda and Isabella. As befits their lower social status, Matilda looks toward the ground, and Isabella stares off into space, her glance directed obliquely across the picture plane. A sustained look directed at the viewer (artist) might be difficult to maintain for these shy maids of Perth. A direct gaze might be considered bold or insulting, while an averted gaze allowed the will of the artist to be imposed: do with me as you will, the proper response of the working-class girl through the centuries.

Within the circle of the Pre-Raphaelite Brotherhood, *Autumn Leaves* was acknowledged as a masterpiece. F. G. Stephens wrote a review of the work for the American art magazine the *Crayon* in which he found the children "fate-like." He built upon a biblical text his own Victorian high church case for deep religious meanings regarding intimations of mortality and final judgment:

> The children's faces are turned from the glowing west, and are in the shadow;—there is a strange impassivity upon them, as if they knew not what they did, senseless instruments of fate, not foolish, but awfully still and composed;—they gather the leaves and cast them upon the pile, half unconscious of the awful threat:
> "For wickedness burneth as the fire: it shall devour the briers and thorns, and shall kindle in the thickets of the forest; and they shall mount up like the lifting up of smoke" (John 9.4). (Warner 128)

Here we see the critic's customary leap from nonlinear visual input to linear, textual output, supported additionally by an exterior textual authority, the Bible. According to Stephens's interpretation the girls are impassive, senseless, still, half-unconscious. Despite Millais's attempt to make them simply beautiful, he has nonetheless conveyed the sense of melancholy in the face of fleeting time. If the girls are impassive and still, it is their ineffectiveness, their inability to stop that passage of time that makes them so. Stephens warns of fire, of possible damnation, but Millais seems to use the girls as the representatives of our human paralysis in the face of time, of the inevitability of the passage of time. This symbolism is based, one presumes, on a more widely held Victorian sense that women were ineffective, passive victims, especially victims of time since their loveliness was so fleeting. After all, Millais had specified that an eight-year-old was the ideal beauty. That brief, perfect moment was something three of his four young models had already passed. What none of the contemporary critics noticed was the sensuality of the scene: the cool light, the textures of leaf and cloth, the Pre-Raphaelite devotion to masses of tumbled hair.

Though *Autumn Leaves* was sold for seven hundred pounds, it was not typical of the readily marketable iconic treatments of girls at mid-century. Its first owner, an industrialist from Lytham named James Eden, soon traded it away, probably for more conventional domestic genre works (Tate 141). Charles West Cope, the "poet laureate of the nursery" as his admirers called him, set the standard for realistic, sentimental portrayals of children (especially one's own offspring) embedded in family life. Cope's highly salable portraits of his daughters in *Evening Prayer* (1850) and *Florence Cope at Dinnertime* (1852) won the critics' plaudits at the very time the Pre-Raphaelites were forwarding their revolt against the academy. Cope was content to record for the art market middle-class children in normative social functions, religion and dinner, two of the mainstays of Victorian life.

Genre painters such as Cope sometimes infused their works with symbolic or philosophical meaning, but their results were more effectively narrative than Millais ever managed to be. John Horsley's *Contrast* (1839) makes a simple, direct comparison between a little girl, young, fresh, and innocent of death, who ignores a newly dug grave by the church door, and the old man who lifts his cap respectfully in anticipation of his own eventual burial. William McTaggart's *The Past and the Present* (c. 1860) paints an old, nearly ruined building and the children who play at building a toy edifice from its ancient bricks, as though history itself were a familiar plaything, though it is the ruin that will remain when the children themselves are dust. The narrative and moral in both these works are easily read.

In contrast, the *Art Journal* ridiculed Millais for including the British lion, the Russian bear, and the French cock as toys in *Peace Concluded* (fig. 4), the picture of a family reading the *Times* announcement of the end of the Crimean war.[4] The animals, of course, symbolized the embattled nations. The picture had originally been intended to criticize the "carpet officers" who arranged to be rotated home to England while less fortunate comrades were still fighting and dying, but peace broke out after Millais began the painting. The direct gaze of the little girl on the left, engaging the viewer, might have been meant to elicit the viewer's judgment had the war still been in progress. The child stands as a witness, beautifully dressed, as purposeful as the angel in Leonardo's *Madonna of the Rock*. She draws attention to the action of the scene by her direct, honest stare, originally intended by Millais as a moral contrast to her father's mendacity. The (powerless) child is used as the embodiment of fair play, the inherent morality of childhood as society's standard. In essence, learning to abide by the rules is a childhood task, one frequently seen in the games or child's play painted by the early genre painters, especially Thomas Webster. Millais gives the figure of the little girl an almost emblematic quality. She becomes an infant image of Justice.

The relationship between the coward on the couch and the toys symbolizing the warring nations would have deepened the moral implications of the painting had the war continued, but Millais had to convert the title of the picture, and thereby its meaning, in time for the Royal Academy exhibition of 1856. The title shift, the text exterior to the visual product, was not enough to save the painting's reputation. The old guard among the Royal Academicians made certain that Thomas Miller of Preston, who had purchased *Peace Concluded* for the prestigious sum of nine hundred pounds, was not invited to the Academicians' dinner, which usually included art patrons, prior to the opening of the exhibition. Despite this snub, all the other paintings Millais exhibited that year sold as well: *Autumn Leaves* for seven hundred pounds, *The Blind Girl* for three hundred pounds, and *Portrait of a Gentleman* for one hundred pounds, according to the report in the *Times* on 27 June.

If Millais found the spring of 1856 a financial success, it was a mixed bag from the critics' point of view. William Rossetti defended his Pre-Raphaelite "brother" in the *Spectator* for his "superlative vigor of color and execution" (Lalumia 94). Ruskin gave *Peace Concluded* unequivocal approval:

> Titian himself could hardly head him now. This picture is as brilliant in
> invention as consummate in executive power; both this and "Autumn

Fig. 4. John Everett Millais, *Peace Concluded*, 1856. 46¼ × 36 in. The
Minneapolis Institute of Arts.

Leaves" . . . will rank in future among the world's best masterpieces. . . .
Note the hint for bringing more of nature into our common work, in
the admirable modelling of the polar bear and lion, though merely
children's toys. (14:57)

But the *Times* called the use of children's toys as symbols of the warring
nations "very puerile," while the *Art Journal* agreed that "These allusions
could not be understood by children of such tender years—hence this passage of the composition becomes caricature" (1856, 170).

Millais beat a retreat from contemporary themes to return to his earlier
medievalism in his 1857 offering for the Royal Academy spring exhibition,
A Dream of the Past: Sir Isumbras at the Ford (fig. 5). Here, for the first
time, Millais's signature girl with the upturned eyes appears: an armored
knight carries her, clasped by his steel-gloved hand, on the front of his
saddle, while a small boy rides behind him, clutching the knight's waist.
Having proved successful when he left behind specific textual references for
the minimal narrative of *The Blind Girl* in the previous year, Millais again
relied on his own visual invention in creating the characters and action
for the scene at the ford. For the Academy catalog, however, a pseudotext
was supplied: a poem by Tom Taylor, editor of *Punch*, provided a narrative
after the fact. But visually *Sir Isumbras at the Ford* is almost devoid of
narrative clues. The viewer is shown a knight as *Ding als sich*, an icon of
knighthood.[5] The two children are perhaps symbols of innocence, but there
are no clues to the painting's motivation or action. There is no smoking
gun. Trained to read paintings like novels, to shift from nonlinear to linear,
from visual to textual, Victorian critics howled at having been cheated of
their task. Satirical cartoons of the work appeared.

Many of the interpretive problems that this work poses center on the
figure of the girl. In the painting, she rolls her large eyes upward in what
might have been meant as a beseeching glance but which can also be read as
one of doubt and uncertainty. As yet, it is a glance, not a gaze, a momentary
check on the competence of her rescuer. She is the first of Millais's girl figures whose intent gazes, intentionally prolonged to encode class levels, will
be directed from their lowly status to the power of the man, seen or unseen,
above them. But if it is the girl's rescue that motivates the painting, Millais
certainly does not clarify that point. She seems at best reluctant and unsure in the grasp of her rescuer. This uncertainty in expression undermines
the dominant role of the massive knight; it can be read as an inadvertent
challenge. She appears unhappy in the clasp of authority. This was not a

Fig. 5 . John Everett Millais, *A Dream of the Past: Sir Isumbras at the Ford*, 1857. 49 × 67 in. Lady Lever Art Gallery, Port Sunlight, Merseyside.

suitable message for the Victorian art market. Ruskin, despite the scandal over Effie, had remained a supporter. But even for Ruskin, who was trying above all to be fair, *Sir Isumbras* "is not merely Fall—it is Catastrophe; not merely a loss of power, but a reversal of principle" (14:107).

Failing to find an appreciative audience for his work, Millais sulked for a year, refusing to submit any paintings to the Academy for public view. Then in 1859, he returned to painting his idea of ideal beauty in *Spring (Apple Blossoms)* (fig. 6), which shows a party of beautiful young girls picnicking in the springtime under the branches of a flowering tree. Hunt commented,

> The demand for representations of trivial incidents was steady, and Millais being encouraged to seek these often displayed great taste in their selection and treatment. His "Apple Blossoms" (1859) was an excellent example of this class. . . . "My First Sermon" and "My Second Sermon" were endearing efforts of his power in this strain; but some which it is needless to instance, however excellent in workmanship, must have been done simply to meet the vulgar demand. (2:179)

Hunt also reports Millais as saying, at the end of his Pre-Raphaelite period:

> I have, up to now, generally painted in the hope of converting them [the British public] to something better, but I see they won't be taught, and as I *must* live, they shall have what they want, instead of what I know would be best for them. A physician sugars his pill, and I must do the same. (2:179)

As a seasonal contrast to *Autumn Leaves, Apple Blossoms* seems a complete inversion of Millais's artistic value system. Reading from left to right, he appears to be painting without meaning: to please, not to inform or uplift. He appears cured of his desire to convert or teach the British public, to paint "what I know would be best for them," and has decided upon the path of aestheticism—almost. He has not yet completely abandoned the role of teacher/physician. This sugarplum contains some symbolic, moral depth. The left side is given over to a kind of communion around a bowl of syllabub. The girls on the left are well dressed in fashionable fabrics. Slightly marginalized to the right are two girls who could be Isabella Nicol in a red cape and Matilda Proudfoot in a black cape. Their dresses, if of poorer quality, are thus concealed. The black-caped figure hands a bowl to the girl in a fashionable yellow dress on the far right (Alice Gray, his

Fig. 6. John Everett Millais, *Spring (Apple Blossoms)*, 1856–59. 43½ × 68 in. Lady Lever Art Gallery, Port Sunlight, Merseyside.

sister-in-law), who reclines on her back, slipping a stalk of grass through
her lips.

Millais places a scythe embedded in the earth behind Alice, and a basket
of cut flowers, flowers that will wither, just above her as a visual barrier
to the threat the scythe may suggest. It appears, when read vertically, that
the point of the scythe is just over the girl's heart. She lies on her back
with one knee raised, her eyes directed at the viewer. She is the seductress
among all the busy young beauties under the tree. Her eroticized body is
positioned nearest the scythe, a not-very-subtle symbol of both death and
a strangely impotent phallicism (the scythe turns downward). Millais thus
returns briefly to the thanatos/eros cycle of his youth. Has the rescue by
Effie turned to a kind of death? Or is sexuality itself condemned? The girl
looks out at us not as witness but as victim. The color yellow, symbolic
of fever and disease, may imply the unhealthiness of abandoned sexuality
in an age of widespread prostitution and venereal disease. It is, perhaps,
Millais's Victorian version of *Et in Arcadia Ego:* there is death in life, even
in Arcadia, even beneath the apple blossoms on a spring day. Threatened
and threatening, Alice is yet another in the series of Millais maidens who
seem at once ensnared by and immune to the controls society imposes on
girlhood.

His need to support a rapidly growing family (six children by 1863;
the eighth and last child was born in 1868) required that Millais produce paintings that could be more easily read—and therefore more readily
sold. His contemporaries were producing endless little amusing narratives
that promised an idealized, moralized slice of life, recognizable and yet
well controlled, a shared set of values neatly contained within the frame.
These recorded for the Victorians the happy activities, pastimes, and ritual
transitions of girlhood. *Apple Blossoms* was Millais's attempt to combine
his own high moral interests with the sort of domestic gathering seen in
William Powell Frith's *Many Happy Returns of the Day* (1856) or Cope's
A Life Well Spent (1860). These were prime examples of the domestic genre
Millais began imitating in the 1860s.

Many Happy Returns shows the dining room of a well-to-do family,
with the women wearing modestly fashionable gowns and the grandfather
reading the *Times.* The birthday girl is at the center of attention, seated
under a wreath of flowers, with a tiny glass of wine at her plate. Her young
brothers are toasting her as her ringleted elder sister waits to have her glass
filled. Another young sister carries a larger glass of wine to her grandfather.
As in Collinson's *Rivals,* the girls are passive or selflessly serving others

while the boys are actively drinking their wine. The grandmother clasps the hands of her daughters, the mother and aunt of the birthday celebrant, in multigenerational gratitude for the ongoing blessings of family life. This emotion contrasts sharply with the indifference of the grandfather, who sits at some distance from the festive board, shielded by his newspaper at the right side of the painting. The father, a self-portrait, sits at the table with his brood, though he may envy the older man's detachment.

Such images of adult supervision and involvement in children's leisure come into art after the middle of the century, Frith's being one of the first examples. The picture of family contentment, however, had for its contemporaries some negative possibilities. Victorian birthday rituals could be something of a trial for the young celebrant, who was expected to recite from memory. And many critics called for "higher" subject matter, preferring history or literature to family life. To the *Art Journal* reviewer the little girl in *Many Happy Returns*

> looks very much frightened; we presume she has not yet made her speech. If this work be a portrait composition, we must say of it that it is painted as well and as brilliantly as the subject can be; but if proposed as a pictorial production, it must be observed that . . . the accomplished artist might easily have selected from a thousand better. (1856, 164)

Cope's *A Life Well Spent* is a glorification, an apotheosis of motherhood, the state to which the Victorian woman was supremely called. It shows an ideal, intently involved mother, modeled by the artist's wife, to whom the children flock to learn their lessons. Cope's epitome of Victorian girlhood is the eldest daughter, who tends the baby in the cradle in imitation of her mother's nurturing example. The entire family is trailing clouds of glory. The lilies on the table and the picture of Christ on the wall indicate the purity of their pious home. The well-appointed furnishings suggest that even a wealthy mother could have this degree of interest in her children.

Such messages were exactly what the Victorian viewing public liked to see. By 1863 Cope testified to the Royal Academy Commission that the domestic genre was so popular that an evening school for life drawing would probably not attract enough art students to make it worthwhile, since they were generally bent on painting fully clothed subjects (354). That year Cope's own entries at the Royal Academy were *The First Music Lesson* (his daughter Emily and son Harry) and *Morning Lessons* (Harry and Arthur). In the same year, seeking to expand his popularity, Millais aban-

doned his aesthetic experiments and joined the ranks of the genre painters
with *My First Sermon* (1863; fig. 7), followed by *My Second Sermon* (1864),
both portraits of his eldest daughter, Effie.

Millais, the sermonizer of the 1850s, must have identified with the
preacher as well as the listener in *My First Sermon*. He is painting his
wished-for audience, those who would have been attentive to his call, anxious for his approval. At the same time, he envisions a captive little girl,
looking up from the penlike box that is her pew, hoping for some prom-
ise of salvation. She is the embodiment, in a high Anglican setting, of the
fear and respect generated by the sort of mid-nineteenth-century religious
upbringing Dickens described in *Little Dorrit* four years later, possibly
remembering Millais's painting:

> There was the dreary Sunday of his childhood, when he sat with his
> hands before him, scared out of his senses by a horrible tract which
> commenced business with the poor child by asking him in its title, why
> he was going to Perdition?—a piece of curiosity that he really in a
> frock and drawers was not in a condition to satisfy. (36)

She is also a type—a schema, as Norman Bryson would say—of a prayer-
ful Baroque saint. She might be, for example, Mary Magdalen in a mode
of remorse, reworked as a respectable little English Protestant girl. The
painting evokes in the viewer the delicious, almost sadistic realization that
one so innocently concerned for her salvation could not have very much
to worry over except, of course, the question regularly put to children by
Parliament's commissioners investigating the extent of their religious education: "Where will you go when you die?" (*Parliamentary Papers* 1842,
16:258–69).

Millais, captured by the social conventions of the art market, creates the
little girl's upward glance as an exaggerated index of subordination. These
pictures are narratives, ostensibly clues to the interaction of one child with
the established church of her day. Dressed in the height of fashion, the little
girl is an isolated figure seated in her parents' rented pew (near the pulpit,
to judge from the upward angle of her attentive glance). Small and timid,
the girl in *My First Sermon* represents the innocent dependency of a female
child on her religious tradition and the social order. Her fear is a guarantee
of the transmission of her culture. Her eagerness to please a range of seen
and unseen authorities (father, painter, patron, Lord) caught the attention
of the Archbishop of Canterbury when he visited the Royal Academy exhibition and admired "The playfulness, the innocence, the purity, and may

Fig. 7. John Everett Millais, *My First Sermon*, 1863. 36 × 28 in. Guildhall Art Gallery, London.

I not add (pointing to Millais's picture of 'My First Sermon') the piety of childhood" (Millais 1:378). With this work, Millais made his peace with the establishment. He was elected to the Royal Academy in the same year.

The following year Millais painted a pendant to this scene. *My Second Sermon* showed Effie falling asleep in church. The Archbishop knew a good joke when he saw one, and at the Academy dinner that year he concluded,

> I beg that when she does wake she may be informed who they are who have pointed the moral of her story, have drawn the true inference from the change that has passed over her since she has heard her "first sermon," and have resolved to profit by the lecture she has thus delivered to them. (Millais 1:379)

But the identification of painter with subject is evident. Enthralled by the authority of the church in the first piece, Effie escapes authority through sheer boredom in the second. Millais, foresaking Pre-Raphaelitism for portraiture and genre, has also fallen into slumber. Something like a death has taken place. The hassock just out of range of her feet appears like a small coffin in the confines of the box pew. By 1867 Millais's entire output for the Royal Academy exhibition consisted of three paintings of little girls, each a portrait of one of his daughters: *The Minuet* (Effie), *Sleeping* (Alice), and *Waking* (Mary).

Sleeping shows a child beneath a satin coverlet. A nurse, seated sewing by the bed, is waiting for her charge to wake. Her presence is a guarantee that this is the picture of a living child, not a memorial.[6] The exquisite rendering of the satin coverlet is the chief painterly feature of the work. There is a memento mori in *Sleeping* in the fading wildflowers that the little girl still clutches. The appeal of this painting and of the portraits of children that Millais and so many other Victorian artists painted must be understood in the context provided by a letter from Taylor, the *Punch* critic, thanking Millais for his painting of Taylor's young son Wyclif:

> I cannot allow the day to pass without thanking you for your beautiful portrait of our boy. It is an exquisite picture of a child, and a perfect likeness . . . a quite inimitable treasure which, long years hence, will enable us to recall what our boy was at the age when childhood is loveliest and finest. Should we lose him—which Heaven avert—the picture will be more precious still. (Millais 2:383)

It is in this context, where the death of any child is so eminently possible, that Millais's "sugar pills" and their market must be understood. Sentimentality seems to arise under conditions of immutability. When the viewer is powerless to change the situation—for example, the mortality rate for children—sentimentality enters as an emotional counterbalance to frustration. Similarly, Millais's own frustration at being misunderstood by his audience produced his most sentimental works.

His paintings of children are now most often viewed only as a sad decline from the high standards of the Pre-Raphaelite years, but from a more general contemporary perspective, paintings of childhood were not to be despised. The followers of the Brotherhood also painted children, and within that larger context, we may redeem Millais's reputation as an exploiter of childhood. If Ford Madox Brown, Frederick Barwell, Robert Martineau, Arthur Hughes, John Brett, and other Pre-Raphaelite associates found children a preoccupying (and highly marketable) topic, Millais could be said simply to have followed a fashion. Millais's talent, however, was such that critics and art historians alike have judged him above fashion. What distressed them and some of Millais's contemporaries was the artist's lack of commitment to his subject matter. While other painters created miniature morality plays using children, Millais either avoided narrative in pursuit of his own aesthetic or made of the narrative an ironic joke. His Royal Academy Diploma picture of 1868 was *A Souvenir of Velazquez,* a variation on the theme of the Infanta. He had struck a vein of gold.

The upward-glancing image in *My First Sermon* became one of the most frequent expressions in Millais's repertoire. The steady upward gaze of his daughter is recycled in *Cherry Ripe, For the Squire,* and other works from the late seventies and eighties. These figures, unlike the girl from *Sir Isumbras,* are tractable, submissive, imagined on a lower visual and social level. With the production of these icons, Millais's work became highly marketable. He crossed the aestheticism of his style with narrative signifiers of submission and passivity in his content, and thereby captured the Victorian art buyer's financial loyalty. And it must be remembered that the buyers of art, the market for these images of young girls, were men. These sentimental signifiers of subordinate behavior were among the most marketable items produced in the second half of the nineteenth century.

Cherry Ripe has recently been the subject of scholarly discussion regarding its sexual implications.[7] While Pamela Tamarkin Reis misreads *Cherry Ripe* as a head-on presentation, in fact we can see from the white areas under the irises of the girl's eyes that she is looking up. A high-status, dominant viewer would read this as subordination, but Reis characterizes the combination of eye contact and smile as a "sexual invitation." Her source for this description, Mark Knapp, only states that "eye contact (usually accompanied with a smile) signals a need for affiliation, involvement or inclusion. Those who have affiliative needs tend to return glances more often. Such affiliative needs may be the basis for a courtship relationship" (132–33). This is scarcely a basis for the slur Reis makes against Millais, though the pose of *Cherry Ripe*'s black-gloved hands between her thighs is indeed unambiguously sexual, as is the title.

For The Squire (fig. 1), less well known, shows a wide-eyed, golden-haired innocent in an old-fashioned bonnet looking up at an unseen authority figure, proffering him a message or gift. It represents a gender/age/size differential between the seen child and the unseen adult male. The title may mean that the letter belongs to the squire and/or that this little girl is being presented to him (and us) with just a titillating touch of nostalgia for the *droit de seigneur*. After 1857, women and children were officially no longer chattel. But in the period implied by the girl's costume, men were the legal owners of their wives and offspring, and the upper class had sexual access to the daughters of the poor. Apart from these possible historic and sexual overtones, the painting shows normative class- and gender-based subordinate social behavior, a central cultural project of the Victorians. The quality of the painting is exquisite, each well-laden brushstroke declaring that the object it helps to create is a luxury good. Millais had no doubts about the marketability of these products. He was willing to supply such sugared pills so long as patrons were willing to buy them. And the point is that in prostituting his art Millais chooses female subjects as the most marketable items in the mid-nineteenth-century English art world. In a way these paintings seem to represent his own innocence and talent offered to the highest bidder. He seems to have despised their content, so sentimental, so much lower than that of his Pre-Raphaelite days, and despised his buyers as well. In this shift of identity from rebel to fashionable artist, he almost punishes himself with these exquisite exercises in paint, abnegating himself in the creation of beautiful little girls. Millais's subjects are icons of innocent vulnerability and subordination with their demure faces and upcast eyes, their youth and their nostalgic costumes. His small, golden-haired girls reinforce the unchallenged, historic authority of the unseen viewer, whether he is the squire of the painting's title or the purchaser of the piece.

Such subordinate, upward-glancing images were not only the creation of men—nor, indeed, did they always take girlish form. Julia Margaret Cameron produced numerous photographs in a Pre-Raphaelite vein. (Many are reproduced in her *Victorian Album*.) In *Prayer* (c. 1866), *Thy Will Be Done* (c. 1866), and *Anticipation* (c. 1866), Cameron has obviously instructed her model Freddy Gould to roll his eyes heavenward, the upward glance presumably indicating subjugation to one unseen divine authority at the direction of another unseen authority, the photographer. It also reduces the individuality of the sitter by enshrouding him or her in stereotypical theatrical behavior. Freddy was the son of a local laborer and sailor, William Gould, and, like Millais's Perth models, authentically poor. Interestingly, in photographing Alice du Cane, age three and a half, the daughter of the Director of Prisons, Cameron records a frontal, direct gaze from the child.

In contrast, Lewis Carroll, known to his sitters as the Reverend Charles Dodgson, almost always insisted that his models be members of his own class. He often called the sitter's attention directly to the camera. Where Cameron imposed her vision on her models, her favorites being her maid and Freddy, Dodgson seems consciously to elicit a response from his girl subjects, who are distinctly from middle-class backgrounds. For example, he recorded *Mary Millais* (1865), the artist's fifth child, with her dark eyes peering into the camera lens, as focused on the viewer as the viewer is on her. The same inquiring look appears on the portrait of Alice Liddell pasted to the last page of the manuscript of *Alice's Adventures Under Ground* (1859). It is a direct, engaging gaze that brooks no nonsense and addresses the person behind the lens in a completely egalitarian manner. Zoe Strong, a relative of the Dean of Christ Church, though backed against a brick wall overgrown with ivy (reminiscent of Millais's *Huguenot*), looks intently at the camera—the cyclops that is Dodgson beneath the cloth—not quite frowning, her firmly determined face framed by the vertical black velvet stripes on her blouse and the fine blonde striations of her hair (1863). A more annoyed, challenging expression may be found on Irene MacDonald's face in *"It won't come smooth"* (1863). She is posed as if brushing her recalcitrant hair. Helmut Gernsheim suggests that Dodgson might be illustrating one of Lewis Carroll's poems, "Those Horrid Hurdy-Gurdies":

My mother bids me bind my hair
And not go about such a figure
It's a bother of course, but what do I care?
I shall do as I please when I'm bigger.

(91)

But the true source of Irene's annoyance seems to be the photographer. His gaze, rather than dominating the subjects, is returned, just as Alice and

Sophie Gray returned the gaze of their brother-in-law Millais in *Autumn Leaves.*

For Dodgson and Millais, the returned gaze acts as a leveling device. Mary Millais, Zoe Strong, and Irene MacDonald focus intently on the exact center of frame. Directly returning the gaze of the lens, and of the adult photographer behind the lens, Mary, Alice, Zoe, and Irene display a level gaze that documents the individuality, the competence, the evident sense of self that some Victorian girls certainly possessed. The same sense of self is also present in the Gray sisters in *Autumn Leaves.* They, too, engage the viewer on an egalitarian footing. Status and self are lost in the eye-rolling episodes of Cameron, the blinded or oblique gaze of Matilda Proudfoot and Isabella Nicol, or the upward glance of Millais's "sugar pills." This choice of direct engagement or escape from confrontation, the directional glances Millais used as an indicator of class in *Autumn Leaves,* is also used as an index of dominance/subordination. The importance of status in gazing has been the subject of a number of studies of nonverbal behavior. Generally, in encoding power or status, researchers have found that "the low status person looked more at the high status person than vice versa" (Patterson 102). And of course looking up implies one is physically at the bottom of some social hierarchy. This explains the upward glance in *For the Squire* and the upward look toward the viewer of *Cherry Ripe.* The exchange of gazes between the photographer and his model, between Dodgson and Alice and the others, may also speak of Dodgson's need for "affiliation, involvement or inclusion," but the seriousness of his young models belies any "courtship relationship." Where the gazes do not meet, where the eyes are turned upward or shifted to the side, exclusion is implied. In Millais's paintings, Matilda and Isabella are marginalized or excluded because of their economic status in *The Blind Girl* and *Autumn Leaves.*

Additionally, however, the upward glance or disengaged glance also provides an opportunity for the voyeur, the one who sees but is not seen—a point that has proved fruitful for contemporary film theorists such as Laura Mulvey, who links viewership with masculinity, control, and consumption. Voyeurism may be the basis of interest in the upward glance of a Millais girl of 1886 who lifts her apron, in a gesture fraught with sexual implications, to catch apples in her skirt. The painting presents multiple indicators of sexuality and availability, though they are seemingly not directed at the viewer/artist.

As icons, Millais's sweet, upward-gazing girls need not represent real objects. Pictures such as *My First Sermon* or *For the Squire* depict societal values, rather than normative behaviors. They are significant not for what they say about girls, since these are imaginary figures without existence, but for the information they transmit about the painter, the art market, and the society in which those two elements interact. As Millais changes from the dominant role of the missionary/teacher Pre-Raphaelite to the more subordinate role of society portrait painter, he chooses to make the transition via an extended series on little girls, a series that is the symbol of his own subordination to the dominant taste of the market. In painting icons and portraits, he also avoids the problematic conflict between verbal and visual, settling comfortably into images of such broad cultural acceptance that words were unnecessary and texts superfluous. His iconic treatments of young girls were meant to be sights and not words. If these images titillated, it was through the teasing sense of power they imply, a power of historic dominance overlain with nostalgia, a sentimentalized image of little girls both sexual and subordinate.

NOTES

1. Christopher Forbes notes that *Sweet Eyes* (1881), *Pomona* (1882), and *Lilacs* (1886) also follow this pattern (108). Additionally, Susan P. Casteras lists *Une Grande Dame* (1883) and the 1887 painting *The Nest* (64).

2. The carpenter's shop itself is closely based on the building scene from the frescos at Campo Santo, Pisa, Italy, c. 1200. Engravings of these were published in 1848. In *Christ in the House of His Parents,* the pose of the assistant on the left, his elbow bent as he measures the table or door upon which he is working, is taken directly from the Campo Santo frescos.

3. See Edwards for an artist's interpretation of the research on the dual nature of experiencing art (453–76). Michael Gazzaniga provides an account of the underlying experiments that confirm this theory. For an interpretation of these issues, see Williams.

4. See Hancher for further discussion of this work.

5. Charles S. Peirce has given the semioticians a clear triad of signs in his definitions of icon, symbol, and index (clue). An icon, according to Peirce, "is a sign which would possess the character which renders it significant, even though its object had no existence;—such as a lead-pencil streak representing a geometric line" (104).

6. Pictures of children in death were a regular part of Victorian art production. Works of this sort by William Lindsay Windus, Thomas Faed, George Harvey, Thomas Brook, and others can be found in the vaults of several major British museums.

7. Laurel Bradley discusses the history of the painting and its widely distributed print in "From Eden to Empire: John Everett Millais's *Cherry Ripe*." She sees the child as innocent. Pamela Tamarkin Reis instead terms the painting a "Victorian Centerfold."

WORKS CITED

Bradley, Laurel. "From Eden to Empire: John Everett Millais's *Cherry Ripe*." *Victorian Studies* 34 (1991): 179–203.

Bryson, Norman. *Vision and Painting: The Logic of the Gaze*. New Haven: Yale UP, 1983.

Cameron, Julia Margaret Prattle. *A Victorian Album: Julia Margaret Cameron and Her Circle*. Ed. Graham Ovenden. New York: Da Capo, 1975.

Casteras, Susan P. *Victorian Childhood*. New York: Abrams, 1986.

Cope, Charles Henry. *Reminiscences of Charles West Cope, R.A.* London: Bentley and Son, 1891.

Dickens, Charles. *Little Dorrit*. 2 vols. 1856–57. New York: Charles Scribner's Sons, 1899.

Edwards, Betty. *Drawing on the Right Side of the Brain*. Los Angeles: Tarcher, 1989.

Forbes, Christopher. *The Royal Academy (1837–1901) Revisited: Victorian Paintings from the Forbes Magazine Collection*. New York: Privately published, 1975.

Freud, Sigmund. *Beyond the Pleasure Principle*. Trans. C. J. M. Hubback. London: Hogarth, 1948.

Gazzaniga, Michael. "The Split Brain in Man." *Perception: Mechanisms and Models*. Ed. R. Held and W. Richards. San Francisco: Freeman, 1972. 29–34.

Gernsheim, Helmut. *Lewis Carroll, Photographer*. New York: Dover, 1969.

Grieve, Alastair. "Style and Content in Pre-Raphaelite Drawings 1848–50." *Pre-Raphaelite Papers*. Ed. Leslie Parris. London: Tate Gallery, 1984. 23–43.

Hancher, Michael. "Urgent Private Affairs: Millais's Peace Concluded 1856." *Burlington Magazine* 133 (August 1991): 499–506.

Hunt, William Holman. *Pre-Raphaelitism and the Pre-Raphaelite Brotherhood*. 2 vols. London: Macmillan, 1913.

Knapp, Mark. *Nonverbal Communication in Human Interaction*. New York: Holt, 1972.

Lalumia, Matthew P. *Realism and Politics in Victorian Art of the Crimean War*. Ann Arbor: UMI Research P, n.d.

Millais, John G. *The Life and Letters of Sir John Everett Millais*. 2 vols. London: Methuen, 1899.

Mulvey, Laura. "Visual Pleasure and Narrative Cinema." *Narrative, Apparatus, Ideology: A Film Theory Reader*. Ed. Philip Rosen. New York: Columbia UP, 1986. 198–209.

Ovenden, Graham, and Robert Melville. *Victorian Children*. New York: St. Martin's, 1972.

Patmore, Coventry. *Poems by Coventry Patmore*. London: George Bell and Sons, 1906.

Patterson, Miles L. *Nonverbal Behavior: A Functional Perspective*. New York: Springer-Verlag, 1983.

Peirce, Charles S. *Philosophical Writings of Peirce*. Ed. Justus Buchler. New York: Dover, 1955.

Pinchbeck, Ivy, and Margaret Hewitt. *Children in English Society*. 2 vols. Toronto: U of Toronto P, 1969.

Reis, Pamela Tamarkin. "Victorian Centerfold: Another Look at Millais's *Cherry Ripe*." *Victorian Studies* 35 (1992): 201–5.

Report from the Commissioners on Employment of Children. *Parliamentary Papers* 16, 1842.

Ruskin, John. *The Works of John Ruskin*. Ed. E. T. Cook and Alexander Wedderburn. 39 vols. London: Allen, 1904–12.

Tate Gallery. *The Pre-Raphaelites*. London: Allen Lane, 1984.

Warner, Malcolm. "John Everett Millais's 'Autumn Leaves': A Picture Full of Beauty and Without Subject." *Pre-Raphaelite Papers*. Ed. Leslie Parris. London: Tate Gallery, 1984. 126–42.

Williams, Leslie. "American Primitives and Luminists: Left-Brained Artists?" *Yearbook of Interdisciplinary Studies in the Fine Arts* 3. Lewiston: Mellen, 1992. 443–74.

CAROL MAVOR

Dream-Rushes: Lewis Carroll's Photographs of the Little Girl

On 25 March 1863, Lewis Carroll compiled a list of 107 names of girls "photographed or to be photographed." The girls are grouped under their Christian names—all the Alices together, all the Agneses together, all the Beatrices together, and so forth, in alphabetical order. Often their birthdates are also given, telltale signs of the girls' true girlishness. The result is a poem of girlhood that rolls off the tongue like a catalog of Victorian flowers. Carroll's prose on this occasion is not unlike one of the most cherished poems of Vladimir Nabokov's Humbert Humbert, Lolita's class list, a poem that Humbert takes pains to memorize:

> A poem forsooth! So strange and sweet was it to discover this "Haze,
> Dolores" [Lolita's full name] (she!) in its social bower of names, with
> its bodyguard of roses—a fairy princess between her two maids of
> honor. I am trying to analyze the spine-thrill of delight that it gives me,
> this name among all of the others. What is it that it excites me almost to
> tears (hot, opalescent, thick tears that poets and lovers shed)? (54–55) [1]

Very few critics have been willing to touch the little girls Carroll photographed. The subject makes them understandably uneasy. When they do enter upon the topic of his curious photographs, they tend to read not the pictures themselves, or the situation of the girl of the period, but rather Carroll. They want to make it clear that Carroll was not a Humbert Humbert.

Helmut Gernsheim, for instance, who was the first to acknowledge the pictures as important to the history of photography and who has written the definitive book on Carroll's photographs, clearly seeks to minimize conflict when confronting the troubling images: "Beautiful little girls had a strange fascination for Lewis Carroll. This curious relationship . . . may be described as innocent love" (18). Similarly, Morton Cohen, the man responsible for publishing the long-lost nude photographs taken by Carroll, argues that Carroll was "drawn *naturally* to them; he revelled in their unaffected innocence, their unsophisticated, unsocialized simplicity;

he worshiped their fresh, pure unspoiled beauty" and was "far from being James Joyce's 'Lewd Carroll' or having anything in common with Vladimir Nabokov's Humbert Humbert" (4, 30).

Cohen's emphasis on purity, innocence, and simplicity is peculiar when one considers what Carroll suggested about childhood in his letters and diaries and in the *Alice* books themselves. Many of the letters revel in the sadistic desires of children, as Carroll-as-child takes sides with all the girl-children of the world, battering his auditor with questions as only children do. Likewise, Alice may try to be polite in Wonderland, but she is downright rude when she goes through the Looking Glass, and Carroll even refers to her as "Malice" in a letter to one of his child-friends. James Kincaid has pointed out the maliciousness of Carroll's children and the impossibility of valuing innocence: "[In the *Alice* books] there is often present a deeper and more ironic view that questions the value of human innocence altogether and sees the sophisticated and sad corruption of adults as preferable to the cruel selfishness of children" (93). The success of Kincaid's useful analysis is not surprising; the literary texts on Carroll are generally more satisfactory than those that focus on the photographs. Although the difference between the critical texts is partly due to different emphases within disciplines and factions, it is also a matter of the problem of confronting the nonfictional Alices—the real Alice Pleasance Liddell and all of her successors.[2] Critics like Cohen try to veil the obvious sexuality that Carroll captured on the photographic plates. Even more than the stories, the pictures "question the value of human innocence"—both Carroll's and his models'.

Cohen argues that Carroll was not of the stern Evangelical tradition that informed the rearing of many Victorian children, but rather inherited his approach to the child from Romantic forebears, who "assumed that the child came into this world innocent and pure" (5). For Carroll the child (especially the female child) was divine, pure, good. Although moments of Cohen's analysis are convincing, he is unreasonably insistent upon washing out any contradictions. At the heart of the argument is not Carroll, but Cohen's own desire to form a general theory of Carroll's sexuality. Cohen is interested in presenting Carroll as "repressed" by Victorian culture, and therefore innocent: "only as repressed human being could he have lived his paradoxical life and worshiped the young girls with a clear, Christian conscience" (31). What Cohen fails to see is how he in turn is repressed by our own society, and how this repression governs his reading of Carroll.

Confronted by the taboo combination of child and sexuality, such critics refuse to "see." In Foucauldian terms, participants in the tradition of modern sexual discourse feel the need to discuss sex in a way "that would not derive from morality alone but from rationality" (Foucault 24). Thus while Carroll himself could lead a double-double life as photographer and clergyman, mathematician/logician and author of nonsense, Cohen forms a *rational* discourse that blocks our way to confronting the contradictions that the pictures play out. In the discussion of Evangelical versus Roman-tic, the difficulty actually lies with the depiction of the girls; like most of the observers of Carroll's pictures, Cohen renders the models as silent and even invisible, solving Carroll's problem by denying the children's sexu-ality. In Cohen's words, "Victorian parents who shared Dodgson's views allowed their innocent offspring to romp about in warm weather with-out any clothes on, particularly at the seaside, and were quite accustomed to seeing nude 'sexless' children used as objects of decoration in book illustrations and greeting cards" (6–7). The telltale words here are "used," "objects," and "decoration." (And is there no difference between playing on the beach and sitting nude before a man and his lens in his studio?) But the larger question remains: Why do we have to insist that children have no sexuality? In pronouncing Carroll's Romanticism, Cohen reveals himself as a latter-day Evangelical, trying to protect his own children (his life's work on Carroll) from falling into evil ways. Ironically, whereas Cohen remarks critically of Evangelical children that they "could hardly be thought to have any freedom . . . these children had to be transmogrified from wicked things into beings of goodness and godliness" (5), Cohen's "children" also lack the freedom of displaying sexuality.

The word "sexuality," indeed, was born at the dawn of the nineteenth century (in 1800) and originally referred only to biology (Heath 7); it was crystallized into its current meaning in 1879, when J. Matthews Dun-can used the term to mean a "possession of sexual powers, or capability of sexual feelings."[3] Duncan reminded his readers that "in removing the ovaries you do not necessarily destroy sexuality in a woman" (223)—a distinction between sexuality and reproduction that Sigmund Freud also drew, this time with specific reference to children:

> To suppose that children have no sexual life—sexual excitations and needs and a kind of satisfaction—but suddenly acquire it between the ages of twelve and fourteen, would (quite apart from any observations) be as improbable, and indeed senseless, biologically as to suppose that they brought no genitals with them into the world and only grew them

at the time of puberty. What *does* awaken in them at this time is the reproductive function, which makes use for its purposes of physical and mental material already present. You are committing the error of confusing sexuality and reproduction and by doing so you are blocking your path to an understanding of sexuality. (311)

Problematic as Freud's readings are, and problematic as it is to use his work in any kind of historical analysis (particularly one outside his own period and culture), he nonetheless remains useful to discussions such as the one at hand—in part, as art historian Griselda Pollock has pointed out, because he gave us a language in which to talk about sexuality (127–28). In particular, we may use this language to talk about sexuality's connection to theories of difference, which, as we shall see, become especially relevant to Carroll's photographs of little girls. Freud not only accelerated the discourse on male and female sexual difference, he also acknowledged both that children are sexual and that they are sexual in a different way from adults. According to him, childhood sexuality is an "instinct" that has been tamed by the time we reach adulthood. To be sure, Freud is essentializing children, and he exacerbates this problem (again in "The Sexual Life of Human Beings") when he equates the child's sexuality with that of the "primitive," the "pervert," and so on. But what is salvageable for our purposes is that he alerts us to the ways in which we have been educated into thinking that children are pure, asexual, and innocent, and to how "anyone who describes them otherwise can be charged with being an infamous blasphemer against the tender and sacred feelings of mankind" (312). I am proposing to be blasphemous: to acknowledge the sexuality of children (and of the Victorian girl at that), while making every attempt *not* to project our oppressive desires onto their bodies—an impossible goal, of course.

Venus of Oxford

Carroll's first reference to photographing a nude child occurs in his diary entry for 21 May 1867: "Mrs. L. brought Beatrice, and I took a photograph of the two; and several of Beatrice alone, 'san habilement'" (*sic;* qtd. in Gernsheim 65). Beatrice Hatch was one of Carroll's favorite models, along with her sister Evelyn; both were at ease in what Carroll referred to as "primitive dress." Of the four nude images that have been rediscovered, we are most surprised by the image of Evelyn Hatch (fig. 1,

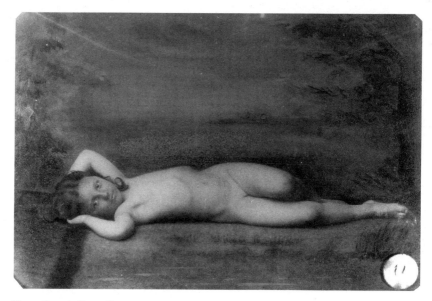

Fig. 1. Lewis Carroll, *Portrait of Evelyn Hatch,* c. 1878. The Rosenbach Museum and Library, Philadelphia.

c. 1878).[4] She catches our eye and confronts us with her own gaze (not unlike Manet's *Olympia,* 1863) as she sprawls before us as a tiny odalisque. As child-woman, posed like a courtesan, Evelyn reminds us also of Titian's *Venus of Urbino*—not only in her pose but also in the treatment of the photograph, which gives it its Venetian quality. It is a portmanteau of "real" photograph and layers of opalescent colors. Evelyn has been "printed on emulsion on a curved piece of glass, with oil highlights applied to the back surface. Beneath it is a second piece of curved glass painted in oil" (Cohen 32). The body glows in a flesh-colored light that gives way to a surrealistically painted marsh of golden moss-greens. In an everlasting sunset, which is strangely muted by the peculiar pink-yellows that shine below the ominous dark violet sky, Evelyn is a modern little Venus of Oxford.

She is also part animal. Her eyes, mildly vampiric, shine like a fox's at night. A closer look reveals tiny highlights that have been painted on the photo-glass, as if her eyes were marbles. Her face, painted darker than the rest of her pure girl-body, indeed gives the sense that Evelyn, like Alice's pig-baby, is part animal and part child. Nina Auerbach has also equated Evelyn with animality, specifically a kind of animal sexuality. In the current Carroll scholarship, Auerbach's is the only discussion that actually confronts this image:

> Since her sexuality is not imaged forth in foils, emblems, or metaphors, Carroll's Evelyn Hatch seems to me a far more healthily realized figure than Beardsley's Salomé, who needs the Baptist's purity to define her lust, or even than Nabokov's sadomasochistic dream of Lolita, for Evelyn Hatch is allowed to be at one with her own implied powers. Thus, the achievement of this photograph lies in its pure acceptance of what Carroll's contemporaries perceived as demonic and dangerous. Unlike Alice, Evelyn Hatch needs no creatures to inform us that she is both animal and dreamer, pig and pure little girl. Carroll as camera eye does perfect justice to the self-transforming mobility of this model. The eroticism, along with the passionate and seditious powers this had to imply, belongs to the child; the artist merely understands it. (168)

Auerbach's analysis, like many of her writings including the ground-breaking *Woman and the Demon* (1982), is exciting for the ways in which it unleashes images (both literary and visual) of supposedly oppressive Victorian stereotypes into subversive power. She relishes the depictions of hungry, aggressive, erotic, violent Victorian women, even if they often "wear the prim pinafore of that supposed Victorian sugarplum, the polite little girl" (xx). Yet in many ways her analysis feels too celebratory and too clear. Though I am sympathetic to her criticism of "sophisticated feminists who purge women of violence and desire with self-imprisoning alacrity" (xxi), like Carroll I prefer to oscillate between celebration and horror. By granting children sexuality, and by suggesting an inventive and girl-empowering reciprocity between artist and model (an idea I will return to later), Auerbach's vision of Victorian feminine subversion transgresses the prudishness of the "innocent" school of readings. At the same time, however, her analysis also covers up other contradictions that might be productive in unraveling the conflicting anxieties of difference in Victorian culture—anxieties that Carroll's photographs of girls make evident.

For example, is Evelyn Hatch really a "beautiful little odalisque," as Auerbach terms her (168)? And if so, what are the standards governing this beauty? She is a beautiful child, in the ways in which our culture and Carroll's is/was sympathetic to the beauty of almost all children, especially little girls. But much of Evelyn's "beauty" in this photograph rests on traditional concepts of beauty as object and as other. The female nude has reigned as the ideal of beauty for centuries, but as feminist art historians (notably Pollock, Rozsika Parker, and Linda Nochlin) have long been pointing out in their explorations of the artistic objectification of the female nude, her passivity is accentuated by the process of her production. In looking at this photograph of Evelyn Hatch, I am reminded of the role of women in Western art: largely absent from the academies and the schools, women artists were not permitted to study from the nude model, while since the late eighteenth century the female nude has been favored over the male (see Parker and Pollock, esp. 114–33). In Carroll's image of Evelyn Hatch, as in so many traditional nudes of the nineteenth century, we find that "woman is present as an image but with the specific connotations of body and nature, that is[,] passive, available, possessable, powerless" (Parker and Pollock 116). Unlike Auerbach, I would argue that Evelyn is Carroll's foil, his other. Stretched across a bed of grass, with trees as her headboard and footboard, Evelyn becomes one with nature; she is metaphor and emblem. In capturing her as odalisque, Carroll is participating in the colonialist visual tradition of Delacroix and Ingres, "orientalizing" Evelyn—as he often did his other girl-models. Besides using the "primitive dress" of nudity, Carroll also "orientalized" such little girls as Xie Kitchin by costuming them as Turk or Chinaman (fig. 2, 1873).[5] The slippage between child, primitive, and other becomes a dance in a looking-glass mirror; the subjects of his photographs collapse together as othered others.

And what does it mean to be a "pure little girl," in Auerbach's phrase? Hélène Cixous has argued that the child is nothing but "an imaginary species, invented by a certain type of psychological literature," and that the little girl is "a complex fantasm" of Carroll's own (234). Why must we always insist that the child is somehow pure, or even "healthy," as Auerbach suggests? Does this formulation not suggest the same mindset that animated the Victorian "cult of the little girl"? Are we so unlike the five hundred thousand people who bought copies of the 1880 *Graphic* Christmas annual for its colorful centerfold (fig. 3): a reproduction of John Everett Millais's famous painting *Cherry Ripe* (Bradley 179)? Laurel Bradley describes the child in *Cherry Ripe* as "Madonna-like" (178), and indeed she is as she sits in a bright glow of purity, tucked into a forested cave as an insipidly sweet modern Madonna of the Rocks. The representation of this little girl in extravagant and strange eighteenth-century dress is actually a quotation from Sir Joshua Reynolds's *Penelope Boothby* (1788)—and can be read as a "reach into the past in order to forge reassuring images for

Fig. 2. Lewis Carroll, *Xie Kitchin as a Chinaman*, 1873. The Gernsheim Collection, Harry Ransom Humanities Research Center, The University of Texas at Austin.

Fig. 3. John Everett Millais, *Cherry Ripe*, 1880. From the *Graphic* Christmas annual.

the present" (Bradley 182). Plainly, as Bradley tells us, "this pretty child in old-fashioned dress is meant to embody the positive attributes of English culture" (179).

But in contrast to a painter like Millais, Carroll the photographer undercut the typical representation of the pure little girl. He exposed her not as a mobcapped girl of preindustrial England, but as neological: sexual and sexualized, childlike and womanly, innocent and knowing. A glance at Carroll's 1879 very different rendition of Xie Kitchin mimicking Reynolds's *Penelope Boothby* (fig. 4) reveals a "strangely vampish image very different in spirit from the original" (Bradley 187). Xie is anything but pure. Though she is clothed, her confrontational gaze and her long, lacy black gloves, pierced by her white fingers, image her, like the nude Evelyn Hatch, as differently sexual.

At the time of the photograph of Evelyn Hatch (about 1878, given that Evelyn was born in 1871 and here looks to be around six or seven), nudes by such artists as Edward Burne-Jones, Frederick Leighton, and Lawrence Alma-Tadema were widely known. Many of them imaged women, like children, as lacking the telltale marks of womanhood: full breasts and (especially) pubic hair. Leighton's *Actaea, Nymph of the Shore* (fig. 5, 1868) is particularly similar to Carroll's photograph, sharing the absence of pubic hair, the unreal background, the reclined pose, and the attachment to the past. The latter characteristic was apparently important to the veiling of what would otherwise have been unacceptable. A case in point is Alma-Tadema's *The Sculptor's Model* (fig. 6, 1877), roughly contemporary with Carroll's photograph. Alma-Tadema's nude was shocking because it was presented as just that—a nude. It was not a Venus, not a Galatea, not a classical masquerade. Worse yet, as the Bishop of Carlisle observed, it was "almost photographic."[6]

Evelyn bears a significant relationship to these painted "pure" (yet sexual) woman-girls of the period; posed as a grown courtesan, she is their mirror image, not woman-girl but girl-woman. Although their bodies have been cleansed of the markings of "sex," they are not unfeminine. Familiar signs of femininity are offered as emblems of reassurance for the male viewer: pose, transparent draperies, flowers, and so forth all connote the womanhood that is not there. As a result, their sexual difference operates like a fetish and is represented as simultaneously absent and present. As Abigail Solomon-Godeau argues of the Western female nude, "patriarchy produces a representation of its desire; sexual difference, like the structure of fetishism, is both there and not there. Nothing to see and nothing to hide" (103).

Fig. 4. Lewis Carroll, *Xie Kitchin as Penelope Boothby*, 1879. The Gernsheim Collection, Harry Ransom Humanities Research Center, The University of Texas at Austin.

Unlike Alice, who is constantly eating and changing size, Carroll's Evelyn will never grow; she is temporally arrested on curved glass, which prevents her from ever growing curves of her own—or pubic hair. At the same time, unlike the models of Manet and Titian, Evelyn can be as rude as Alice and has no need to cover her pubic area politely. There is "apparently" nothing there but pure little girl, a "complex fantasm" of Carroll's own. Likewise, what Auerbach describes as the "animal" hidden in Evelyn Hatch not only gives the image power but also plays into the Victorian fear of the animal in woman. Animality ran riot in the bodies of the hysteric and the prostitute; it was the source of inspiration in Dante Gabriel Rossetti's snaky fantasy portraits of the femme fatale; it was the culprit in the stories surrounding John Ruskin's failed marriage to Effie Gray.[7] But it also hibernated in the womb of the secular female angel. This effort to catch hold of the ungraspable sexuality of good and bad woman alike was the impetus for an astonishingly wide (and sometimes bizarre) range of suggestions about the feminine, from the belief that women should not eat meat while menstruating for fear that their flow would increase, to the induction of sleep during birth as a form of combat against the gravid uterus. The manifestations of such anxiety are endless and have been well documented by such historians as Thomas Laqueur, Mary Poovey, Londa Schiebinger, and Elaine Showalter, among others.[8]

The conventions of the female nude in art, the animality of women in medicine and popular belief, are all part of a complex web of social history that Auerbach's powerful celebration spins over, but that is predicated by her constant slippage between (fictional) Alice and (real) Evelyn Hatch. While such sliding between imaginary and real girls may have been the rule of Carroll's world, one must step outside Wonderland when coming face to face with the image of a real girl: she *lived* in an actual cultural moment. For example, one might consider the possible relationship between the picture of Evelyn Hatch and the hideous Victorian folk belief that a man could be cured of venereal disease through intercourse with a virgin. What dis-eases did the voyeuristic tendencies of this picture cure for Carroll? (We know that he lost his stutter in the presence of little girls; what happened in the presence of their pictures?) Similarly, to what extent can the photograph serve as a commentary on the legal system that governed all the little girls of the period?

The Victorian girl-body was being contested as Evelyn was sitting (reclining) for her portrait. Carroll's photographic years, 1856–80, roughly correspond to the years of greatest Victorian debate over the female body: the Contagious Diseases Acts of 1864, 1866, and 1869; the Offenses Against

Fig. 5. Frederick Leighton, *Actaea, Nymph of the Shore*, 1868. 57.2 × 102.2 cm. National Gallery of Canada, Ottawa.

Fig. 6. Lawrence Alma-Tadema, *The Sculptor's Model*, 1877. Christie's Images, London.

the Person Act of 1861; and the Criminal Law Amendment Act of 1885.[9] In her important article "The 'Maiden Tribute of Modern Babylon' Re-Examined: Child Prostitution and the Idea of Childhood in Late-Victorian England," Deborah Gorham has unveiled the ideological contradictions hidden underneath William Stead's famous exposé (in the *Pall Mall Gazette* of 6–10 July 1885) of "white slavery" and the traffic in virgins. The debates leading up to the Criminal Law Amendment Act or the so-called Stead Act (which raised the age of consent from thirteen to sixteen) suggest the difficulty the Victorians faced in determining the parameters of "girlhood."[10]

Part of the problem was that the Victorians did not possess the category of adolescence, which did not begin to come into existence until the end of the nineteenth century. (Thus, for instance, Carroll was once horrified to discover that he had kissed a young woman of fourteen, thinking that she was merely a child.) Likewise, the problem of who and what a child was also animated the legal discourse of the period. Because, as Monique Wittig has argued, only females are "sexed," the laws only referred to those beings who were problematically sliding between the categories of girl and woman; male children were outside of "sex," a division set up both to mark women from girls and to mark females from the rest of society. As a result—like Carroll's letters—the various age-of-consent amendments were only addressed to girls. They were about "sex," not about childhood. As Gorham points out, the legislation was significant because it regarded women as less than full citizens, while inscribing them as so different that special laws were required to protect them (the rhetoric of "protection," of course, was merely a thin veil for "control"). Like a female nude by a Great Master, the law painted decency over itself through a highly developed and contradictory rhetoric.[11]

The discourse of the law, which supposedly sought to prevent harm to young girls but actually sought to control female sexuality, is also aptly illustrated by the Offenses Against the Person Act. This piece of legislation not only defined as a felony a man's sexual intercourse with a girl under ten and as a misdemeanor his intercourse with a girl between ten and twelve, but also contained special provisions that controlled her economic position and ensured that she would be governed by her guardians far past "childhood." For example, Gorham notes,

> If a girl under sixteen entered into a relationship with a man, her parents could charge her "abductor" with depriving them of the services of their daughter. If a young woman had property, her parents or guard-

ians could even prevent her marriage up to the age of twenty-one, if they could prove that the suitor had used "false allurements." (363–64)

Then as now, "sex is a category which women [and girls] cannot be outside of" (Wittig 67).

Given the law of the period, then, it is hard to conceive that Evelyn Hatch would ever be successful (as Auerbach suggests) in producing an erotic energy of her own, let alone any seditious power. How could she overcome the odds against it? Her pose suggests that she has "fallen" away from the Victorian guardianship of the values of middle-class girlhood. There were laws against such traveling. Possibly it is not the viewers who are embarrassed, but Evelyn herself. Her darkly painted face may indicate a blush.

The Myth of Everlasting Flowers

As both sexual and nonsexual, the body of the little girl marked her as simultaneously different from the male viewer and (according to cultural conventions) lacking the marks of true womanhood. As "pure little girl," she was supposedly nonsexual. Yet given the work of Freud and Foucault, the "cult of the little girl," the artistic treatment of her image, the uneasy law of the period, and so forth, we cannot read her as anything but sexual. She was thus both woman and not-woman; she played safely *and* dangerously. In this regard she imaged what Louis Marin describes as the *neutre*, a space of unresolved contradiction that exposes oppositional forces without ever synthesizing them, and played in his supplementary category, the *ne-uter*. Of the latter Marin writes that "grammar defines it as neither masculine nor feminine. It is, rather, outside gender; neither active nor passive, but outside voice. In botany or zoology a flower or insect is 'neuter' if it lacks organs for reproduction, unable to mate or reproduce itself" (12).

For the Victorians, the little girl was outside gender until she grew (in the most literal sense) to be a woman. Perhaps this was part of the appeal of many of Julia Margaret Cameron's photographs, which present overtly sexual representations of children while shrouding them not only in Christian typology but also in androgyny. In her portrayals of John the Baptist and Jesus Christ, Cameron inscribed the infant/child figures as *neutre*. In at least one instance, when Jesus' genitals are exposed, they are clearly female (fig. 7, 1865).[12] Similarly, John the Baptist was regularly modeled by

Fig. 7. Julia Margaret Cameron, *Spring*, 1865. Collection of the J. Paul Getty
Museum, Malibu, California.

a young girl, Florence Fisher (fig. 8, 1872). But although Cameron imaged her figures of Christ and John sensually, with seductive looks and exposed shoulders, and made their gestures and poses even more sensual through her controversial printing techniques, her pictures are dreamy, blurry, and otherworldly.[13] Cameron's work has magically escaped the labels of "perversion" that have encumbered Carroll's photographs. Clearly she has been saved by her "angel in the house" lifestyle, which included a house full of children. She has been safely defined as heterosexual and productive, in opposition to the common reading of Carroll as a repressed homosexual. No dangerous penises have appeared in her work. And no one has imagined any homoeroticism between Cameron and her maid/model, Mary Hillier, or between the young women who frequently and lovingly embrace each other in many of her images. Like good Victorians, historians have preferred to bathe in the "neutrality" and "purity" of the little girl.

Carroll too preferred his little girls (if not invariably their images) to lack female sexuality, always intimately connected with death. He ensured that his subjects would remain beautiful and everlasting by capturing them on the photographic plate, before they could wilt. Pasted into his albums, Carroll's little girls were not unlike spring flowers pressed in a flower press and preserved in a Victorian scrapbook. Carroll wanted his child-friends to be forever little, to remain "unpicked"; he longed to avoid the disappointment and anxiety that Alice experiences when she tries to hold onto her plucked "dream-rushes" in *Through the Looking Glass*. The "darling scented rushes" are symbols of Carroll's girls:[14]

> with bright eager eyes she caught one bunch after another of the darling scented rushes.
> "I only hope the boat won't tipple over!" she said to herself. "Oh, *what* a lovely one! Only I couldn't quite reach it!" And it certainly *did* seem a little provoking ("almost as if it happened on purpose," she thought). Though she managed to pick plenty of beautiful rushes as the boat glided by, there was always a more lovely one that she couldn't reach.
> "The prettiest are always further!" she said at last, with a sigh at the obstinacy of the rushes in growing so far off, as with flushed cheeks and dripping hair and hands, she scrambled back into her place and began to arrange her new-found treasures.
> What mattered to her just then that the rushes had begun to fade, and lose all their scent and beauty, from the very moment she picked them?

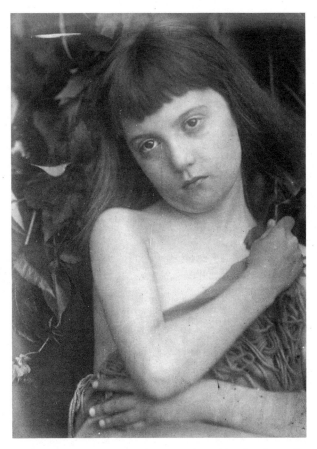

Fig. 8. Julia Margaret Cameron, *Florence/Study of St. John the Baptist,* 1872. Collection of the J. Paul Getty Museum, Malibu, California.

Even real scented rushes, you know, last only a very little while—and these, being dream-rushes, melted away almost like snow. (256–57)

The photograph became for Carroll the contradictory "neuter" medium to hold the little girl as forever young in the looking glass. We can see the image as temporal in that it records a specific moment, a split second in the young sitter's life, yet as eternal in that it is everlasting and not subject to change. The little girls become Marinesque flowers without the organs to generate themselves; their only reproduction is photographic reproduction, infinitely repeated as sameness. The infinitely duplicatable quality of the photograph is hauntingly demonstrated in the bottom right-hand corner of the picture of Evelyn as odalisque. We are confronted with an incongruous number "11," penned in on a tiny white orb that casts a tiny dark shadow on the glass behind. This number "11" is what has always troubled me the most about this photograph; it seems to suggest that not only are such images reproducible, but they are also disposable, like Carroll's own girl-child friends. Their moments with him were fleeting, despite the everlasting nature of their images.[15]

But the split between temporality and eternity is not the only contradiction within the photograph. There is also a play between "real" and "unreal"—much as the little girl is "sexual" and "nonsexual" or "woman" and "not woman." Roland Barthes addresses the paradox of the photographic medium in "The Photographic Message," where he argues for

> the coexistence of two messages, the one without a code (the photographic analogue), the other with a code (the "art" or the treatment, or the "writing," or the rhetoric, of the photograph); structurally, the paradox is clearly not the collusion of a denoted message and a connoted message (which is the—probably inevitable—status of all the forms of mass communication), it is that here the connoted (or coded) message develops on the basis of a *message without a code*. (19)

In the case of Carroll's photography, we can see that the photograph is a portmanteau of the art object and reality. Like the invented portmanteau double-words of his *Looking Glass* world, the photograph is the "baggage" encasing the two: the photographic "analogue" (the denoted message) and the connoted message/the treatment of the photograph—its "art." That the photograph presents itself as both "real" and "unreal" allows Carroll to believe in the myth of everlasting flowers, the myth that such girls as Alice Liddell will remain "forever little."

The Photographic Condition of the Girl

Despite my earlier criticisms of Auerbach's gloss of the Evelyn Hatch photograph, my intention has not been to obscure the level of performance that her discourse unleashes. Carroll's contradictory (*neutre*) photographs certainly document something of the "girl's own." Part of his art was to tap into the child who played within all the Alices, Evelyns, and Xies. One senses this talent within his sensitive and lovely letters, within the *Alice* books (which turn readers of any age into children), within the unencumbered delightful memories that a number of his girl-child friends recorded as adults. But how much of this has to do with the medium itself? For one also suspects that *all* photographs harbor the sitter's own presence; that is what makes them photographs.

Photographs literally transport light from days gone by to the modern viewer, a time travel that itself ensures a certain resonance between the sitter and the viewer. The light that touched Evelyn or Alice now touches us. Photography is a visual caress between the viewer and the subject(s) of the picture—a silent performance. Consider how the sitter resonates when Barthes is brushed by light suspended in collodion since 1852:

> One day, quite some time ago, I happened on a photograph of Napoleon's youngest brother, Jerome, taken in 1852. And I realized then, with an amazement I have not been able to lessen since: "I am looking at eyes that looked at the Emperor." . . . I was overcome by an "ontological" desire: I wanted to learn at all costs what Photography was "in itself," by what essential features it was to be distinguished from the community of images. (*Camera* 3)

For Barthes photography is born not of painting but of the theater; it is "a kind of primitive theater, a kind of *Tableau Vivant,* a figuration of the motionless and made-up face beneath which we see the dead" (*Camera* 32). On a less poetic level, Ben Maddow remarks, "It's the special naiveté of the twentieth century to think that the artist alone determines the subject; in examining a succession of photographic portraits one is struck instantly by the will and the force of the sitter" (qtd. in Gordon and Guiliano 12).

Recalling the discursive play of Marin, I want to suggest that the girl-models figured on Carroll's photographic plates often oscillate in a performative space; they are "not artist," yet they are also "not, not artist." The spatial play represented here is uniquely active, and different from the non-play suggested in other child photographs of the period. The stilted nature of the children imaged by the professional photographers O. G. Rejlander and Henry Peach Robinson (whom Gernsheim calls "The High Priests of Photographic Art" [13]) speaks primarily to the pair's interest in the science of photography—making "composite" pictures—and in the task of illustrating a story. Unlike Carroll, they did not seek to capture some essence of childhood. And unlike him again, they had neither the desire nor the talent to entertain children. Carroll's gift in this line, in contrast, enabled him to capture the performances of *his* child-subjects.

Agnes Grace Weld, in *Little Red Riding Hood*, treats us to such a performance (fig. 9, 1857). Her gaze, not unlike Evelyn Hatch's, confronts us and draws us in with a seductive charm reminiscent of Greta Garbo's sultry, wounding eyes. Red Riding Hood/Agnes grows from the strangling ivy bower, caught in some magical, mystical trance, as if she were in the process of overcoming the hold of the vegetation behind her. Hers are the eyes of the wolf that has presumably just eaten her grandmother; we wonder whether she has eaten the wolf, and whether she is considering eating us. The open basket, which displays one delicious bun, is sexually suggestive and undoubtedly Carroll's doing, but the eyes are Agnes's own.[16] In a four-part series of 1858, Robinson, too, portrayed Little Red Riding Hood (fig. 10). However, his version is essentially caught up in the narrative, and goes so far as to display a wolf in bed (thanks to the work of a taxidermist). Strangled by the conventions of the story, it is only when Robinson's Little Red Riding Hood stands at her grandmother's door that the model can exhibit herself as "child." In contrast, one could argue that Carroll's/Agnes's reciprocal play interrupts the narrative by conflating the characters, making it impossible to say just what might happen next.

The performative nature of these prints is intensified when one views them in the actual albums as Carroll arranged them. A large collection of these albums is found in the Gernsheim Collection, housed at the University of Texas in Austin; it includes one of his most notable, *Photographs Vol. III*, the title written in gilt on the front cover. Inside are 115 of Carroll's photographs, remarkable for the fact that nearly all are autographed by their subjects. The signatures (all different and often highly individual) are reminiscent of an artist's signature at the bottom of a painting. Like footprints in the sand, both picture and autograph display the subject's touch: the picture records the body's touch of the light, and the ink records the hand's touch of the page.

I am particularly drawn to the page featuring Irene MacDonald splayed before us as a portmanteau of odalisque and Victorian girl (fig. 11, 1863).

Fig. 9. Lewis Carroll, *Agnes Grace Weld as Little Red Riding Hood*, 1857. The Gernsheim Collection, Harry Ransom Humanities Research Center, The University of Texas at Austin.

Fig. 10. Henry Peach Robinson, from the *Little Red Riding Hood* series, 1858.
The Royal Photographic Society, Bath.

Fig. 11. Lewis Carroll, *Irene MacDonald*, 1863. The Gernsheim Collection, Harry Ransom Humanities Research Center, The University of Texas at Austin.

Eyes dreamy (one eye more closed than the other), shoulders bare, an Oriental cloth or carpet heavily veiling her absent bodice, Irene lies on pelts, one visibly that of a tiger, as if she were a bacchante. Her charming and voluminous white cotton skirt, however, and the clean white socks and black "Baby Janes" that trim her schoolgirl legs, confront the "Orientalism" of the pose, marking her image as taboo and thereby heightening its eroticism. There is nothing particularly fresh in this play of contradictions; they have long been subsumed by Western culture. But this image extends beyond the picture's edge and onto the album page, where we find a small piece of paper glued below the scene, collage-fashion. The paper carries Irene's signature, a fanciful and undeniably original parade of letters. Irene's almost-realized attempt to spell out her name unfreezes the image by introducing her voice. Two backward *N*'s, an *E* that should be an *L*, compete against the singularity of Carroll's authorship. He may be a man of letters, but hers are the ones I take in.

Little/Liddell Fetishes

Because of its smallness and its ability to permit a long, lingering look, the photograph is wonderfully suitable as a fetish object (Metz
81). The liveliness and individuality of Carroll's photographs of his child-
friends turn them into pocket versions of the real thing, just like Alice after
she drinks from a bottle *not* marked "Poison." Carroll had always been
obsessed with the idea of life in miniature. As a boy he made his own
marionettes and theater. On another occasion he fashioned for a sister a
tiny set of tools, complete with case; at one inch long, they were probably too small even for Lilliput (Greenacre 316). The catalog for Carroll's
estate sale after his death in 1898 lists a stationery set consisting of very
small notepaper and matching envelopes, all collected in a larger envelope
marked "Lilliputian Stationery" in Carroll's own hand (Stern, *Library* 79).
Constructing miniature worlds, writes Susan Stewart, is a way of making
"an 'other' time, a type of transcendent time which negates change and the
flux of lived reality" (65). Carroll ensured such an "other" time by cement-
ing a tiny photograph of Alice Liddell inside his telescope; one gaze and
the world would stop, every star would be Alicious. The "Pleasance" of
this heavenly image served to protect Carroll from the brutality of time, as
if he too were an eternal star, an "everlasting flower."

Like the Victorian girl, the fetish is always double-edged. In psycho-
analytic terms as in its everyday usage, it "means both loss (symbolic castration) and protection against loss" (Metz 84). Whether it works in the
Freudian sense of stopping the look of what has already been seen (the
mother without a penis) "retrospectively," by fixating on an object that
was near before the horrifying primal glance, or whether it means carrying
a rabbit's foot to avoid failing a logic test, both systems embody contradictory functions. They both avert danger while acknowledging the reality
of that danger; they both are signs of an everlasting anxiety (fear of loss)
that sleeps in all of us (Metz 86). In this context Carroll's photographs of
the little girl—especially Evelyn Hatch as the nude odalisque—become the
perfect fetish objects. "There and not there," the little nude is a souvenir
of days gone by. She is a keepsake of the sexual indifference that Carroll
wants to believe in. At the same time, however, she embodies sexual difference, a possibly dangerous difference that he involuntarily acknowledges
and fears. He must therefore simultaneously ward off this acknowledgment
by fetishizing her as not different at all.

The photograph also works with and against Carroll's preoccupation with time, aging, and development.[17] As has been touched upon already, the photograph is indexical, because of its "actual contiguity or connection in the world"; it is a print of a *real* object, as "lightning is the index of the storm" (Metz 82). The indexical aspect of the photograph, the basis for its "message without a code," serves to grant a "reality" to the connoted message (which is based on the "art" of framing, composition, printing techniques, scale, lighting, coloring with oils). This paradox allowed Carroll to believe that little girls remain forever little. But the reality of his photographic Never-Never Land was double-edged. For on the other side of the photographic plate is the fact that because "Photography . . . remains closer to the pure index [we find that it is always] stubbornly pointing to the print of what *was*, but no longer *is*" (Metz 83). In the photograph a "tiny piece of time brutally and forever escapes its ordinary fate," as Christian Metz puts it (paraphrasing Philippe Dubois), while at the same time it must indicate that all time is forever lost (84). This is why photography—and not merely our photographs of our dead loved ones—is associated with death: every photograph indicates the death of a moment, the fact that we are that much closer to our own deaths. For Carroll, who noted in his prefatory poem to *Through the Looking Glass* that "We are older children, dear, / Who fret to find our bedtime near," the photograph of the little girl served as a fetish simultaneously to ward off death and to express Carroll's anxiety about that death. Possibly this is why he himself had such a horror of being photographed.

No Boys, No Women, No Time, and No Street Urchins

In this last section, I would like to turn back to an early photograph (1859) of Alice Liddell posed as a beggar. A special version of it was discovered in the possession of Alice's granddaughter. Tinted, like Evelyn Hatch, Alice is presented in an oval of gold, centered in a black-lacquered traveling photograph mount (fig. 12). Once again we see bare shoulders, this time exposed by a torn shirt signifying the "beggar"'s nonexistent poverty. Her crimson rag skirt, tinted with visible brushstrokes, takes on the air of velvet. The reds and greens, the pinkness of her cheeks, the gold and black of the frame, add to the preciousness of the image. The wall behind her suggests a garden wall, as if she had somehow crept into the yard of the Liddell family. Alice as Cinderella. Only the rich could believe such a story. But even beyond photography's usual attachment to death, this image is attached to despair. "Alice as Beggar" operates as further evi-

Fig. 12. Lewis Carroll, *Alice Liddell,* c. 1858. The Governing Body of Christ Church, Oxford.

dence of Carroll's uneasy relationship with children outside the utopian circles of Oxford or the Pre-Raphaelites. Carroll's camera operated like the "cult of the child" industry as a whole; both were directed at the children of the upper classes. Nevertheless, in Carroll's case there was an exception to this rule, a little girl named Coates—though I doubt that she ever received a special letter from him containing an acrostic of her name.

Daughter of one of the Croft employees, Coates was the subject in one of Carroll's rare pictures of working-class children (fig. 13, 1857). Unlike Alice, she is not simulating another class—she *is* another class. Heavy work boots peek out from under her plain, plaid dress. In stark contrast to Alice's whimsical bob, her hair is pulled severely back from her face. Coates is not lovingly plastered against a garden wall; instead, she is seated on some steps going down to the ground. Wire-covered basement windows, with all their metaphorical baggage, serve as her backdrop. Gernsheim has celebrated this picture for its intentional naturalness, its lack of pompous setting. Yet what comes through is the difference of Coates's life, Coates's class—a subject of difference not usually apparent in Carroll's work.

Working-class children, with their truncated childhoods, must have been particularly unnerving for Carroll. In a letter to an adult Beatrice Hatch, he reveals that his utopia was not only free of boys and time but also drew a line at a certain level of class:

> I should like to know, for curiosity, who that sweet-looking girl was, aged 12, with a red nightcap. I think she had a younger sister, also with a red nightcap. She was speaking to you when I came up to wish you goodnight. I fear I must be content with her *name* only: the social gulf between us is probably too wide for it to be wise to make *friends*. Some of my little *actress*-friends are of a *rather* lower status than myself. But, below a certain line, it is hardly wise to let a girl have a "gentleman" friend—even one of 62! (*Letters* 82)

This letter raises the contradictions of "class" that afflicted the age-of-consent legislation. For not only was "immoral" sexuality connected with the lower classes, economic patterns also ensured that by age twelve many lower-class children would leave home and enter the workplace. The poor child was dangerously outside the protective surveillance provided by the bourgeois parent. "Below a certain line," the risk that the child might really be an "adult" must have become an unbridgeable difference for Carroll.

Similarly, on 18 July 1893 Carroll wrote to his artist friend Gertrude

Fig. 13. Lewis Carroll, *Coates*, 1857. The Gernsheim Collection, Harry Ransom Humanities Research Center, The University of Texas at Austin.

Thompson, requesting her to photograph a nude child for him. The letter reveals Carroll's desire for the body of the *upper-class* girl:

> If *I* had a dry-plate camera, and time to work it, and could secure a child of a really *good* figure, either a professional model, or *(much better) a child of the upper classes,* I would put her into every pretty attitude I could think of, and could get, in a single morning, 50 or 100 such memoranda. (Cohen 29, third emphasis mine)[18]

Alice *posed* as a little beggar allowed Carroll to play in a simulated difference of class that was not really different at all, in much the same way that he played with her and Xie as Chinamen, Turks, and Danes.[19] The oils that tint the photograph of Beggar Alice signify culture and fantasy and ensure that we classify the scene as art and not life. But how different the effect might have been if Alice were of the working classes! One understands why Carroll never dressed Coates in seductively ripped clothes.

The effect was indeed very different when the controversial philanthropist Dr. Barnardo used "artistic fiction" to image the children brought to his home for destitute children. The pictures were employed to advertise the homes, with the hope of raising both sympathy and revenue. The bodies of the children turned over to Barnardo's care, desperate and without rights of their own, became suitable blank slates for his cause. Consider the case of Florence and Eliza Holder. The sisters were brought in by their mother around 1876, "poorly but decently clad" (fig. 14)—possibly in clothes borrowed for the occasion in order that they might be properly dressed for this important moment of their lives (Wagner 140). Much to Mrs. Holder's alarm, she was later confronted with a photograph of Florence without the shoes that she had come in with, her hair disheveled, wearing a tattered dress. To top matters off, Florence was posed as if she were selling newspapers in the street, something she had never done in her life (fig. 15). Barefoot, with her petticoat skirt mysteriously hiked up on one side, she is reminiscent of Carroll's "Beggar Alice." But her unbelievably disheveled hair and her sad, angry face hold no seduction for the viewer. There are no fairy tales for Florence. A portrait of her sister Eliza was also taken; the picture was placed on a collecting box with the legend, "A little waif six years old, taken from the streets." This text, which suggested that she had been living on the street without her mother, was a lie, but the story was made believable through the reality-effect of the photograph (its message without a code). The tale came out in an arbitration case in 1877.

Maybe it is because I know Florence's story that I cannot see anything

Fig. 14. Anonymous photographer, *Florence and Eliza Holder*, c. 1876. The Barnardo Photographic Archive, The University of Liverpool Library.

Fig. 15. Anonymous photographer, *Florence Holder*, c. 1876. The Barnardo
Photographic Archive, The University of Liverpool Library.

of the girl's own in the portrait ordered by Barnardo. However, I hear the
screams of her mother in court. And I see the manipulation of her and her
body for the causes of an upper-middle-class man.

The impetus behind Carroll's fading Victorian prints may be traced to
a general "cult of the little girl" that was invoked in a range of cultural
spaces: by the artists who portrayed her as "pure" (sexualized but not actively sexual), as in Millais's *Cherry Ripe* or Arthur Hughes's *Girl with
Lilacs* (1863), the painting that Carroll chose to hang over the fireplace in
his own study (Stern, "Pre-Raphaelite" 174); by the children's illustrated
books and greeting cards typified by Kate Greenaway's little "dollies"; by
the law of the period, which sought to determine the parameters of girlhood. But Carroll's actual images remain atypical. His photographs record
a representation of the little girl that feels undecided, as if he too were
caught, with the Victorian girl, in an act of blushing and nonblushing at
the same time.

This "undecidability" is poignantly demonstrated in a scene (neither fic-
titious nor true) from Gavin Millar's film *Dreamchild* (1985). The scene features Alice, her mother, one of Alice's sisters, Mr. Dodgson, and Mr. Duck-
worth, seated in a rowboat that is floating down a beautiful flower-lined
river. Alice stories have been told. It has been a perfect summer day . . .
until now. Mr. Dodgson has begun to *stare* at Alice. His eyes are filled
with an overwhelming, uncomfortable sort of love. His gaze, painful for
all involved, does not go unnoticed by Alice. It is clear that she has experienced it before and that her sister has seen it before. Without warning,
Alice puts a stop to the look by giving Mr. Dodgson a cold splash of river
water right in the eyes. Humiliation washes over his face. If he were not
utterly speechless, he would be stuttering. Mrs. Liddell sternly insists that
Alice apologize to Mr. Dodgson. Then, with unnerving knowledge and defiance, Alice not only apologizes but also uses her white lace handkerchief
to dry Mr. Dodgson's pathetic face—sensually drawing the moment and
the beads of water out, until we and Alice's mother can take it no longer.
His gaze, a white lace handkerchief, a performative little girl, a sexuality
without parameters: these are the (filmically frozen) contradictions at play
in those photographs of Carroll's that feature *his* "complex fantasm" that
we call "the girl."

NOTES

I am grateful to Helene Moglen, Stephen Heath, and Hayden White for their
provocative questions, insightful criticisms, and generosity during various stages of

this project. I would also like to thank Jennifer Fiona Ragheb and Thomas Moore for their invaluable work as research assistants.

1. Without drawing any conclusions, I would note that it was Nabokov who translated *Alice in Wonderland* into Russian in 1923. Several authors have written about the literary connections between Carroll's writings and those of Nabokov; see, for example, Prioleau.

2. *Alice's Adventures Underground,* of course, was first narrated during a boat trip on 4 July 1862 and was written down, at Alice's request, and given to her on 26 November 1864 as a Christmas present. This copy contained Carroll's own illustrations and ended with an oval portrait (taken by Carroll) of Alice herself. *Alice's Adventures in Wonderland,* with illustrations by Tenniel, was first published by Macmillan in 1865.

3. I use the date 1879 on the authority of the *Oxford English Dictionary,* although it is actually not until the fourth edition of *Duncan's Clinical Lectures* (1889) that the passage that uses and discusses the word "sexuality" appears. I am indebted to Stephen Heath for pointing out the birth and development of the word in the nineteenth century. For a rich discussion of this topic, see Heath, esp. 7–9.

4. Three of the four nudes have been painted over. The fourth is actually a watercolor only, probably made from laying a piece of watercolor paper over one of Carroll's photographs. The picture of Evelyn is at once the most photographic and the most sexually explicit.

5. Nancy Armstrong has dealt with the interesting and conflicting ideas of occidentalism that arose during this period of orientalism, as reflected in the anxieties found in the *Alice* books (and elsewhere) as well as in a small selection of Victorian photographs. While I find Armstrong's feminist, literary, and historical arguments enlightening, her discussion of the visual images falls short. For example, one wonders why Carroll's photographs of Xie Kitchin and the Liddell girls as Chinamen were not discussed in relation to the photograph of Alice Liddell as a (British) beggar. Even more troublesome is the absence of a discussion of how Julia Margaret Cameron's photographs of Ceylonese peasants relate to Cameron's other images (Cameron posed both her English maid and her Ceylonese peasants as Madonnas, for instance, and tried to photograph an English friend as a Ceylonese, although the latter images are now lost).

6. "My mind has been considerably exercised this season by the exhibition of Alma-Tadema's nude Venus . . . [there might] be artistic reasons which justify such public exposure of the female form. . . . In the case of the nude of an old master much allowance has been made . . . for old masters it might be assumed knew no better . . . but for a living artist to exhibit a life-size, life-like, almost photographic representation of a beautiful naked woman strikes my inartistic mind as somewhat if not very mischievous" (qtd. in Wood 115).

7. Ruskin, Alice Liddell's art teacher and an acquaintance of Carroll (he appears in *Alice in Wonderland* as the "drawling master" who taught "drawling," "stretch-

ing," and "fainting in coils"), is another frequently cited devotee of the Victorian "cult of the little girl." Like Carroll the author of many letters to young girls, Ruskin also wrote a fairy tale—*The King of the Golden River*—to one, thirteen-year-old Effie Gray. When the two finally married and Ruskin was faced with Effie's matured body, the relationship soured, perhaps over his "disgust" for her womanly curves and pubic hair (see Millais, esp. 21). Ruskin divorced Effie (who then married Millais) and subsequently fell in love with ten-year-old Rose La Touche. Stranger still, however, was his long epistolary seduction of Kate Greenaway, the children's illustrator. His interest was not in her but in her drawings of little "dollies"; Ruskin even requested that she draw these girls without clothes: "As we've got so far as taking off hats, I trust we may in time get to take off just a little more—say mittens—and then—perhaps—even shoes! and—(for fairies) even . . . stockings—and then—. . . . Will you—(it's all for your own good—!) make her [a drawing of a sylph] stand up and draw her for me without a cap—and without her shoes,—(because of the heels) and without her mittens, and without her—frock and frills? And let me see exactly how tall she is—and how—round. It will be so good of and for you—And to and for me" (qtd. in Engen 93–94).

8. See especially the essays by Laqueur, Poovey, and Schiebinger in *The Making of the Modern Body* (edited by Laqueur and Catherine Gallagher), as well as Showalter's *The Female Malady*.

9. Speculation over why Carroll gave up photography in 1880 is rife. Cohen has argued that Carroll abandoned his favorite hobby for two reasons: the victory of the new dry plate process over the wet collodion process that Carroll preferred, and Carroll's desire to devote more time to scholarship in order to finish his many projects before he died (22–25). Gernsheim, in contrast, contends—after discussing the situation with many of Carroll's models in their old age—that "despite his precaution of photographing girls in the nude only in the presence of the mother or another adult woman, a scandal did develop in Oxford in 1880, which decided Lewis Carroll to abandon his hobby altogether. This bears out my feeling that the reason for his decision lay outside the field of photo-technique" (v).

10. The age of consent was raised to thirteen in 1875. Prior to that year, the age of consent had been twelve, which reflected legislation of the thirteenth century.

11. Similarly, Judith Walkowitz has explored Josephine Butler's campaign against the Contagious Diseases Acts, in which Butler fought against the inevitability of prostitution as a cultural institution while still maintaining, importantly, that women had a right not to be harassed and even to choose to prostitute themselves. Walkowitz's discussion of Butler demonstrates what Michel Foucault has suggested—that sexuality was *not* repressed in the Victorian world, but was in fact at the center of their discourse.

12. Here I differ slightly from Armstrong's readings of Cameron's child-images as participating in a Victorian penchant for photographing prepubescent girls. Despite Cameron's general focus on the maternal figure, her photographs of the

prepubescent are consistently androgynous or *neutre* (in Marin's sense). This is not to say that they are not feminine. In the two photographs that Armstrong features (*Study of a Dead Child* and *Cupid*), there is no way of knowing the gender of either child without knowing the model. It is interesting that Armstrong should read both as female, based solely on the feminine aestheticization of each, especially given that Cupid is a male figure in mythology. (Incidentally, the child modeling as Cupid here—Freddy Gould?—also appears as Christ or John the Baptist in a number of Cameron's Madonna pictures.) I have not seen any raised garments on this little Cupid, so I prefer to keep his/her gender at "play" (as Marin would say); and indeed, it is imaged as such by Cameron.

13. Carroll and many other critics of the day were unsympathetic to Cameron's technique; they felt that she was not being true to the medium. (Carroll was a great fan of Lady Hawarden's *clear* photographs.) Gernsheim writes of one of the occasions when Carroll and Cameron met: "In August 1864, when he [Carroll] was on holiday at Freshwater, Isle of Wight, they spent a happy evening at Mrs. Cameron's house looking at each other's photographs. She had then been photographing for only a few months, but characteristically already spoke of her pictures 'as if they were a triumph in art,' as Lewis Carroll records with a touch of mockery, adding more critically, 'Some are very picturesque, some merely hideous. *She* wishes she could have had some of *my* subjects to do *out* of focus—and *I* expressed an analogous wish with regard to some of *her* subjects' " (30).

14. According to Gardner's annotation (Carroll 257), "It is possible that Carroll thought of these dream-rushes as symbols of his child-friends. The loveliest seem to be the most distant, just out of reach, and, once picked, they quickly fade and lose their scent and beauty."

15. Consider the following letter written by Carroll to one of his few child-friends to remain a friend past puberty: "I always feel specially grateful to friends who, like you, have given me a child-friendship and a woman-friendship. About nine out of ten, I think, of my child friendships get shipwrecked at the critical point, 'where the stream and river meet,' and the child-friends, once so affectionate, become uninteresting acquaintances, whom I have no wish to set eyes on again" (Collingwood 368–69).

16. Similarly, Auerbach reads Carroll's photograph of Alice Price "caught" holding a doll face to face as a mockery of proper motherhood; she comments, "The pensive sensuality of the child's pose, the erotic hunger of her expression, become more apparent to us as we look, until the doll becomes less a thing to nourish than a thing to eat" (167).

17. The difference/indifference or absence/presence that is utopically contained in Carroll's photographs is not unlike the "Podsnappery" in Charles Dickens's *Our Mutual Friend* (1864–65). In the famous satire (which speaks to the period's obsessive devotion to the innocence of the girl), "the cheek of a young person" becomes a fetishized testing site for impossible sexual contradictions. But since Georgiana

Podsnap is in the habit of blushing whether it is appropriate or not, all tests are fallacious. There is no way of demarcating her guilt from her innocence. Like Carroll's images, "[Mr.] Podsnap's idea of his young person is that of a creature who cannot in fact exist" (Yeazell 343).

18. This letter is omitted from Cohen's edition of Carroll's letters.

19. While Rejlander also photographed "simulated" poor children, they were represented sentimentally and without the sexuality of Carroll's "Beggar Alice."

WORKS CITED

Armstrong, Nancy. "The Occidental Alice." *Differences* 2.2 (1990): 3–40.

Auerbach, Nina. *Romantic Imprisonment: Women and Other Glorified Outcasts.* New York: Columbia UP, 1986.

Barthes, Roland. *Camera Lucida: Reflections on Photography.* Trans. Richard Howard. New York: Farrar, Straus and Giroux, 1981.

———. "The Photographic Message." *Image/Music/Text.* Trans. Stephen Heath. New York: Hill and Wang, 1977. 15–31.

Bradley, Laurel. "From Eden to Empire: John Everett Millais's *Cherry Ripe*." *Victorian Studies* 34 (1991): 179–203.

Carroll, Lewis [C. L. Dodgson]. *The Letters of Lewis Carroll.* Ed. Morton N. Cohen with Roger Lancelyn Green. New York: Oxford UP, 1979.

———. *Through the Looking Glass and What Alice Found There.* In *The Annotated Alice.* Ed. Martin Gardner. New York: Meridian, 1960.

Cixous, Hélène. "Introduction to Lewis Carroll's *Through the Looking-Glass* and *The Hunting of the Snark*." *New Literary History* 13.2 (Winter 1982): 231–51.

Cohen, Morton. *Lewis Carroll, Photographer of Children: Four Nude Studies.* New York: Potter, 1978.

Collingwood, Stuart Dodgson. *The Life and Letters of Lewis Carroll.* London: T. F. Unwin, 1898.

Duncan, J. Matthews. *Clinical Lectures on the Diseases of Women.* 4th ed. London: J. and A. Churchill, 1889.

Engen, Rodney. *Kate Greenaway: A Biography.* New York: Schocken, 1981.

Foucault, Michel. *The History of Sexuality. Vol. 1, An Introduction.* Trans. Robert Hurley. New York: Pantheon, 1978.

Freud, Sigmund. "The Sexual Life of Human Beings." Lecture 20. *Introductory Lectures on Psychoanalysis.* 1917. Standard Edition. Trans. James Strachey. New York: Norton, 1977. 303–19.

Gernsheim, Helmut. *Lewis Carroll, Photographer.* New York: Dover, 1969.

Gordon, Jan B., and Edward Guiliano. "From Victorian Textbook to Ready-Made: Lewis Carroll and the Black Art." *Soaring with the Dodo: Essays on Lewis Carroll's Life and Art.* Ed. Edward Guiliano and James R. Kincaid. Charlottesville: UP of Virginia, 1982. 1–25.

Gorham, Deborah. "The 'Maiden Tribute of Modern Babylon' Re-Examined: Child Prostitution and the Idea of Childhood in Late-Victorian England." *Victorian Studies* 21.3 (Spring 1978): 353–79.

Greenacre, Phyllis. "The Character of Dodgson as Revealed in the Writings of Carroll." *Aspects of Alice: Lewis Carroll's Dreamchild as Seen Through the Critics' Looking-Glasses 1865–1971*. Ed. Robert Phillips. London: Gollancz, 1972. 316–31.

Heath, Stephen. *The Sexual Fix*. London: Macmillan, 1982.

Kincaid, James R. "Alice's Invasion of Wonderland." *PMLA* 88.1 (January 1973): 92–99.

Laqueur, Thomas, and Catherine Gallagher, eds. *The Making of the Modern Body: Sexuality and Society in the Nineteenth Century*. Berkeley: U of California P, 1987.

Marin, Louis. *Utopics: The Semiological Play of Textual Space*. Trans. Robert A. Vollrath. Atlantic Highlands: Humanities, 1990.

Metz, Christian. "Photography and Fetish." *October* 34 (Fall 1985): 81–90.

Millais, Euphemia. *Effie in Venice: Unpublished Letters of Mrs. John Ruskin Written Between 1849–1852*. Ed. Mary Lutyens. New York: Vanguard, 1965.

Nabokov, Vladimir. *The Annotated Lolita*. Ed. Alfred Appel, Jr. New York: McGraw-Hill, 1970.

Parker, Rozsika, and Griselda Pollock. *Old Mistresses: Women, Art and Ideology*. New York: Pantheon, 1981.

Pollock, Griselda. *Vision and Difference: Femininity, Feminism and the Histories of Art*. New York: Routledge, 1988.

Prioleau, Elizabeth. "Humbert Humbert Through the Looking-Glass." *Twentieth Century Literature* 21.4 (December 1975): 428–37.

Showalter, Elaine. *The Female Malady: Women, Madness and Culture in England, 1830–1980*. New York: Pantheon, 1985.

Solomon-Godeau, Abigail. "The Legs of the Countess." *October* 39 (Winter 1986): 65–108.

Stern, Jeffrey. "Lewis Carroll and the Pre-Raphaelite: 'Fainting in Coils.' " *Lewis Carroll Observed*. Ed. Edward Guiliano. New York: Potter, 1976. 161–80.

———. *Lewis Carroll's Library*. Charlottesville: UP of Virginia, 1981.

Stewart, Susan. *On Longing: Narratives of the Miniature, the Gigantic, the Souvenir, the Collection*. Baltimore: Johns Hopkins UP, 1984.

Wagner, Gillian. *Barnardo*. London: Weidenfeld and Nicolson, 1979.

Walkowitz, Judith. *Prostitution and Victorian Society: Women, Class and the State*. Cambridge: Cambridge UP, 1980.

Wittig, Monique. "The Category of Sex." *Feminist Issues* 2.2 (Fall 1982): 63–68.

Wood, Christopher. *Olympian Dreamers: Victorian Classical Painters, 1860–1914*. London: Constable, 1983.

Yeazell, Ruth. "Podsnappery, Sexuality, and the English Novel." *Critical Inquiry* 9 (1982): 339–57.

JOYCE SENDERS PEDERSEN

Life's Lessons: Liberal Feminist Ideals of Family, School, and Community in Victorian England

In 1889, Maria Grey published *Last Words to Girls on Life in School and After School.* A feminist of liberal persuasion, Grey and her sister Emily Anne Shirreff pioneered reforms in girls' education, promoting the establishment of academically oriented secondary schools for girls.[1] The sisters also actively supported the women's suffrage campaign. Despite her undoubted commitment to women's rights, however, Grey's testament to girls primarily emphasized their future duties: "the governing purpose of your school life is to prepare you by its teaching and discipline for the service society will demand of you after school" (*Words* 10). She did not, she stated, wish to encourage "asceticism" in girls. However, she cautioned, "Self must take the second, not the first place . . . the welfare of the whole must come before the welfare of the individual" (5–6).

Anticipating, then, that well-educated, emancipated women would exercise self-restraint and look first to the welfare of "the whole" and only secondarily to their own, Grey directed girls' attention to the service that might be required of them by family, society, the nation, and all humankind (*Words* 6 and passim). Her thinking suggested no radical disjunction between private and public life. The same education that prepared girls for family responsibilities, she assumed, would also fit them for participation in the public sphere.

Whether women in fact opted primarily for a domestic or for a public role did not strike Grey as particularly important so long as they were free to choose. She wished all manner of employments to be opened to women and urged her readers—"you, the first generation of public school girls"—to prove women capable of public virtues (*Words* 53). She left no doubt, however, that she considered a happy marriage, especially if it produced children, to be women's "happiest and most natural sphere of action," and if she dismissed the notion that "idleness and dependence" were essential to "ladyhood," she also rejected the idea that paid employment and a life apart from home were essential to "honourable womanhood" (270, 239–40). Convinced that motherhood would always be women's first function,

Grey predicted that few women would ever participate actively in public life beyond exercising the vote (320–21). She regarded the prospect with apparent equanimity.

Grey's views (such as her emphasis on duty and self-restraint; her tendency to conflate public and private virtues and duties; her broad acceptance of the current sexual division of labor, in which women functioned primarily as homemakers) were common to many Victorian reformers who, like Grey herself, were at once feminists and liberals.[2] These orientations have sometimes been represented as failures of a Victorian feminist imagination not fully emancipated from traditional norms of class and gender.[3] I would certainly not deny that in practice these emphases may have helped perpetuate women's subordination, or that they were informed by elitist values. I would suggest, however, that to understand their meaning for Grey and her contemporaries, we must view these orientations not as rooted in a regressive feminine ideal but as grounded in the same liberal paradigms of self-development and social progress that inspired these reformers' commitment to women's emancipation. While certain of these ways of thinking may today appear repressive, for Victorian feminists they were integrally related to their hopes for a better future not just for individual women but for all humankind. This essay, then, examines the ideals of family, school, and community held out to girls by Maria Grey and other liberal feminists in an effort to provide a better understanding of the assumptions that informed both their liberal and their feminist commitments.

Private Character and Public Virtue: Liberal Paradigms of Progress

The advice that Maria Grey and other liberal feminists addressed to girls should be understood in the context of what might be termed the higher liberalism of the mid- and late-Victorian years. Most eloquently and influentially elaborated by John Stuart Mill, this strand of liberal thought emphasized qualitative aspects of individual happiness and sought to reconcile individual self-development with the pursuit of broader social ends. Concerned primarily with individual well-being on the one hand and the general utility of the whole society on the other, liberal analysts drew few distinctions in principle along the lines of sex or class. Further, conceiving education as a lifelong process of individual development, such distinctions as they drew between youth and adulthood related to differences of degree more than kind. When Maria Grey and other liberal feminists turned their attention to girls, they were thus disinclined to view them as a separate caste. The advice they proffered girls rather mirrored their general convictions concerning individual and societal development.

Liberal feminists took as their point of departure a rationalist, libertarian, individualist ethos that identified individual improvement as the source of progressive social change. Their feminist vision encompassed both individual and social ends. As the suffrage leader Millicent Fawcett asserted: "Women need education, need economic independence, need political enfranchisement, need social equality . . . mainly because without them they are less able to do their duty to themselves and to their neighbours" (Introduction 29). Liberal feminists such as Grey and Fawcett favored women's emancipation neither solely that individual women might improve their lot nor that they might promote progressive social change. They believed in both processes, and they saw the two as integrally related.

Individual character development was the linchpin linking essentially self-serving goals to wider social ends in liberal feminist thought. Freedom, according to liberal lights, was improving to the character. As the feminist publicist and suffragist Frances Power Cobbe declared, "it is in the firm faith that women will be *more* dutiful than they have ever been, more conscientious, more unselfish, more temperate, and more chaste, that I have joined my voice to the demand for their emancipation" (*Duties* vii). In his classic liberal manifesto "The Subjection of Women" (1869), John Stuart Mill explained that freedom was educative. Conditions of freedom promoted rational decision-making, enabling and obliging individuals to assume responsibility for the consequences of their choices.[4] Freedom, Mill argued, stimulated not only intellectual but also moral development, expanding individuals' mental and moral frames of reference, encouraging social awareness. Thus freedom, reason, and social responsibility tended to develop hand in hand: "the communities in which the reason has been the most cultivated, and in which the idea of social duty has been the most powerful, are those which have most strongly asserted the freedom of action of the individual" (336). Consistent with these assumptions, Mill and other liberal feminists favored women's emancipation not least as a means of furthering their moral and mental development:

> Whatever has been said or written . . . of the ennobling influence of free government . . . the larger and higher objects which it presents to the intellect and feelings, the more unselfish public spirit, and . . . broader view of duty, that it engenders, and the generally loftier platform on

which it elevates the individual as a moral, spiritual, and social being—
is every particle as true of women as of men. (Mill, "Subjection" 337)

Similarly, although in the 1850s Shirreff had feared the "lowering tendencies of active life," by the 1880s she too was emphasizing "the mental and
moral discipline gained by a higher and wider range of work" (*Education*
26, "Work" 37).[5]

Freedom, liberal feminists tirelessly insisted, would make women better.
"The free woman makes the best wife and the most careful mother,"
Fawcett categorically declared (*Suffrage* 41). One might find Mrs. Jellybys
in novels, Cobbe commented, but her own experience indicated that women
who exercised "Public Spirit" also made admirable daughters, wives,
and mothers (*Duties* 158).[6] Shirreff deplored the "frivolous idleness" and
thoughtless extravagance of many girls and advised public involvement
as an antidote. Civic rights and duties, she explained, would lead women
to cherish civic virtues and the public interest ("Work" 53). In expanding
women's mental and moral horizons, liberal feminists argued, women's
emancipation would encourage wives to sympathize with their husbands'
higher interests, mothers to keep in mind principled, large-minded goals
when rearing their children, and woman philanthropists to be more judi-
cious in doling out charity to their neighbors (see Mill, "Subjection" 329–
33; Cobbe, *Duties* 99; Shirreff, "Work" 71; Davies, *Thoughts* 72–76). In
short, they believed that freedom would encourage socially responsible
behavior in both the private and the public spheres.

In Mill's case the conviction that freedom promoted moral and intellectual improvement was further underwritten by the belief that the higher
individual happiness was to be found in the promotion of socially beneficial
ends—such as the improvement of humankind, intellectual endeavors, or
artistic pursuits.[7] Free to choose their own goals, Mill considered, rational,
enlightened, experienced individuals would prefer these activities to narrowly self-seeking ends.[8] Couching her argument in Kantian terms, Cobbe
reached similar conclusions. She rejected theories that treated woman as an
"adjective" (whose "final cause" was to be defined only relative to others'
needs). Instead she considered two theories of woman as a "noun" (having
purpose as an individual): the "selfish" theory, which made woman's private happiness her end in life, and the "divine" that she should live for
God. Cobbe plumped for the latter theory, observing that the "selfish" life
was inadequate because if one sought only one's own pleasure one would
be unhappy ("Cause" 6–24).

If liberal feminists promoted women's emancipation particularly with

an eye to their mental and moral development, they were certainly not indifferent to questions of material well-being. Their demands for the vote,
for an end to legal restrictions on women's employment, and for improved
educational opportunities for women were motivated in part by concern
for women's material interests. They considered, however, that ultimately
well-being was a function of mental and moral culture. Thus Mill viewed
"self-respect, self-help, and self-control" as "the essential conditions both
of individual prosperity and of social virtue" ("Subjection" 330), while
Shirreff argued, "In point even of mere money . . . as regards the real
needs of the working population, a higher tone of habits, character, and
intelligence would do more than a rise of wages" ("Hindrances" 86).

This said, however, it is true that these Victorian moralists viewed
the direct pursuit of material self-interest—or indeed any directly self-
aggrandizing behavior—as inferior to disinterested intellectual and social
commitments. The more enlightened the individual, they considered, the
less narrowly self-interested his or her outlook was apt to be. As Emily
Davies (a leading light in the movement for women's educational reform)
declared:

> I believe the best women think more of duties and responsibilities than
> of rights and wrongs, and care comparatively little for any "right" but
> that of giving their best in the service of God and humanity, by the
> free development of whatever capacities of usefulness they possess.
> (*Thoughts* 5)[9]

The disinterested motivations associated with individual character development in turn helped sustain a free, progressive social order. Only if
individuals developed principled commitments to larger social ends could
society avoid anarchy on the one hand, despotism on the other. Mill and
Harriet Taylor reflected on the problem:

> Does not all experience shew that when people care only for them-
> selves and their families, then unless they are held down by despotism,
> every one's hand is against every one, and that only so far as they care
> about the public or about some abstract principle is there a basis for
> real social feeling of any sort? (385)

Consistent with this stance, Grey explained to girls that a principled,
dispassionate outlook was essential for constructive participation in public life:

The first condition of fitness for useful influence or action in public matters, is the power and habit of looking at them from above our personal standpoint, and with the earnest *desire*, at any rate, to see them unbiased by our personal likes and dislikes, in the light of principle, not prejudice. (*Words* 311)

What, she demanded, would become of the society that had no other tie or loyalty than individual self-interest? (48).

For liberal feminists such as Maria Grey and John Stuart Mill, individual improvement and social melioration appeared to be mutually reinforcing. Individual character development, however, was crucial. Accordingly, they judged all manner of institutions with an eye to their educative potential.

Progressive Principles of Family Life

While Victorian antifeminists (like the structural-functionalists of a later era) viewed home and public life as separate spheres with distinctive norms and values, liberal feminists emphasized the linkages between the two.[10] To liberal feminists, the family was above all a setting for character formation. Mill considered that for the parents the family should serve as "an exercise of those virtues which each requires to fit them for all other association." For the children, he continued, family life should be "a model . . . of the feelings and conduct which their temporary training by means of obedience is designed to render habitual . . . to them" ("Subjection" 295). Laying as it did the foundations of character, the family seemed to liberal feminists to constitute the cornerstone of national life. Josephine Butler (who was active in women's educational reform before she became leader of the crusade against state regulation of prostitution and the double standard of sexual morality) declared, "Home is the nursery of all virtue, the fountain-head of all true affection, and the source of strength of our nation" (xxv). Grey agreed: "The home . . . is the real seed-ground of life. What is planted and cultivated there will determine, in all but rare cases, the general quality of the future crop" (*Words* ix). On liberal feminists' reading, the quality of family life and that of public life appeared integrally related.

Consistent with this view, Grey suggested that over the long run private and public relations tended to converge. She distinguished three types of marriage corresponding to three stages of civilization: the barbarous, where women were treated as chattel; the legal/familial, where women were cast as passive partners in a legal contract aimed at perpetuating the family; and the individualist, where marriage was based on the free choice of two individuals. These stages corresponded to an evolution away from a society based on force toward a society ruled by law in which authority rested increasingly on voluntary assent rather than coercion ("Sequel" 778–80).

Mill pursued a similar line of thought. The family as currently organized was, he considered, an atavistic institution. Such anomalies were characteristic of transitional times: "Institutions, books, education, society, all go on training human beings for the old, long after the new has come; much more when it is only coming" ("Subjection" 294). At present, Mill charged, at a time when libertarian, meritocratic principles based on a recognition of individual rights increasingly prevailed, the family remained a "school of despotism," geared to a moribund age when authority rested on force or on accident of birth (294–95).

Mill and other liberal feminists suggested that the lessons of contemporary family life were often far from improving. The legal subjection of wives, they argued, had a corrosive influence on the character of both sexes, promoting selfishness and tyranny in men, narrow sentiments, deviousness, and want of judgment in women. In their current subject state, women's influence on family and society was by no means entirely beneficial. Ill educated, impulsive, dependent, knowing little of the world and caring less, unable to conceive of issues except in personal terms, women, they charged, all too often discouraged husbands from focusing on anything other than the family's worldly interests; condoned ignorance, idleness, and frivolity in their daughters; and (through ill-judged charity) promoted improvidence in their neighbors (Mill, "Subjection" 288–89, 329–33; Davies, *Thoughts* 72–76; Cobbe, *Duties* 99; Butler xxxviii).

If individuals were to be educated to participate in a progressive society, liberal feminists concluded, family relations must conform to progressive principles. Mill explained: "The moral training of mankind will never be adapted to the conditions of life for which all other human progress is a preparation, until they practise in the family the same moral rule which is adapted to the normal constitution of human society" ("Subjection" 295).[11] Family life, he believed, must be reformed that it might become "the real school of the virtues of freedom." Grey concurred that

> when men and women stand . . . equal [as] helpmeets in the work of
> life . . . then only, may we hope to see the moral cesspools of society

cleansed away, and the human family advancing with steady step
and even front to the final conquest of civilisation over barbarism.
("Men" 685)

According to this analysis, then, an alteration of private, family relations
was necessary for the full realization of progress in the public sphere.

If the family were to become a "school of the virtues of freedom," marriage, liberal feminists considered, must be grounded in the free choice
of potentially self-dependent individuals.[12] Arguing that women too often
married not from love but from material necessity, they urged that women's
educational and employment opportunities be extended to enhance their
freedom of choice. Cobbe explained that "it is only on the standing ground
of a happy and independent celibacy that a woman can really make a free
choice in marriage" (*Essays* 67–68; see also Butler xxxi, H. Mill 403).
Viewing freedom of choice as a precondition for individual moral development, Shirreff asserted that extending women's employment opportunities
would promote "self-reliance and increased dignity of character." At the
societal level, she predicted, the result would be

> honourable independence for women who remain single; true honour
> for those who have voluntarily placed themselves under the yoke of
> marriage. . . . more equal companionship between husbands and wives;
> higher influence for mothers. . . . a larger place as citizens . . . more
> influence on the life of the nation. ("Work" 72)

Liberal feminists such as Shirreff anticipated that freedom of choice would
enhance women's status and authority in both the domestic and the public
domain.

Associating freedom with self-government and the rule of reason, liberal
feminists considered that both within the family and in society at large,
order must be secured chiefly by voluntary deference to an authority perceived as reasonable, not by compulsion. Grey explained: "Obedience . . .
not of the outward act only, but of the inward mind . . . that *respects*,
not merely fears the authority to which it bows,—is the foundation of all
social order, which could never be maintained by force alone" (*Words* 39).
In a progressive society authority must rest primarily on merit, particularly intellectual and moral merit. As society advanced, Grey noted, not
force but law increasingly ruled, and for the higher purposes of life (beyond the simple preservation of the species), she suggested, moral purpose
and intellect were decisive ("Men" 675). Likewise, Mill anticipated that

in practice a variety of factors would influence authority patterns within a marriage, including age and contribution to the family's material support. He assumed, however, that intellectual and moral qualities—mental superiority, decisiveness—would tell heavily ("Subjection" 291–92). Modern principles of social virtue, Mill asserted, required that individuals be fitted "to live together as equals; claiming nothing for themselves but what they as freely concede to every one else; regarding command of every kind as an exceptional necessity" (294). Thus the family should ideally be "a school of sympathy in equality [for man and wife] . . . without power on one side or obedience on the other. . . . It would then be an exercise of those virtues which each requires to fit them for all other association, and a model to the children" (295). In a similar vein, Davies, too, argued that the influence exercised by men and women alike, whether in the state or the family, must rest on a "moral and spiritual" rather than a "physical and legal" basis (*Education* 183–84).

Such a meritocratic vision did not necessarily assume that authority would ultimately be distributed equally between the sexes. Liberal feminists differed in their estimates of the relative potential capabilities of men and women. Mill and Davies emphasized that nothing could be known with certitude of either sex's native abilities (Mill, "Subjection" 313; Davies, *Thoughts* 48–49), while Grey was of the opinion that the sexes had different natural orientations deriving from their paternal and maternal functions. She left open the question of relative intelligence, although she pronounced male and female intelligence to be "precisely similar" in kind (*Words* 67, "Sequel" 787). Shirreff, on the other hand, believed women to be on the average innately inferior to men ("Work" 54). None of these reformers, however, considered that women's possible general inferiority mandated legal or customary restrictions on their civil rights. There were no grounds for compulsion. In a free society, they hoped and believed, merit would ultimately tell.

Within the family, liberal feminists distinguished sharply between the status of children and that of adults. Children, they emphasized, must be trained to obedience. Mill anticipated that the family "will always be a school of obedience for the children, of command for the parents" ("Subjection" 295).[13] Shirreff took a similar tack, arguing that "absolute unquestioning obedience must be the rule of childhood, if we hope to form later a habit of obedience to the voice of duty" ("Hindrances" 19). The child habituated to obedience was not, Shirreff considered, the slave of coercion. Instead, she contended, that child was acquiring the habit of self-control:

"The willing submission to the rule felt to be lawful and wise is the germ of self-government" (*Training* 14). Representing obedience to parental authority as a form of voluntary submission based on the child's trust and reverence for its parents rather than as a concession to force, Shirreff depicted such obedience as laying the foundation for "a habit of obedience to the voice of duty" ("Hindrances" 19–20). She viewed such internalization of discipline as the precondition for the moral life.

Gradually, as habits of discipline were internalized, external constraints might be relaxed. Thus Shirreff distinguished between the "obedience of the child" and the "willing docility of youth." Warning that "in educating girls to submission we have too often educated them to nullity," she urged the merits of "rational freedom" for older girls (*Education* 296–97, 301). Similarly, addressing her attention to "the direction of the young during the intermediate stage between boyhood or girlhood and manhood or womanhood," Davies advised "the strengthening and development of character by a discipline combining subordination to rule with a considerable amount of self-government" (*Home* 11–12). Character training aimed, then, at creating self-directing individuals.

Self-government was closely linked with self-restraint—with the rule of reason—in Victorian liberal feminist thinking. Mastery of the passions by the reason was considered crucial in establishing individuals as free moral agents, enabling them to realize their full humanity. Discussing the "essential principle of self-control," Grey told girls that

> only in so far as you learn to be a "law unto yourselves" are you raised above the lower animals, the creatures of their instincts, appetites, and outward circumstances, to the level of human beings, endowed with the glorious privileges of freedom and self-government. (*Words* 21) [14]

Cobbe likewise considered sexual self-discipline central to women's status: "The woman who is the slave of her passions is everywhere the slave of man,—the woman whose moral nature is supreme over her passions everywhere obtains a certain modicum of freedom" (*Duties* 8).

Victorian feminists' ideals of marriage reflected these priorities. They wished the voice of reason to prevail in the domestic as in the public sphere. While their attitudes toward sexual passion varied, they were broadly agreed that marriage ought not to be entered into primarily for sexual gratification.[15] Not passion but principle offered the best foundation for a happy marriage, as Grey and Shirreff sought to demonstrate in their 1853 novel, *Passion and Principle*.

These Victorian reformers were not unmindful that what Cobbe termed a "well-ordered life" required an adequate material basis. To this end, Cobbe approved, when possible, of dowries, and Davies recommended that women gain professional qualifications in part as a means of facilitating otherwise imprudent marriages (Cobbe, *Essays* 48; Davies, *Education* 107–9). However, just as they disapproved of the pursuit of narrow private or sectional interests in the public arena,[16] these liberals deplored marriages rooted in the hope of worldly gain. Marriage, they agreed, must be hallowed by disinterested affection. Otherwise, they considered, it was but a form of prostitution.[17]

Liberal feminists were broadly agreed that family life must promote individual development. Thus, for example, Davies hoped for "a development of the family ideal which shall make room for, and even cherish, individuality" (*Home* 12). Similarly, Susan Mendus has shown how central was the goal of self-development to Mill's ideal of married life. Their ideals, however, were far from self-indulgent. Mill's vision of marriage emphasized shared beliefs and the development of altruistic attitudes in the partners.[18] Davies was particularly concerned that parents not stifle their daughters' aspirations for a higher mental culture and greater social usefulness (*Home* 10, 16; *Education* 57–58).

Associating individual development with the acquisition of unselfish attitudes, these reformers looked to family life to instill high ideals of service at the same time that it nourished individuality. As Davies demanded, "Why, should not our English homes be animated by a spirit of truth and of sacrifice ... in which all high thoughts and generous impulses should ... grow, all mean and selfish ends be, by common consent, disowned[?]" (*Thoughts* 77). Similarly, Cobbe looked to marriage to foster "higher modes of thinking and a nobler and more devoted life than either man or woman can attain alone" (*Essays* 43). To these Victorians, individual development, individual happiness, and generous impulses appeared likely to advance hand in hand.

Associating character development with sympathetic attitudes toward others, liberal feminists saw good grounds for hope that, properly ordered, family life would foster public as well as private virtue. Mill considered that having learned to cultivate sympathy toward their families and immediate associates, individuals might then extend these unselfish sentiments to others (Robson 130). Generous principles, Davies hoped and believed, would radiate out from the family, eventually influencing the whole quality of national life. Eventually, she predicted, there would be little need for philanthropic schemes for elevating the poor. Gradually, the ideals of the "employing class" would be "unconsciously communicated to their subordinates" and leaven all the classes below them; the "want of hearty sympathy" among the different classes (which Davies saw as "one of the most serious impediments to social progress") would be assuaged (*Thoughts* 77–78).

Given their family role, Grey considered, women might play a special part in promoting social happiness and virtue. Women, she suggested, had a natural bent (by virtue of their maternal qualities) for welfare-related employments ("Sequel" 791). They were, she thought, the natural educators of the race, comforters of the helpless, carers for the poor, ministers of charity. Echoing sentiments shared by many conservatives, she proposed that women (whose primary sphere was, she thought, apt in most cases to remain the home) would be inclined to take a more disinterested, principled view of public issues than men, who were actively engaged in the fray. This, she informed girls, was "the true refining and purifying influence which the more instructed and cultivated classes should exercise on politics" (*Words* 321).

Butler likewise envisioned the establishment of a virtuous circle wherein generous home impulses would make themselves felt in the world and the reforms realized there would in turn redound to the benefit of the home. She explained that "giving forth of the influences of Home . . . for the community good, would ultimately result in the restored security of all the best elements in our present ideal of Home" (xxviii). Far from being "separate spheres," home and public life were intertwined. Progressive principles, Butler and other liberal feminists hoped and believed, would gradually win their way in both, promoting individual happiness and social harmony.

Educational Ideals/Educational Settings: School, Home, and Public Life

Individual character development thus constituted the crux of the educational enterprise as liberal feminists envisioned it. Focusing on individual mental and moral improvement, they evoked an educational ideal that made no distinctions as to sex or future function. Girls' education, Davies asserted, like that of boys should aim to produce "the best and highest type, not limited by exclusive regard to any specific functions hereafter to be discharged" (*Education* 14). Similarly, Grey declared that "education in its only true sense, as moral and intellectual training, is equally indispensable to [girls and boys], and must be conducted on the same prin-

ciples and by the same methods" (*Requirements* 4–5). Contending that
vocational training was easy in proportion as general moral and mental
education had been accomplished, Shirreff argued that the latter served as
a preparation "for all the practical work of life, from common household
duties to the study of any special branch of art or trade" (*Union* 18).

On a practical level, consistent with their libertarian, individualist, rationalist commitments, Victorian liberal feminists lent their support to reforms in girls' education with an eye to promoting individual development,
enhancing women's freedom of choice, and strengthening their intellects.[19]
Valuing mental training not only in its own right but also for the moral
benefits that they considered it entailed, liberal feminists promoted the
establishment of girls' secondary schools and women's colleges that provided a more rigorous course of intellectual studies than had been usual
for girls.[20] In keeping with their meritocratic outlook, they also supported
the introduction of examinations in girls' education, aimed at establishing
a common standard for certifying achievement. In qualifying girls for a
wider range of desirable occupations than had formerly been open to them,
liberal feminists hoped that these reforms would extend women's freedom.

While they encouraged the creation of new-model schools and colleges
for girls, the reformers did not consider that these formal institutional
settings offered unique educational advantages. The lessons learned in
school might—in favorable circumstances—be learned as well or better
elsewhere. Shirreff considered that ideally home education was preferable
to that which might be found in school: "Those who hold that the highest aim of education is the formation of character . . . who believe . . .
that original individual power is more precious than a high average of attainments, will always feel that home education, if good, ought to be the
best" ("Home Education" 65). Likewise, explaining that the same principles should govern the organization of a household of young people and
a college, Davies declared, "I believe that many of the advantages of a college might, in a greater or less degree, be attained in a well ordered home"
(*Home* 10–11, 12). Public pursuits might offer analogous advantages, also
enabling women to extend their mental and moral horizons. Thus Butler
lumped together "education, earnest work in trades and professions, and
a share in grave national interests" as all tending to correct the "foolish
sentimental tendencies of the women whose chief literature at present is
the sensational novel" (xxxiii).

While school and college did not offer girls unique opportunities for
character development, liberal feminists considered that, given the defi-

ciencies of many homes and women's limited experience of public life, such institutions often had a vital part to play. Thus, while acknowledging that homes might provide similar opportunities, Davies argued that college usually offered a more promising setting for meeting "the claims of the higher life." Home discipline, she explained, was often lax and offered little support for a systematic course of study. In contrast, she considered that college life inculcated the view that intellectual cultivation was "among the *duties* of life," fostered habits of self-control, and offered girls both precious freedom from casual interruption and the stimulus of sympathetic companionship (*Home* 10–12).

Taking this argument a step further, Grey suggested that girls might acquire a more developed sense of their domestic responsibilities in school than they were apt to do at home. Home discipline, she considered, had become too relaxed in latter years. She noted disapprovingly that children were now allowed to feel themselves the first objects of the mother's love, if not the father's: "Their [children's] health, their education, their pleasures, are the first things considered in all family arrangements" (*Words* 226–27). In these circumstances, Grey believed, the discipline of school might play a compensatory role, instilling in girls a nicer habit of obedience to duty—including that owed to parents—than they were apt to gain at home (*Words* 226–28).[21]

School and collegiate life, reformers indicated, might compensate not only for the shortcomings of home but also for girls' limited experience of the world. Shirreff suggested that a rigorous course of intellectual training was especially necessary for those who lacked the discipline of regular public employment:

> those who inevitably possess leisure [including the "comparatively small number of men of fortune" and "the whole mass of women of the upper and middle classes"] require, not less but more education, and of a higher and more severe cast than those who will be kept at school, in some measure, all their lives by the enforced labour of a profession. (*Education* 23)

Davies took a similar line in urging the provision of improved secondary schools and colleges for girls. While acknowledging that a literary education could not entirely replace a knowledge of the world gained from observation and experience, she considered that it would help women "of the higher class" acquire the varied knowledge, mental and moral discipline, and impartial, deliberative outlook that their duties required. A large and liberal culture such as might be gained in college was, she suggested, probably the best corrective of women's tendency to take a petty view of things (*Thoughts* 80, *Education* 74–76).

In extending women's moral and intellectual range, schools and colleges, reformers argued, would prepare women to function more effectively in both the private and the public sphere. Elaborating on this point, Davies explained that the same varied knowledge, the same qualities of mind and character were required in the home as in public life. The chief domestic duties of women of the upper and middle classes, she contended, were those of government and administration. Thus, for example, the same abilities that made for economical domestic management promoted success in business. Indeed, she suggested, under the conditions of modern society, a liberal education and the pursuit of a profession perhaps provided the best training for success in the special functions of mistress of a household (*Education* 100–104).

In providing girls with access to a culture similar to that of boys, reformers proposed, educational institutions might foster happier, more companionate relationships between the sexes, improving the quality of life both within and outside the family. Urging the advantages of coeducation, Grey considered that shared pursuits and interests would help eliminate young men and women's "morbid excitement and curiosity" about the opposite sex, and she hoped this circumstance would discourage young men from adopting a predatory attitude toward women ("Sequel" 792–93). Less absorbed by petty familial concerns, more likely to be motivated by principled ideals, well-educated women, liberal feminists predicted, would be more inclined to adopt disinterested commitments. This trend would in turn promote happier marriages, with men and women's life together being enriched by shared ideals (Mill, "Subjection" 335–36; Cobbe, *Duties* 99; Davies, *Education* 122–23).

School life, Grey told girls, was a preparation for the larger life beyond the school and for the service owed society (*Words* 39). While warning girls that they must never lose their individuality or independence of character, she informed them that they would learn a dual lesson from the social side of school life: "The unimportance of your individual selves as compared with the community. . . . [and] its correlative . . . the importance of each individual share in the collective action of the community" (56, 53). Thus while Grey directed girls' attention to the wide range of public activities in which women might engage—in the professions, in charitable work, in local government, in party organizations—she did not view such pursuits as requiring fundamentally different motivations or orientations from those required for domestic life. Whether girls opted chiefly for domestic or public pursuits, the lessons of school were the same; in either case individuality was best expressed in a life of disinterested service.

Similarly, whether girls ultimately chose the public or the private realm as their chief area of endeavor seemed to Grey, and other liberal feminists, of secondary importance so long as the choice was a free one. Nor did they distinguish sharply within the public sphere between paid employment and unpaid volunteer work.[22] Identifying self-development above all with intellectual and moral growth, these reformers considered that potentially home and public life, paid and unpaid work, offered equivalent opportunities for character training. Convinced that public life and home life were equally honorable, Grey urged girls to do the duty closest to hand (*Words* 240). Cobbe took a similar line. Viewing the perfecting of individual souls as the "end" of creation (*Duties* 18), she argued that "disinterested labour of any kind"—whether it took the form of fulfilling family obligations, pursuing artistic or scientific ends, or involving oneself in philanthropic activities—was equally work for God (*Essays* 141).

In practice, Victorian liberal feminists were broadly agreed that domestic duties had a special claim on wives and daughters. Adopting an extreme stance, Cobbe argued that daughters who were required at home by parents ought neither to marry nor to seek employment outside the home (*Duties* 89–90).[23] While Mill urged that individuals should be allowed great latitude in their domestic arrangements, he regarded the customary division of labor wherein the husband earned the income and the wife undertook to manage the household and bring up the children as, in general, satisfactory ("Subjection" 297–98). Taking a somewhat more radical line, Davies questioned whether the wives and daughters of the property-owning classes had adequate serious employment at home and suggested that in homes with servants women might combine marriage and a profession or serious voluntary work (*Education* 109–10).[24] In cases of conflict, however, she also assumed that home duties came first for women.

Certainly in some respects these Victorian liberals were applying a double standard. They did not envision that men would often choose between marriage and a career. Nor did they entertain the possibility that sons, like daughters, might have special obligations to their parents. However, this aspect of their thought must be understood in the context of their other commitments. They did not wish women's lives to be bounded by narrow family claims. Rather, they viewed home life as potentially consistent with the pursuit of individual utility on the one hand and public interests on the other. Associating self-development and the higher happiness with disinterested ideals, they saw no conflict between the domestic obligations they urged on women and their commitment to women's individual well-being. Home life, they insisted, would be the happier when infused with larger public commitments. Ultimately, the ideal of happiness and virtue that they held up to women was the same as the one they held up to men: the principled pursuit of high ideals.

Assuming that freedom was improving to the character, these Victorian reformers and educators believed that women's emancipation would ultimately enhance familial solidarity and communal well-being. Their assumptions were located in a now largely unfamiliar historical and moral landscape. Few today can unequivocally share their faith in progress either at the individual or at the aggregate level, and the disinterested, self-repressive motivations that they so admired have but limited appeal to most contemporary advocates of women's freedom. However, the problem that these liberal feminists addressed—that of reconciling individual claims for freedom with family commitments and public responsibilities—remains alive and well today. In this respect, if there has been a failure of imagination, it has perhaps belonged as much to our generation as to theirs.

NOTES

1. See Edward W. Ellsworth, *Liberators of the Female Mind,* for an account of the Shirreff sisters.

2. The term "liberal feminist" is used here to denote a general ideological orientation rather than a partisan commitment to the Liberal Party. For another approach to this strand of feminist thought, see Olive Banks's discussion of "equal rights" feminism in *Faces of Feminism: A Study of Feminism as a Social Movement.* I have preferred the term "liberal feminism," as I do not believe that this strand of thinking can be understood apart from liberal theory generally in the context of Victorian England. Susan Moller Okin offers a good introduction to John Stuart Mill as a "liberal feminist" in *Women in Western Political Thought* (197–220).

3. Various constructions have been placed on these attitudes. For example, Zillah R. Eisenstein argues in chapter 7 of *The Radical Future of Liberal Feminism* that failing to address the sexual division of labor, John Stuart Mill and Harriet Taylor's views were at once sex-biased and elitist, condemning all but the exceptional woman to de facto dependency and inferior status. Similarly, Susan Mendus

has criticized Mill's analysis of women's circumstances for its insistence on the centrality of moral issues as opposed to practical/material constraints.

In "The Contradictions in Ladies' Education," Sara Delamont describes educational reformers such as Grey as caught in a snare of double conformity to traditional norms of ladylike behavior and elite male educational standards. Deborah Gorham's study *The Victorian Girl and the Feminine Ideal* suggests that the self-sacrificing feminine ideal held out to middle-class girls persisted even while the normative standards concerning their education, employment, and leisure activities changed. Ellen Jordan has emphasized that it was politically inexpedient for educational reformers to challenge a domestic ideology that required that education should fit women for domestic roles. Stifling debate over key issues, their approach, she contends, contributed to the practical success of the reforms they promoted in women's education, but at an ideological price.

4. Mill declared that "freedom of individual choice is now known to be the only thing which procures the adoption of the best processes, and throws each operation into the hands of those who are best qualified for it" ("Subjection" 273).

5. Although individual moral and mental improvement remained central to her vision, Shirreff's ideas as to women's proper role broadened substantially over the years. By the 1880s, as her "Work of the World" series demonstrates, she was demanding that women be granted the same civic rights and work opportunities as men.

6. Mrs. Jellyby, a character in Charles Dickens's *Bleak House* (1852–53), was an avid philanthropist who neglected her family.

7. Chapter 5 of John M. Robson's *Improvement of Mankind* provides an unrivaled account of Mill as a social moralist. See also Okin 209.

8. Jonathan Riley discusses the ultimate harmony that Mill posited between individual happiness and the general happiness (231–34).

9. For Davies's life and ideas see Barbara Stephen, *Emily Davies and Girton College*.

10. Brian Harrison and Joan N. Burstyn both explore the ideology of "separate spheres." Okin offers some interesting reflections on functionalist thought in chapter 10 of *Women in Western Political Thought*.

11. Mill considered that citizenship (which functioned partly as "a school of society in free countries") offered similar lessons but that it filled too small a place in modern life and did not sufficiently affect the "daily habits or inmost sentiments" to serve as the major agency of the resocialization that he envisaged ("Subjection" 295).

12. While they agreed that marriage must initially be based on free choice, liberal feminists differed in their views as to the conditions under which a marriage, once established, might be dissolved. While Grey considered that marriage should be dissolvable only when there was a breach of the marriage vow, Mill (who viewed marriage in the light of "a voluntary association" not unlike a business partner-

ship) was of the opinion that divorce should be granted at the will of either party. However, convinced that freedom fostered an enhanced sense of responsibility toward others, he anticipated that "in a tolerably moral state of society" divorce would be rare, especially when children were involved (Grey, "Sequel" 784; Mill, "Subjection" 290–91 and "Marriage" 48).

13. Victorian liberal feminists, of course, had every interest in distinguishing the status of adult women from that of children. As Cobbe remarked, while men might easily be coaxed "to pet us like children," it was more difficult to persuade them to "treat us like responsible human beings" (*Duties* v).

14. See Robson (151–52) for a discussion of the primacy of reason in Mill's social and moral thought.

15. If, as Mendus indicates, Mill considered sex in the light of a low, animal function, Grey maintained that perfect love must embrace both the spirit and the flesh (Mendus 189 and passim; Grey, "Sequel" 781). For a more general consideration of feminist attitudes on these matters, see Constance Rover, *Love, Morals and the Feminists.*

16. Thus Mill considered that ideally voters and their representatives should be guided by their sense of the general interest of the community, not by their own individual or class interests (see "Government" 444–47, 490, and passim; see also Grey, *Words* 311).

17. "Women," Harriet Taylor [Mill] declared, "are educated for one single object, to gain their living by marrying—(some poor souls get it without the church-going in the same way—they do not seem to me a bit worse than their honoured sisters)" ("Marriage" 375). It was a familiar theme. See also Grey, *Old Maids* (17), and Cobbe, *Duties* (44–45).

18. Mill explained: "When two persons both care for great objects, and are a help . . . to each other in whatever regards these . . . there is a foundation for solid friendship, of an enduring character, more likely than anything else to make it . . . a greater pleasure to each to give pleasure to the other, than to receive it" ("Subjection" 334).

19. Accounts of the reforms introduced in girls' education include Margaret Bryant's *Unexpected Revolution,* Carol Dyhouse's *Girls Growing Up in Late Victorian and Edwardian England,* and my own *Reform of Girls' Secondary and Higher Education in Victorian England.* I have considered the relationship between liberal ideology and the content of girls' education in these reformed institutions in greater detail in "Education, Gender and Social Change in Victorian Liberal Feminist Theory."

20. "Mental training," explained Shirreff, ". . . is no less powerful in its influence on the character than on the intellect" (*Union* 16).

21. See also Shirreff, "Hindrances" (19–20). Davies also promoted reformed secondary schools for girls in part with an eye to improving their performance of their domestic duties (*Thoughts* 73–74).

22. Thus Grey advised girls who did not need the money and who were not strongly attracted to a profession that they would do better to take up volunteer work and not crowd into already overcrowded fields (*Words* 247), while Davies viewed unpaid public service when seriously undertaken as nearly equivalent to a profession (*Education* 110–11).

23. At the same time, however, she emphasized that daughters not required by parents at home should be equally free to devote themselves to work or to marriage.

24. Davies, it should be noted, urged disinterested standards of behavior on parents as well as daughters, warning that it was "only natural" that parents should be slow to encourage their daughters' aspirations after duties besides those of ministering to their own comfort (*Education* 57).

WORKS CITED

Banks, Olive. *Faces of Feminism: A Study of Feminism as a Social Movement.* Oxford: Martin Robertson, 1981.

Bryant, Margaret. *The Unexpected Revolution: A Study in the History of the Education of Women and Girls in the Nineteenth Century.* London: U of London Institute of Education, 1979.

Burstyn, Joan N. *Victorian Education and the Ideal of Womanhood.* London: Croom Helm, 1980.

Butler, Josephine E. Introduction. *Woman's Work and Woman's Culture.* Ed. Josephine E. Butler. London: Macmillan, 1869. vii–lxiv.

Cobbe, Frances Power. "Celibacy *v.* Marriage," "Female Charity: Lay and Monastic," and "What Shall We Do with Our Old Maids?" *Essays on the Pursuits of Women.* London: E. Faithfull, 1863. 38–57, 102–41, 58–101.

———. *The Duties of Women.* London: Williams and Norgate, 1881.

———. "The Final Cause of Women." *Woman's Work and Woman's Culture.* Ed. Josephine E. Butler. London: Macmillan, 1869. 1–26.

Davies, Emily. *The Higher Education of Women.* London: A. Strahan, 1866.

———. *Home and the Higher Education.* London: Printed for the London Association of Schoolmistresses, 1878.

———. "The Influence of University Degrees on the Education of Women," "Letters Addressed to a Daily Paper at Newcastle-upon-Tyne, 1860," and "On Secondary Instruction as Relating to Girls." *Thoughts on Some Questions Relating to Women, 1860–1908.* Cambridge: Bowes and Bowes, 1910. 41–62, 1–18, 63–83.

Delamont, Sara. "The Contradictions in Ladies' Education." *The Nineteenth-Century Woman: Her Cultural and Physical World.* Ed. Sara Delamont and Lorna Duffin. London: Croom Helm, 1978. 134–63.

Dyhouse, Carol. *Girls Growing Up in Late Victorian and Edwardian England.* London: Routledge and Kegan Paul, 1981.

Eisenstein, Zillah R. *The Radical Future of Liberal Feminism*. New York: Longman, 1980.

Ellsworth, Edward W. *Liberators of the Female Mind: The Shirreff Sisters, Educational Reform, and the Women's Movement*. Westport: Greenwood, 1979.

Fawcett, Mrs. Henry [Millicent Garrett]. Introduction to *A Vindication of the Rights of Woman*. By Mary Wollstonecraft. London: Unwin, 1891. 1–30.

——. *Women's Suffrage: A Short History of a Great Movement*. 1912. New York: Source Book, 1970.

Gorham, Deborah. *The Victorian Girl and the Feminine Ideal*. Bloomington: Indiana UP, 1982.

Grey, Maria. *Last Words to Girls on Life in School and After School*. London: Rivingtons, 1889.

——. "Men and Women." *The Fortnightly Review* n.s. 26 (1 November 1879): 672–85.

——. "Men and Women: A Sequel." *The Fortnightly Review* n.s. 29 (1 June 1881): 776–93.

——. *Old Maids: A Lecture by Mrs. William Grey*. 2d ed. London: Ridgway, 1875.

——. *On the Special Requirements for Improving the Education of Girls*. London: Ridgway, 1872.

Grey, Maria, and Emily Shirreff. *Passion and Principle: A Novel*. London: Routledge, 1853.

Harrison, Brian. *Separate Spheres: The Opposition to Women's Suffrage in Britain*. London: Croom Helm, 1978.

Jordan, Ellen. "Making Good Wives and Mothers? The Transformation of Middle-Class Girls' Education in Nineteenth Century Britain." *History of Education Quarterly* 31.4 (Winter 1991): 439–62.

Mendus, Susan. "The Marriage of True Minds: The Ideal of Marriage in the Philosophy of John Stuart Mill." *Sexuality and Subordination: Interdisciplinary Studies of Gender in the Nineteenth Century*. Ed. Susan Mendus and Jane Rendall. New York: Routledge, 1989. 171–91.

Mill, Harriet Taylor. "Enfranchisement of Women." *The Collected Works of John Stuart Mill* vol. 21. Ed. John M. Robson. Toronto: U of Toronto P, 1984. 393–415.

[Mill], Harriet Taylor. "On Marriage." *Collected Works of John Stuart Mill* vol. 21. Ed. John M. Robson. Toronto: U of Toronto P, 1984. 375–77.

[Mill], Harriet Taylor, and John Stuart Mill. "Papers on Women's Rights." *The Collected Works of John Stuart Mill* vol. 21. Ed. John M. Robson. Toronto: U of Toronto P, 1984. 378–92.

Mill, John Stuart. "Considerations on Representative Government." *The Collected Works of John Stuart Mill* vol. 19. Ed. John M. Robson. Toronto: U of Toronto P, 1984. 371–577.

————. "On Marriage." *The Collected Works of John Stuart Mill* vol. 21. Ed. John M. Robson. Toronto: U of Toronto P, 1984. 35–49.

————. "The Subjection of Women." *The Collected Works of John Stuart Mill* vol. 21. Ed. John M. Robson. Toronto: U of Toronto P, 1984. 258–340.

Okin, Susan Moller. *Women in Western Political Thought*. Princeton: Princeton UP, 1979.

Pedersen, Joyce Senders. "Education, Gender and Social Change in Victorian Liberal Feminist Theory." *History of European Ideas* 8.4/5 (1987): 503–19.

————. *The Reform of Girls' Secondary and Higher Education in Victorian England*. New York: Garland, 1987.

Riley, Jonathan. *Liberal Utilitarianism: Social Choice Theory and J. S. Mill's Philosophy*. Cambridge: Cambridge UP, 1988.

Robson, John M. *The Improvement of Mankind: The Social and Political Thought of John Stuart Mill*. Toronto: U of Toronto P, 1968.

Rover, Constance. *Love, Morals and the Feminists*. London: Routledge and Kegan Paul, 1970.

Rubenstein, David. *A Different World for Women: The Life of Millicent Garrett Fawcett*. New York: Harvester/Wheatsheaf, 1991.

Shirreff, Emily. "Home Education and Private Governesses." *Journal of the Women's Education Union* 3 (15 May 1875): 65–66.

————. *Intellectual Education, and Its Influence on the Character and Happiness of Women*. London: Parker and Son, 1858.

————. *Moral Training: Froebel and Herbert Spencer*. London: Phillip and Son, 1892.

————. "Some Modern Hindrances to Education: No. III, Love of Wealth," and "No. VII, Relaxation of Home Discipline." *Journal of the Women's Education Union* 5 and 7 (15 June 1877, 15 June 1879): 84–88, 19–22.

————. *The Work of the National Union*. London: Ridgway, 1872.

————. "The Work of the World and Women's Share in It," nos. 1–3. *Journal of the Women's Education Union* 9 (15 March, 15 April, 15 May 1881): 37, 52–56, 68–72.

Stephen, Barbara. *Emily Davies and Girton College*. London: Constable, 1927.

Strachey, Ray. *Millicent Garrett Fawcett*. London: John Murray, 1931.

SHERRIE A. INNESS

"It Is Pluck, But—Is It Sense?":
Athletic Student Culture in
Progressive-era Girls' College Fiction

This essay focuses on the representation of athletics in popular Progressive-era stories about student life at women's colleges,[1] an aspect of the genre that has been largely overlooked by scholars.[2] "Few well-drawn female characters are part of the world of play and sport," Christian K. Messenger comments in his recent study, *Sport and the Spirit of Play in American Fiction;* "women in play and sport are not fully characterized. . . . The representation of play and sport in American fiction remains a distorted masculine preserve" (xiv). But Messenger fails to examine girls' college stories, in which a chapter or a short story about the athletic woman is almost *de rigueur.* His misrepresentation is particularly noticeable because he provides an extensive analysis of Progressive-era boys' college fiction (chiefly the Frank Merriwell at Yale saga). One might argue that Messenger ignores women athletes in college novels because they "are not fully characterized," but I fail to see how these women are any less fully characterized than Frank Merriwell or other heroes of boys' sport stories.

What does this exclusion do? Most important, it establishes an artificially cohesive image of team sports and the societal approval they received in the 1890s. Messenger suggests that "college sport in the 1890s was a cultural adaptation of the predatory Darwinian spectacle of self-assertion and survival with military, hence societal, sanction" (153). Furthermore, a "young [athletic, male] hero could work for himself and for the goals of society at the same time without conflict" (154). Although I do not refute Messenger's characterization of the importance of organized games for males, this description is not appropriate for women's college athletics. Women did not receive societal sanction for pursuing competitive team sports; they were more likely to meet with disapproval, from the reproofs of college administrators to the negative comments in many popular periodicals. Also, metaphors of war, which could so easily be applied to men's team sports, could not desirably be attached to women's. Male athletic rivalry could be justified because it fostered the self-assertive and aggressive qualities needed in capitalism and in war (a view commonly accepted in the 1890s). Men's college team sports supported the capitalist system by training males to act as units within a larger structure.[3] But if male athletes enhanced their ability to function as breadwinners, the role of women as mothers seemed threatened by the competitive spirit promoted in team athletics. Training women for capitalist competition would do nothing to prepare them for their duties as wives and childbearers.

The aggressive female athlete posed a problem for women's college officials, who were openly concerned with denying the alleged masculinity of their students and with discrediting critics who claimed that women graduates had too few children to do their part in maintaining the Anglo-Saxon race. Physical education, however, could also provide an arena for administrators to refute the image of the masculine college woman and to assert the femininity of their students. Gymnastic exercises could be promoted as upgrading a woman's "ultimate maternal capacities" (Smith-Rosenberg 21). Simultaneously, if these activities were carefully individualized, they would have the potential to prevent women from organizing in a peer group based upon the team, which might offer resistance to administrative regulations.

But as we shall see, these beliefs about the benefits of gymnastic exercises and the dangers of team athletics are undermined by the writers of Progressive-era girls' college stories, who create a college environment in which gymnastics instruction rarely appears and is made to seem less important than a team sport such as basketball. In these books, the focus of physical education instructors on the individual woman whose physical flaws are corrected by regulated gymnastics instruction is replaced by an emphasis on the entire student community. Student opposition to the "correct" gymnastics becomes legitimate in these texts in which female muscularity is praised and the "athletic girl" is one of the heroines of her peer community. Thus the stories promote a cohesive student group that is represented as undermining both the authority of college administrators and the goals of a physical education system aimed at producing more efficient mothers.

Gymnastics and Hygiene: Designing the Efficient Mother

Gymnastics were part of the required curriculum at Mount Holyoke, Vassar, Smith, Wellesley, and Bryn Mawr when these colleges first opened (Mount Holyoke in 1837, Vassar in 1865, Wellesley and Smith in 1875, Bryn Mawr in 1885).[4] Each school insisted that all of its students should engage in light physical exercise. Sometimes this exercise was nothing more strenuous than a twenty-minute stroll under the shelter of Vassar College's arcade, built to protect students in inclement weather, but simple gymnastics also were included in the educational program. Students did calisthenics (similar to the exercises promoted by Catharine Beecher at her Hartford Female Seminary as early as 1827) at the new Mount Holyoke. In the 1870s, the colleges required students to perform the nonstrenuous gymnastics of the Dio Lewis system (which included such exercises as the beanbag toss).

I will bypass these early years in favor of a close analysis of the gymnastics instruction of the 1890s for two reasons: At its outset, physical education instruction was less highly regimented and controlled by educational specialists than it would be in the 1890s. Also, it was not until the 1890s that team sports established themselves to any great extent at women's colleges, when they quickly developed into a threat to what physical education departments considered their "real" work: gymnastics instruction.[5] Before this time, women college students had engaged in athletic pursuits other than gymnastics or calisthenics (long tramps in the woods and bicycle rides were particularly enjoyed), but competitive team sports did not become widely popular until basketball was introduced to the colleges in the mid-1890s.

Basketball, invented in 1891 by James Naismith, was a phenomenal success at women's colleges.[6] Smith had its first interclass freshman-sophomore game on 22 March 1893; the sport was introduced at Vassar in 1894, with class teams forming that same year. Other women's colleges were quick to follow Smith's lead, and basketball was soon played at many of the women's colleges in existence at the turn of the century. Interest in individual exercise waned, while basketball skyrocketed in popularity. In 1901 Lavinia Hart, an observer of college life, remarked that "college girls are enthusiastic athletes. Basketball is the universal favorite sport" (193).

Although basketball caught on quickly with students, physical educators and commentators on athletic culture questioned college women's interest in this sport. Basketball threatened the importance of gymnastics instructors since gymnastics instruction was regulated primarily by departments of physical education, while basketball teams were formed and coached by students. Thus it is not surprising that basketball was often depicted by physical education teachers and the popular media as dangerous to the goals of gymnastics.

An example of this division between gymnastics and team sports appears in Edith Rickert's 1912 article for the *Ladies' Home Journal* entitled "The Athletic Side That Threatens Danger":

> Echoes of the old-time hatred of "class drill" are still heard from alumnae; but this is now being largely replaced by individual exercises based upon the special needs of each girl, as determined after a thorough physical examination by a resident physician, or by the director of the gymnasium.
>
> In this way the round-shouldered girl does not have to do exercises for strengthening the ankles; but each girl is made to work to overcome her own defects and to strengthen her weak points in a way that is wholly admirable.
>
> Yet there is another side to modern physical training in women's colleges, and one that threatens danger. . . . the spirit of athletics has crept into gymnasium work, and . . . muscularity is encouraged at the expense of the kind of development that is especially needed by women. (12)

Here the "efficiency" associated with Taylorism in industry invades women's gymnastics. A person's weak points and physical defects are emphasized; the body is reduced to an endless multiplicity of points that can be mapped, charted, and ultimately corrected. Using this blueprint, it is possible to "design" the woman best suited to efficient motherhood, altering any individual parts that fail to come up to par. The measurements taken of every part of a woman's body, which were vital to the gymnastics discipline of the 1890s, created an exact mapping to ensure that no part of the physique escaped a systemized discipline. Women's colleges employed gymnastic activities as a constraining and shaping force on the female form. Society sought to mold or design the female body into a more perfect form for the good of the Anglo-Saxon race. As Patricia Vertinsky comments, "exercise prescriptions were most often designed for women to improve their functioning in their traditionally appointed tasks of childbearing and childrearing" (39).

Carefully regulated gymnastics instruction was particularly successful at women's colleges.[7] In 1898 a commentator on college life noted: "The college officers [at women's colleges] are as a rule more alive to the importance of the [gymnastics] department. . . . the disturbing element of athletics does not enter so largely into competition with efforts at systematic physical training" (Leonard 628). Why was gymnastics exercise encouraged at such women's colleges as Smith, Mount Holyoke, Vassar,

Bryn Mawr, and Wellesley? One would suppose that these colleges, which so strongly supported the right of bourgeois women to pursue the same intellectual goals as men, would reject a physical education system that emphasized that a woman's main function was physical.[8] But in fact such schools, although they encouraged women's academic pursuits, did not always lend their support to the same women's attempts to redefine the image of proper femininity in other ways. At some of the more traditional women's colleges (such as Mount Holyoke), gymnastics had a history of acting as a conservative force, constraining women to their domestic roles. For example, in 1881 a gymnastics drill team at Mount Holyoke presented a performance while dressed in caps and aprons, with dustpans strapped to their backs. Of course, they drilled with brooms (Rota 158). We can only presume that such an exercise made Mount Holyoke students better able to do the weekly domestic chores that the college required of them.

There is another reason for the colleges' acceptance of applied gymnastics instruction: its scientific image often managed to conceal its traditional goals. In an era when science was commonly perceived as contributing to the Darwinian improvement of humankind, gymnastic instructors sought to lend prestige to their discipline by emphasizing and developing its connection to science. For example, physical education teachers used graphs, statistics, and close measurements in an attempt to turn their profession into a scientific discipline. Administrators at women's colleges thus saw an exercise system that seemed up-to-date and progressive. Scientific gymnastics appeared to be the perfect vehicle to display a college's belief in the beneficial powers of science.

The decade of the 1890s was an era of professionalization in the United States; physical education was only one of many fields to gain professional status in this period. The gymnastics teacher was raised from a rank considerably lower than that of an academic instructor to become "part of a powerful coalition of professionals in the educational arena who cooperated in the close surveillance of students' physical performance and well-being" (Atkinson 41). Associating herself with a scientific field, the educator increased her prestige: "By creating an institutional complex in which teaching was 'scientific,' [women physical education instructors] ... conveyed the view that physical education was a serious subject" (McCrone 121). Kathleen McCrone considers this trend a liberating one for the teachers of women's physical education, but I question whether students also felt liberated by the new scientificism of gymnastics. Because of their desire to appear scientifically advanced, women's colleges encouraged gymnastic work that promoted "the kind of development . . . especially needed by women"—that is, development aimed at making women better mothers rather than at giving them "an exhilarating awareness of physicality and the potential significance of body control" (McCrone 49).

Gymnastics instruction established a continuous system of observation and discipline. Women students were first subjected to analytical anthropometry when they arrived at college; Vassar, Wellesley, Smith, Mount Holyoke, Bryn Mawr, and other women's colleges all took exacting measurements of their recruits. Influenced by various physicians (for example, Dr. Sargent at Harvard and Dr. Hitchcock at Amherst), both physical education instructors and medical doctors at women's colleges considered careful measurements of the body to be an essential first step in categorizing and curing individual female "deficiencies." Even before beginning gymnasium work, the students had to submit to having their physical attributes charted in excruciating detail. A file was created that followed women even after they had graduated: college physicians contacted them after graduation to see how they were holding up under the strain of life outside the college.[9]

One of the most widely used systems of gymnastic instruction was the Sargent system (gymnastic exercises using small dumbbells and other gymnasium equipment); in 1894 Bryn Mawr, Wellesley, Vassar, and Smith all claimed allegiance to this method. At Vassar the exercises were required three times a week; also, "careful measurements [were] taken periodically, and. . . . [showed] clearly the valuable effects of systematic physical training" (Burstall 157). With Sargent's routines, time became a fetish; a woman could be improved if she accepted the "religion" of confessing and charting her physical flaws at regulated intervals. To make this system even more complete, Vassar students had to pledge under an honor code to take at least one hour of exercise a day in addition to their gymnastic classes.

In women's colleges, various systems of gymnastic instruction (such as Swedish gymnastics)[10] using anthropometry were ardently proclaimed by instructors and administrators to be good for the individual. As Dorothy S. Ainsworth remarks in her history of physical education in colleges for women, "It was believed that all students had some defects and that they could and should be remedied by individual attention" (17). Each woman was singled out to be graded and measured. We can better understand the purpose of this individual attention if we look at it in the light of a statement that Michel Foucault makes in *Discipline and Punish:* "Individualization appears as the ultimate aim of a precisely adapted code" (99). I would alter

Foucault's statement to read concurrently, "[De-]individualization appears as the ultimate aim of a precisely adapted code." With such a precisely adapted code as the highly regulated gymnastics instruction of the 1890s, both individualization and de-individualization could be applied to the subject of the code simultaneously. At the same time that physical education instructors sought to individualize students and categorize them according to particular weaknesses, they also assigned them to the undifferentiated category of future mothers. The codifications of gymnastic instruction sought to create a bourgeois woman who conformed both as an individual and as a member of a group to the dictates of the dominant cultural values that prescribed the maternal role as the only one acceptable for women.[11]

Gymnastics, however, was only one side of physical education at women's colleges; another was team athletics, which subverted the "correct" feminine molding that was the aim of gymnastics work. As I noted above, team athletics received a less than enthusiastic reception from physical educators, college administrators, and many commentators on college life. For example, Lucille Eaton Hill, the influential director of physical training at Wellesley, disapproved of basketball and feared that it would teach women how to compete at the expense of their femininity. In "Women and Basket-Ball," published in the periodical *Mind and Body* in 1900, an anonymous critic was even more severe than Hill about competitive games of basketball between college women: "Such public exhibitions of infuriation on [the] part of young ladies . . . should neither be encouraged or tolerated by college authorities" (60). Basketball was subject to careful control and regulation by college administrators intent on denying the masculinizing influences ascribed to higher education for women.[12] To these individuals, as to outside observers, the muscular, competitive woman athlete posed a distinct problem.

From the college's point of view, the woman basketball player represented a failure of the gymnastics department, because she would not turn her enthusiasm "into the directions in which women need special training." Instead, she cheerfully risked androgyny on the basketball court. Her acceptance of muscularity and her display of competitiveness were not the only ways in which she deviated from the norms considered desirable for women. The close identification between the individual athlete and her team and college class also posed a problem for Progressive-era women's college administrators intent on improving individual students. Rickert noted the deplorable loyalty of the athlete to her team:

In games and field contests particularly the danger [of athletics] is increased by a sense of loyalty that tries to overcome physical weakness. Rather than lessen the chances of victory for her team a girl will play at the risk of permanent injury to her health. Sometimes she will be hurt and still will play on, as she has seen her brother do, until the game is finished, without counting the possible cost to herself. It is pluck, but— is it sense? (12)

The threat of team athletic activities is clear: "the individual character of the work is lost in sight of the keenness of competition" (Rickert 12). Individual, noncompetitive gymnastic exercises are largely ignored in favor of "copying the boys." The college woman, when free from administrative constraints, can easily be seduced by the competitive thrills of group athletics and thus "get in with a set of girls who rebel against every law of hygiene, and so go on from bad to worse" (11). Rickert does not care to explain what lies in the dark depths of going from bad to worse. It seems evident, however, that the danger lies in affiliation with a set of girls who promote class and clique loyalty rather than obedience to the authorities and their gymnastics requirements. This set of girls threatens to become a peer group that has more influence upon its members than do school authorities. Presumably, the members of this group neither care about their role as future American mothers nor worry about their masculine image on the playing field.

It is the representation of this set of girls, apparently unconcerned with the possibility that they could be made less womanly by team sports and little impressed by the benefits of gymnastics instruction, that I examine in girls' college stories. We will find that the Progressive-era reader of these stories, most likely already aware of the conflict between the exciting new game of basketball and the more socially acceptable gymnastics, was encouraged to resolve her ambivalence in favor of team sports.

Fictional Resistance to Individual Specification

In the idealized world of girls' college stories, gymnastics instruction, as well as other areas of school life, can be remolded. Individuals who might undermine the importance of team sports—gymnastics instructors, for example—are simply left out of the stories. Not a single physical education instructor appears as a character in any of the texts I have examined, although Bryn Mawr, Mount Holyoke, Smith, Vassar, and Wellesley had organized physical education departments by the middle 1890s. In comparison, almost every novel or short story does include the portrait of an academic professor.

Gymnastic exercises are also usually omitted, replaced by the basketball story or chapter. A few authors mention gymnasium work briefly, but only to mock or downplay its supposed corrective powers. For example, Madeline Ayres, the only student in Margaret Warde's *Betty Wales, Sophomore* (1909) to use gymnastic instruction as a medical corrective, is more than slightly sarcastic about its effectiveness; she comments to her friend Helen:

> You ought to go in for gym. . . . It would straighten you up, and make you look like a different person. I'm going in for it myself, hard. I'm hoping that it will cure my slouchy walk, and turn me out "a marvel of grace and beauty," as the physical culture advertisements always say. (*Sophomore* 45)

The reaction of Jean Webster's Patty (in *When Patty Went to College*, 1903) is more typical of the attitude of college students toward gymnasium exercise. When asked by a shocked friend whether she had actually gone to the gym, Patty quickly denies that awful possibility: "Goodness, no! I'm not so far gone as that" (70).

Myra (*Elinor's College Career*, 1906) is more conscientious about her required gymnasium activities:

> Myra hurried methodically through her prescribed exercises till she reached the rowing-machine. She always lingered at this for more than the requisite flexions; because she enjoyed sitting there while she watched the score of blue-suited girls variously busy at the poles and ropes, the rings and bars. (Schwartz 302–3)

The efficient ordering of exercises is undermined by Myra's initial haste and subsequent lingering. The time-discipline of the administration is replaced by student control over how much time is to be spent on the various exercises. Nor does Myra linger to pursue her corrective activities—she is more interested in watching the "blue-suited girls." Gymnastics fails to make Myra more aware of her individual defects; instead, she is lost in the pleasure of viewing her peers.

The subversive quality of Myra's gaze should be emphasized. We must remember that when Julia Schwartz's novel was published, corsets, long dresses, gloves, and hats were required attire for bourgeois women outside their households. The female body was typically concealed from the view of both men and women. Even in sports played between men and women, such as golf and lawn tennis (both popular at the turn of the century), women wore long dresses, although it is true that they were cut six or seven inches above the ground. Thus the gym uniform of baggy bloomers and loose tunic must have seemed remarkably revealing to Myra or any of the young readers of this book. Instead of being shocked at such a display, Myra takes delight in it, while paying little attention to the Taylorized exercises she is supposed to pursue.[13]

The Benefits of Basketball · The college administrators' and gymnastics instructors' negative portrayal of the athletic, masculinized woman outside of fiction is radically transformed in girls' college stories, where the basketball player's muscular physique and athletic vigor are considered desirable traits. These texts envision a world dangerous to the established social order—an insular women's community in which students can actively participate in team athletics or play an equally important role as spectators (who cheer on the athletes and write songs and chants for their teams).

The emphasis of these stories on the importance of both the athletes and the women watching the game is crucial because it provides the precollege reader with a tantalizing glimpse of her future at a women's college. Although we should not regard such novels as offering a realistic view of college life, I would suggest that they did help to socialize their precollege readers into life at a women's college. The stories stress the camaraderie of the whole student population rather than of an elite, tight-knit clique composed exclusively of team members. Although a reader who is only five feet three might not be able to imagine herself on the basketball team, she can still picture herself cheering from the gallery or gaining fame and popularity as the writer of a college song. Hence girls' college stories gained subversive potential against the dominance of gymnastics because they were able to create an image of sports that unified all students. The idealized nature of this scenario is evident; it is unlikely that the perfect cohesion of the fictional student community happily united over a basketball game ever existed in reality. Yet I suggest that this mythical community did provide the precollege reader with an idealized image of how her own academic career could be structured, particularly in respect to the positive, supportive attitude that she should adopt toward team sports.

The athlete I examine in these stories is the basketball player participating in a game against a different college class: for example, the freshmen play the sophomores in the big game of the year while the juniors play the seniors.[14] These class games are composed of all the elements that physical educators were so eager to keep out of women's sport: spectators are rowdy and insist upon cheering; the athletes display a most unladylike physical prowess and interest in winning. An interclass basketball game provides an ideal scenario to demonstrate the wholehearted student affirmation of all aspects of sport that women are expected by society most to deplore.

Girls' college fiction affirms a girl's right to be both athlete and spectator, while questioning the views of a society that considers women's sports frivolous (McCrone 51). These texts refuse to legitimate the physical education strategies of college officials who concerned themselves with a social-Darwinist system of gymnastic exercises with its two unstated goals: the first, of providing an acceptable form of physical activity for college women without emphasizing the dangerously self-sufficient, all-female team; the second, of strengthening American women for their role as future mothers. In these stories, the affiliation with the student community that team athletics provides is much more important to the students than any potential duty they might have to ensure a stronger race.

Here the team is an allegory for the cohesive student community and is capable of subsuming every woman into a single organization. Although certain players may shine in their performances, it is the team that is truly important. Even the star athletes, like Christine Arnold in Caroline M. Fuller's "The Basket-Ball Game," are submerged in the group identity. This does not mean, however, that the team is the ultimate authority within these texts. The members of the team recognize that they only play basketball as representatives of their college class—a much larger, more important group. By understanding the less-powerful location of the team as a smaller image used to represent the cohesive nature of the class, we can understand why the class, not the team, is called upon to inspire athletic performance. For instance, to encourage her teammates, Christine holds up the class flag:

> She gathered her team around her, lifted the green flag . . . and . . . with one fierce gesture of love and loyalty, said,—"Girls, it is for this!"
> Her classmates understood her, and clenched their fists in silent determination. (121)

Similarly, when Christine dislocates her shoulder in the game, she asks her friend Ruth to "take down our flag,—the flag of Ninety-five. Hold it where I can see it, and then I shall not scream when my shoulder is set" (123).

Why does Christine have such a seemingly fanatic attachment to her class flag, while paying little attention to the importance of performing for her teammates? Because these girls' college stories stress that the student athletic subculture is not limited to the players on the gymnasium floor but also includes every student who watches the game. Thus the members of the team, instead of feeling isolated from the spectators, feel a close bond with them. Spectators and players are both working for the good of their entire class.

Christine's use of a particular class flag (the flag of Ninety-five) also can be understood as Fuller's use of nostalgia to rally support for women's team athletics. Thus far I have concentrated upon how girls' college stories present to precollege students an alluring image of the team athletic culture at women's colleges. We must, however, also understand Christine's plea as being addressed to women who have concluded their college careers. (This point is supported by the fact that Christine defends the flag of Ninety-five in a novel published in 1899, when presumably a more up-to-date flag would appear more relevant to younger students. Not coincidentally, Fuller was herself an 1895 graduate of Smith College.) Women who have left their athletic days far behind them are encouraged to remember the pleasure of their own involvement in college team sports. Even women who have never participated in athletics are reminded of their loyalty to their college and to their college class. In the Progressive era, presumably this technique would have influenced the post-college readers of a novel such as *Across the Campus* to support rather than oppose athletics at women's colleges. College graduates who persist in condemning team sports for women are openly disparaged. For example, in Anna Chapin Ray's *Sidney at College* (1908), the captain of the freshman team criticizes "old croakers of alums" who think that basketball is not an appropriate sport for girls (206). We cannot locate the subversive influence of these girls' college stories only among a juvenile readership.

Since the emphasis of such narratives is on the cohesion of the peer community, it is not surprising that any playing by an individual that threatens to undermine the importance of the team's group nature is openly discouraged. In *That Freshman* by Christina Catrevas, Tommy condemns a sophomore basketball player, Anna Walker, for being "too sure of herself and not of anybody else. She spoils the chances of her whole team by her individual playing" (291).[15] This style of play fails dismally. Anna "would not again trust the ball to another" (294) and thus loses the ball when she attempts to make a basket. Her failure does more than simply demonstrate

her lack of basketball finesse. When Anna is too sure of herself, she repudi-
ates her peers—something that must be firmly discouraged. Here Catrevas
also implicitly criticizes the women's colleges that emphasize the development of the individual through gymnastic exercises, so that students have
no opportunity to learn the importance of subordinating their desires to
the good of the peer community.[16] Group cooperation is depicted as a more
effective mechanism for achieving success than solitary effort.

The emphasis girls' college stories place on the members of the college
student body working together goes much further than a simple criticism
of gymnastics culture. One can also understand the emphasis on the group
as an attempt to transform the stereotypical "feminine" community (that
is, the family) into something more radical. While the family is traditionally structured around the patriarch, there is no center at all to the all-
women's community that is structured around the basketball game. When
an individual (such as Anna) attempts to become the focus, she is firmly
discouraged. Thus the authors of girls' college stories go beyond simply
replacing a male center of influence with a female. Instead, they raise the
question of whether a group needs an autocratic figure at all.

Individual athletic excellence, however, is not completely repudiated in
these stories. The star athlete is an important figure as long as she realizes that she is playing for all her classmates, not just for her personal
glory. She metaphorically represents the best of the whole community, and
she is emulated by her classmates, who admire her for qualities—such as
brawn and beauty—that have nothing whatsoever to do with the aims of
Progressive-era gymnastics instruction. By creating an ideal, idolized athlete with whom the entire student population can identify, these fictional
texts reformulate the Progressive-era aim of designing a more efficient
mother into that of designing a glamorous heroine who will encourage
readers to pursue team athletics.

In these texts, what actually constitutes an attractive star athlete is not
just brawn. In Schwartz's short story "That Athletic Girl," a student wonders why the unnamed athlete is so attractive: "I do not know whether
it is because she has not yet learned to mount neat cross-sections of her
heart under a mental microscope, or because she looks so well in her gym
suit" (*Vassar* 204). Good looks and muscularity are important; but a certain amount of stoicism is called for, too. Janet, a star athlete in "At the
First Game," hides the fact that she shrinks from physical pain because
"The class [was] proud of her as a model athlete, strong, cool, and brave"
(Gallaher 234). Janet's true feelings matter less than being a suitable repre-

sentative of her class. Why can this particular star athlete gain approval for her individual athletic prowess, which, as we have just seen, is denied to other characters such as Anna Walker? Simply because the acceptable star never forgets that she is a member of a team. No matter how well she may perform, she remembers that her glory reflects more on the team and on her college class than on herself. Thus when she is successful on the court, her achievement is shared by her teammates and watching classmates.

This conceptualization of leadership was one way in which girls' college novels had a socializing effect that extended beyond the basketball court. Readers were encouraged to view athletic activities not primarily as training for domestic duties but as preparation for careers outside the home. Yet these stories do not depict the athlete as readying herself for existence in the competitive, male marketplace. Janet is not a Frank Merriwell, shouldering aside all obstacles in a solitary dash down the football field—ideal preparation for advancing to a position as captain of industry. She would undoubtedly disapprove of Frank's pathway to success, preferring a profession such as settlement work or social work in which her sense of social responsibility could be expressed. Thus although girls' college stories do undermine the conservative ideology implicit in gymnastics activities, it is too reductive to see them as texts that completely reshape popular ideology about feminine roles.

The Spectators · During a basketball game, the watching student crowd is differentiated only by class color. Theodora (heroine of Josephine Daskam's "Emotions of a Sub-Guard") observes that the auditorium is divided into two color groupings: "[she] pushed through the yellow and purple crowd, [and] caught a glimpse of the red and green river that flowed steadily in at the other door" (1); "The galleries were crowded with the rivers of color that poured from the entrance doors" (3). The transformation of individuals into a color-coded mob allows the class to demonstrate its cohesion.[17] In this "river," no boundaries exist between individuals; just as it is impossible to separate the elements of a river's flow, it is impossible to identify the individuals who make up this stream. The reader receives the impression that the whole student community is coming to watch the basketball game; resistance to supporting team sports seems almost impossible, at least within this textual universe.

Class colors have three other purposes. They are colors chosen by the students, not the faculty members; thus an allegiance to one's colors represents an adherence to one's peer group. They strengthen the link between

the spectators wearing one color and the team wearing the same color.
And, as I shall discuss later in more detail, class colors can also pinpoint
the outsiders (such as faculty members) who are unable to understand the
importance of colors as a signifier of student identity.

In order to make the bond between the teams and the spectators more
explicit, college cheers and songs are "belted out" at every possible occasion by the watching students. Outside of fiction, observers of women's
college life had mixed feelings about the nature of these cheers.

> Within [Bryn Mawr] each year has its cry. . . . The class practices the
> cheer in private until it can be shouted by all at the top of their voices,
> absolutely in unison; the effect is most remarkable, rather agreeable at
> a little distance out of doors, but within doors distinctly the reverse.
> (qtd. in Atkinson 642; the comment dates from 1907)

> I sincerely envy the feeling of the girl who joins in the college yell and
> takes part in the rollicking college song, entirely unconscious of her
> own personality, entirely carried away by the collective excitement.
> ("The American College Girl" 174)

Both of these quotations emphasize the unity that is achieved in a class
song or cheer. In the chorus, the class presents a unified front; no one voice
stands out in the collective roar. Faculty members at women's colleges were
explicit about the undesirability of cheering at athletic competitions: students were supposed to do nothing more rambunctious than sing their class
songs as a group at basketball games whenever their team was winning.
In theory, this would have provided a harmonious display of the students'
ladylike decorum: one class would sing its song, followed by the next class
singing its song. In reality, this system often broke down. For instance, in
the excitement of a game, the two opposing teams would both sing their
songs at the same time, resulting in cacophony, not harmony. Although administrators might have deplored such a display of emotion getting out of
control at a game, in fiction cheering and yelling is encouraged rather than
discouraged, even if faculty members might be offended by the uproar.

In "Emotions of a Sub-Guard," for example, Theodora, an alternate on
the Smith freshman basketball team, which is playing against the sophomores, describes the spectators as anything but controlled—although the
team's coach does remind them, "Girls, remember not to wear yourselves
out with kicking and screaming. You're right under the President. . . . Miss
Kassan says this must be a quiet game! She will not have that howling!"

(Daskam 4). Theodora hears "shouting to be heard of [*sic*] her parents in Pennsylvania" (5). The class songs are "shouted out" "well and . . . loud and strong," causing the sophomores and the audience to clap vigorously (5).[18] Cheering, like the spectators' clothing with its absence of frills, projects a desirably masculine image; for example, in "At the First Game," a student admonishes her cheering cohorts: "Keep your voices down like a man's, and don't shriek." In spite of this admonition, the cheer is shrill: "Just as much loyalty goes with it as if it were in double-bass, however" (Gallaher 227). This passage integrates team loyalty (a quality usually ascribed to males) with shrillness (an attribute socially ascribed to females). Obviously, the belief of such prominent educators as G. Stanley Hall that education should strive to bring out all that is most masculine in a man and all that is most feminine in a woman has little currency in these texts, especially on the athletic field. Rather than avoiding identification with masculine traits, women students actively embrace them.[19]

Even the songs are punctuated by howls, shouts, and cheers and show little feminine reserve. The classes that produce the most interesting scraps of doggerel to greet new occurrences in the game are praised and cheered; the athletic sisters Martha and Kate Sutton are regaled with:

Here's to Sutton M. and K.
And they'll surely win the day,
Drink 'em down, drink 'em down, drink 'em down, down, down!
(11)

This comes closer to a male drinking song than one of female transcendence over the spirit of competition. Even the names of Martha and Kate take on masculine overtones: they are called by their patronyms.[20] Melodic and harmonious singing is replaced by competition over who can shout the loudest. Similarly, in "The Basket-Ball Game," "competitive knots of spectators sang their class songs in rival keys" (Fuller 120). Even that aspect of sports in which audience participation is encouraged—singing— is subverted and transformed into competition rather than "safe" feminine melody.

It is difficult for us to comprehend fully what a revolutionary activity cheering was for a bourgeois woman living during the Progressive era. Even in the 1890s, middle-class women were not expected to cheer or yell at any social event. When men were shouting at a boat race or a football game, the most violent display of emotion ladies were allowed was a frantic fluttering of their handkerchiefs. Thus the idea of women cheering as wildly as men suggested an entirely new mode of behavior for bourgeois women. These college cheers can also be understood metaphorically as the sign of Progressive-era women college graduates literally gaining a voice. These women did not confine their voice to the gymnasium; they were also vocal and outspoken outside the college. Whether it was Gail Laughlin campaigning for suffrage, Lillian Pettengill examining the domestic work system by writing about her own experiences working as a maid, Elva Young Van Winkle joining the Massachusetts Bar in 1898 and helping to found the American Association of University Women, or Mary K. Conyngton investigating the conditions of women workers in industry, many women graduating from women's colleges were speaking out at the turn of the century, being aggressively vocal about the social ills of the time. Whether they only read about the joys of cheering and yelling at athletic games or whether they participated in such games themselves, women were encouraged by team sports to be vocal and outspoken rather than to maintain a ladylike reserve.

Outsiders: Teachers and Men · Does anyone dare confront these boisterous and dangerously cohesive young women? Does anyone dare suggest that this athletic culture based on vigorous participation as either athlete or spectator might not be entirely desirable? In these texts, a few individuals do denigrate the importance of athletics for women. These people, however, are typically such outsiders to the student community as teachers and men. Rather than weakening the control of the student community over its members, criticism by these aliens helps reaffirm the desirability of membership.

The teachers in these stories frequently show little concern for the significance of various athletic rituals. For example, in contrast to Christine's melodramatic devotion to the class flag in *Across the Campus,* teachers are indifferent when it comes to class membership. During a basketball game, a student reacts angrily when she overhears a professor saying her team will lose, and is furious that the teacher has accepted flowers from both of the opposing teams: "[The faculty member] had a bunch of violets . . . pinned to her dress, and her hands were full of daffodils. That was like the Faculty! To take their flowers and talk that way!" (Daskam 121). Professors and administrators are represented as unconcerned about the outcome of athletic contests. Here, in Kaja Silverman's formulation, convention plays its central role in iconic signification (24). For the students, the flowers represent their college class and their loyalty to it; the professors, however, do not consider this system of signification important. They are outsiders

to the students' conventions. Because it is the students' ordering of signification that shapes these texts, the faculty members will always appear as
outsiders, as they do not understand the students' language.

While faculty members are located at the margins of the games, men
are either entirely excluded or barely tolerated; in both cases they are considered a hindrance to female enjoyment.[21] For example, in "At the First
Game," a student, Ruth, is unable to foist off a visiting male on someone
else and must remain with him: "Poor Ruth! Behold her skirting the edge of
things with a man. He is only [a secondary interest], and she has struggled
to foist him off on somebody, anybody. Men are dear and desirable beast-
ies, but, oh! not at Vassar" (Gallaher 225). Having one's own man on
campus is a poor second to joining in the excitement of the game. Like the
professors, men do not understand the system of signification within this
insular community. They are dispensable.

What a reversal this is from the construction of physical education under
gymnastics instruction! Implicit in the gymnastics program was the understanding that its aim was to prepare a woman for marriage. In women's
team sports, in contrast, there is no role for men to fill. The athletes and the
student spectators organize activities and compete on their own, without
any male help. From there, it is only a step to the next logical question:
if women can do this in the sports arena, why not in other areas? Hence
these texts propagate the radical idea of female self-sufficiency.

When a man does dare to question the soundness of sports for women,
retribution is swift. The best example of this occurs in the short story
"Revenge" (Goodloe, *College Girls*, 1895), in which a young newspaper re-
porter is roundly condemned for writing an article that stereotypes women
at "girls' colleges" as having far less ability than men at competitive sports.
Katharine Atterbury, who is captain of the senior crew and a respected
tennis player, reads Jack Newbold's article and scornfully remarks:

> To read this article one would imagine that we were imbecile babies.
> One would think that a girl was as weak as a kitten, and didn't know
> a boat from an elevator, or a five-lap running track from an ice-wagon,
> or a golf club from a sewing-machine. He . . . seems to think that all
> our training and physical development is a huge joke. (167)

Katharine postulates an answer to Jack's misguided article:

> I'm tired of reading this sort of trash about women's colleges. It is time
> the public was learning the true state of things—that girls can and do
> swim, and row and play golf and tennis, and run and walk about, just

as their brothers do, and that we have courage and muscle enough to go in for football even, except that we have some little regard for our personal appearance. (168)

Curiously enough, even before mentioning sports, Katharine mentions women's colleges; why does she do this when Jack is talking principally about athletics, not condemning women's higher education overall? Katharine criticizes far more than Jack's story; she also questions the popular linkage between women's colleges and corrective gymnastics. Here she connects the college to many of the athletic activities in which students engage outside the gymnasium, associating women's higher education positively with activities such as swimming, playing golf, and running. Katharine radically reinscribes the desirable relationship between women's colleges and physical education. She even dares consider football, that bastion of male prowess, a potential activity for women.

Here the masculinizing influence of team athletics comes to the forefront. Katharine stresses the similarities between women athletes and their brothers. This creates what McCrone calls a parallel world of female athletic culture:

[Sport's] masculinity makes it an obvious sphere for women to attempt to penetrate—or at the very least to challenge by creating parallel worlds of their own—in their efforts to counter external definitions of female physical and emotional frailty. (2)

I agree about the parallel nature of men's and women's sports, but I emphasize that they are not necessarily governed by the same rules or concerns. As Katharine mentions, she finds an opportunity in this new realm of team sports for women to play as well as their brothers, and at the same time to have regard for personal appearance. Although at first she seems to be concerned with preserving her proper femininity, actually she is heading in a dangerous direction. Personal appearance is to be preserved for an audience that is chiefly, if not entirely, female. In this parallel world the male is superfluous, having no role as either athlete or spectator.

When Katharine and her friends discover that Jack is a terrible athlete and invite him to campus, the not-so-innocent suggestion is made that he have a try at golf, under the eyes of Katharine's friend Miss Yale (her name showing the topsy-turvy nature of this all-female world where even the name of such a stronghold of male athleticism as Yale University can be feminized) and a group of other college women: "He would greatly have preferred not trying before Miss Yale and the knot of young women who had drawn together at some little distance, and were obviously watching him. . . . He felt desperately nervous" (177). As Jack is forced into demonstrating his manly prowess in many different sports, the female scrutiny is constant and relentless. Miss Yale remarks that she wants Jack to try the track: "I want to see just how you hold your head and arms" (182). The categorization and identification of body parts that women were expected to accept as part of a good gymnastics program are now directed at Jack, and he cannot escape:

> It was a rare and pleasingly curious sight that Miss Yale and Miss Thayer and a great many other young women assembled near the track . . . looked upon. . . . It occurred to Newbold as he dashed around and around that it would be far preferable to keep going until he fainted away or dropped dead, than to stop and encounter the remarks and glances of those young women. (182)

A complete role reversal exists here. In this instance, Jack is going to faint, while the women casually talk about him among themselves. The dominant cultural views of the acceptable roles for men and women are openly satirized: Jack presents a ludicrous image on the athletic field or track, while the women watching act as critical judges of his ability.

An even greater threat to a stable social order is that Jack's race around the track is a *"pleasingly* curious sight" (my emphasis). Not only do the women force Jack into a role that thoroughly undermines his male prestige, but they enjoy doing so. Instead of being uneasy with the role reversal, they glory in it. The question arises of whether these women will ever give up the pleasure of their new role. Similarly, the Progressive-era girl reader of this story is encouraged to assume a more masculine persona, to become the athletic Katharine rather than the "frilly, ribbony" roommate who is relegated to the sidelines. Again, we see the students in these stories moving further and further away from nurturing, feminine roles.

In conclusion, these stories challenge and subvert the scientific gymnastics instruction that was part of the curriculum at most women's colleges during the Progressive era. Instead of gymnastics, team athletics are held up as the desirable model of physical activity for women. The most popular team sport for women, basketball, becomes in girls' college stories the ideal sport to represent resistance to the social emphasis on the benefits of individualized physical activities for women. In an era in which women's team sports were often condemned by critics as leading to a loss in femininity and a gain in masculinity and competitiveness, the readers of these stories were encouraged to display aggression in athletics. In the student community created in these texts, women can "act like men" as both athletes and spectators and be praised rather than censured for doing so.

The influence of these stories reaches far beyond the athletic field. The student who experiences the lack of constraint of a gymnastics uniform is likely to question why she must ever submit to the restraints of a corset and a long dress. The girl who shouts and stomps her feet at a basketball game might no longer be content to be silent about her social rights. The athlete who has experienced the support of her female classmates might realize she does not have to be dependent upon men for support. Even readers of girls' college fiction who never themselves played in a basketball game or went to college were still provided with a subversive representation of how women could rebel against the social ideology that considered women's bodies as little more than baby-making machines. I am not saying that the turn-of-the-century readers of these texts became social revolutionaries, but they were provided with a framework for resistance whose significance could carry over to the world outside the story. Certainly, girls' college sport stories must have encouraged their readers to question the ideology of femininity in many areas other than the gymnasium.

NOTES

I am grateful for the suggestions of Judith Halberstam, Carolyn Haynes, Nicole Hoffman, Kathryn Shevelow, Shawn Smith, and the editors of this volume.

1. Fiction about student life at women's colleges was tremendously popular from the 1890s to the 1930s. Targeted at a teenage, female audience, hundreds of novels and collections of short stories about student life at the Seven Sister colleges, as well as at mythical women's colleges, were published by dozens of publishing companies. In the same period, boarding school novels were published for younger girls, while boys had an even greater number of books to read about student exploits at Harvard, Yale, Princeton, and other universities. A few novels addressed the experiences of women students at coeducational colleges and universities, but women's colleges were far more frequently depicted, probably because the fictional students could be portrayed as more engaged in the student culture than at coeducational schools where males dominated athletics, government, publications, and other student activities. Although there were more than a hundred other women's colleges in existence during the Progressive era, the Seven Sisters were the best known and most written about schools. These texts, however, were not aimed solely at a market

of Smith or Wellesley graduates or potential Smith or Wellesley students. Instead, college fiction reflected the generic "women's college," which explains the many novels based on fictional schools. Thus, in many ways, college fiction represented the total women's college experience to readers—not only the experience at a few select institutions.

2. An exception is Jane S. Smith's "Plucky Little Ladies and Stout-Hearted Chums: Serial Novels for Girls, 1900–1920" (166–67), which briefly mentions the importance of the college athlete and the dominance of basketball in several serial novels.

3. Theodor Adorno remarked that sports simply prepared men for their lives in an industrial system: "Modern Sports, one will perhaps say, seek to restore to the body some of the functions of which the machine has deprived it. But they do so only in order to train men all the more inexorably to serve the machine" (qtd. in Mrozek 11).

4. Although my selection of women's colleges is limited, many of the statements that I make about these institutions can be applied to the physical education programs at other women's colleges such as Elmira, Mills, Rockford, Simmons, Trinity, and Wells.

5. It was not until 1906 that Wellesley pioneered the decision to make any activities besides gymnastics a part of its required, supervised physical education program. Bryn Mawr followed Wellesley's lead in 1907; Mount Holyoke and Vassar followed in 1917, with Smith trailing in 1925.

6. Women's basketball was also popular at coeducational universities. In 1896 Berkeley and Stanford had their first women's basketball competition, at which only female spectators were allowed (Guttmann 95). These schools, however, already had entrenched male team sports such as football and baseball, which drew large crowds. Thus women's team sports at the coeducational institutions were never as prominent as they were on women's campuses.

7. For information on the required gymnastics instruction at Mount Holyoke, Smith, Bryn Mawr, and Wellesley, see Alice K. Fallows, "Athletics for College Girls," 63–64, and Alys W. Pearsall Smith, "A Women's College in the United States," 920–21. For the importance of women's colleges in creating a scientific system of physical education, see Sara A. Burstall, *The Education of Girls in the United States,* 148.

8. For other essays on the traditional aims of physical education programs, see Paul Atkinson, "The Feminist Physique: Physical Education and the Medicalization of Women's Education"; Messenger, *Sport and the Spirit of Play in American Fiction,* 136–60; and Carroll Smith-Rosenberg and Charles Rosenberg, "The Female Animal: Medical and Biological Views of Women and Their Role in Nineteenth-Century America."

9. The system of discipline operating through gymnastics instruction establishes a Foucauldian frame of indeterminate scrutiny: "The ideal point of penality today

would be an indefinite discipline: an interrogation without end, an investigation that would be extended without limit to a meticulous and ever more analytical observation, a judgement that would at the same time be the constitution of a file that was never closed" (Foucault 227).

10. Swedish gymnastics emphasized drill work, the sparing use of apparatus, and physical correction. As Theodore Hough wrote in his early-twentieth-century text on gymnastics, the "most distinctive feature of Swedish work is the fact that it never loses sight of the corrective element" (13). See also Baron Nils Posse's *Handbook of School-Gymnastics of the Swedish System.*

11. Margaret Sherwood made the connection between gymnastics and racial progress explicit when she described Vassar's gymnasium in 1898: "Here is complicated apparatus—rings for swinging, horses for jumping, chest-weights, clubs—all those devices that an untoward generation has been obliged to make in order to retrieve the physical blunders of its ancestors" (646). Compare this with Arabella Kenealy's disparagement of the racial energy lost in team athletics: "it is the laboriously evolved potentiality of the race they are expending on their muscles" (643). See also Anna J. Hamilton, "What Kind of Education Is Best Suited for Girls?," 69.

12. One way in which college authorities curtailed the competitiveness of basketball was by adopting women's rules at all the eastern women's colleges in 1899. These rules confined the players to certain areas of the court, required that the ball be dribbled no more than three successive times, and stated that the ball could not be held longer than three seconds. They were implemented to alleviate the physical strain of basketball on women and to make the sport suitable for ladies. At the same time, they limited the possibilities for effective teamwork.

13. Nevertheless, to read this passage as signifying Myra's overt or latent lesbianism would be ahistorical. As we shall see, Myra is not alone in her admiration of athletes; other students also view athletes as physically attractive. At the turn of the century, this admiration was only gradually beginning to be categorized by medical professionals as potentially lesbian. For more information on how the attitude toward women's affectionate relationships was changing in this period, see Nancy Sahli, "Smashing: Women's Relationships Before the Fall."

14. Other organized athletic pursuits appear not at all (hockey) or only rarely (golf and field day events) in these stories. This is particularly interesting since by 1901 Bryn Mawr, Smith, Wellesley, and Vassar had all established hockey teams. Individual athletic pursuits, such as cycling and walking, also seldom appear in these texts. These activities, which did not stress competition, were more widely accepted by the public than team sports. See Rosalind Rosenberg, *Beyond Separate Spheres,* 54, and Caroline Ticknor, "The Steel-Engraving Lady and the Gibson Girl," 106.

15. Similarly, in Helen Leah Reed's *Brenda's Cousin at Radcliffe: A Story for Girls* (1903), a student remarks about basketball that "a girl who thinks only of

her own ability to make a wonderful throw may make a throw that will gain great applause, but she generally sends the ball into the hands of the enemy" (259). Such passages recall the famous comment of Thomas Hughes's Tom Brown (1857) that it is the "unselfish" nature of football and cricket that places them above games "where the object is to come in first or to win for oneself, and not that one's side may win" (271); unlike the college girls of the Progressive-era stories, however, Tom's recognition of this point shows his newly achieved unity of mind with his teachers.

16. I would also add that the criticism of individual gymnastics activities might reasonably be extended to include a critique of the emphasis of the women's college on individual success in other areas, such as academics. Administrators and faculty members at women's colleges who desired to demonstrate that their institutions were as academically rigorous as male universities and colleges encouraged their students to adopt the capitalist model of the brilliant individual scholar, prepared to do battle in the marketplace. The prominence of this model of academic production exerted (and still exerts) a hegemonic control that allows little room for communal scholarship to achieve equivalent prestige.

17. What about the other team? Is it not established as an anticommunity to the school class with which the reader is aligned? I suggest that the structure of girls' college stories encourages us not to think of the two teams and classes in such a static fashion. Remember, the freshmen playing against the sophomore team are going to become sophomores themselves later in their educational careers. Every student has the chance to experience every level of the student hierarchy (freshman, sophomore, junior, and senior). Also, the texts are careful to dissipate the competition between the two teams by the end of the game. Basketball stories frequently conclude with both teams congratulating the opposing players for their superior play; there appears to be little lingering antagonism from the losers.

18. Similarly, in Catrevas's *That Freshman,* cheering is described as "raucous" (274), "ripped out" (275), and "rough [and] 'manly' " (88).

19. Another example of the masculinized female image in these texts is the use of nicknames. Many of the most prominent athletes have boys' nicknames; for example, Theodora (Daskam, *Smith College Stories,* 1900) is "Theo," and the star basketball player in *Betty Wales, Sophomore* (Warde, 1909) is "T. Reed." In *Betty Wales Decides* (Warde, 1911), Madeline defends the use of boys' names for girls to let girls escape from being confined to a limited female identity. When Madeline hears a student commenting that it is "certainly queer how many of the nicest girls get nicknamed Bob and Bill and Dickie," she replies: "The reason . . . is that the very nicest girls are all-around nice—not sissy nice, or young-lady nice, or clever nice, but nice every way,—and just as good fun to play about with as any man in the world. And the rest of us notice that, without stopping to analyze it, and call them Bob or Billy" (244–45). Unlike Erving Goffman, who discusses the in-

stitutional loss of one's name as a potential "great curtailment of the self" (18), I perceive the students in these stories who are given nicknames as losing one self and gaining another. The male nicknames show that these young women belong to a community that allows its members to transgress typically feminine ways.

20. Similarly, female hockey players at the English schools Girton and Newnham are referred to as "men" (McCrone 36).

21. For college stories in which men are the focus of athletic events, see Joy Lichtenstein, *For the Blue and Gold,* and James Gardner Sanderson, *Cornell Stories.* In these texts about coeducational schools, women do not even cheer to encourage the men's teams, and certainly do not participate as athletes.

WORKS CITED

Ainsworth, Dorothy S. *The History of Physical Education in Colleges for Women.* New York: Barnes, 1930.

"The American College Girl: By a European University Girl." *Outlook* 76 (16 January 1904): 171–75.

Atkinson, Paul. "The Feminist Physique: Physical Education and the Medicalization of Women's Education." *From "Fair Sex" to Feminism: Sport and the Socialization of Women in the Industrial and Post-Industrial Era.* Ed. J. A. Mangan and Roberta J. Park. London: Cass, 1986. 38–57.

Burstall, Sara A. *The Education of Girls in the United States.* 1894. New York: Arno, 1971.

Catrevas, Christina. *That Freshman.* New York: Appleton, 1910.

Daskam, Josephine Dodge. *Smith College Stories.* New York: Scribner's, 1900.

Fallows, Alice K. "Athletics for College Girls." *Century* 66 (May 1903): 58–65.

Foucault, Michel. *Discipline and Punish: The Birth of the Prison.* Trans. Alan Sheridan. New York: Pantheon, 1977.

Fuller, Caroline M. *Across the Campus: A Story of College Life.* New York: Scribner's, 1899.

Gallaher, Grace Margaret. *Vassar Stories.* Boston: Richard G. Badger, 1900.

Goffman, Erving. *Asylums: Essays on the Social Situation of Mental Patients and Other Inmates.* Chicago: Aldine, 1962.

Goodloe, Abbe Carter. *College Girls.* New York: Scribner's, 1895.

Guttman, Allen. *Sports Spectators.* New York: Columbia UP, 1986.

Hamilton, Anna J. "What Kind of Education Is Best Suited for Girls?" *Addresses and Proceedings of the National Educational Association.* Washington, D.C., 1906. 65–71.

Hart, Lavinia. "A Girl's College Life." *Cosmopolitan* 31.2 (June 1901): 188–95.

Hough, Theodore. *A Review of Swedish Gymnastics.* Boston: Ellis, 1901.

Hughes, Thomas. *Tom Brown's Schooldays.* 1857. New York: Puffin, 1983.

Kenealy, Arabella. "Woman as Athlete." *Nineteenth Century* 45 (April 1899): 633–45.

Leonard, Fred E. "Physical Training in the Colleges." *Popular Science Monthly* 52 (1898): 622–28.

Lichtenstein, Joy. *For the Blue and Gold.* San Francisco: Robertson, 1901.

McCrone, Kathleen E. *Playing the Game: Sport and the Physical Emancipation of English Women, 1870–1914.* Lexington: UP of Kentucky, 1988.

Messenger, Christian K. *Sport and the Spirit of Play in American Fiction.* New York: Columbia UP, 1981.

Mrozek, Donald J. *Sport and American Mentality, 1880–1910.* Knoxville: U of Tennessee P, 1983.

Posse, Nils. *Handbook of School-Gymnastics of the Swedish System.* Boston: Lothrop, 1891.

Ray, Anna Chapin. *Sidney at College.* Boston: Little, 1908.

Reed, Helen Leah. *Brenda's Cousin at Radcliffe: A Story for Girls.* Boston: Little, 1903.

Rickert, Edith. "What Has the College Done for Girls?" *Ladies' Home Journal* 29 (January–April 1912): 11–12; 9, 52; 15–16; 23–24.

Rosenberg, Rosalind. *Beyond Separate Spheres: Intellectual Roots of Modern Feminism.* New Haven: Yale UP, 1982. 13–37.

Rota, Tiziana F. "Between 'True Women' and 'New Women': Mount Holyoke Students, 1837–1908." Diss. U of Massachusetts, Amherst, 1983.

Sahli, Nancy. "Smashing: Women's Relationships Before the Fall." *Chrysalis* 8 (Summer 1979): 17–27.

Sanderson, James Gardner. *Cornell Stories.* New York: Scribner's, 1898.

Schwartz, Julia Augusta. *Elinor's College Career.* Boston: Little, 1906.

———. *Vassar Studies.* New York: Putnam's, 1899.

Sherwood, Margaret. "Undergraduate Life at Vassar." *Scribner's* 23 (1898): 643–60.

Silverman, Kaja. *The Subject of Semiotics.* New York: Oxford UP, 1983.

Smith, Alys W. Pearsall. "A Women's College in the United States." *Nineteenth Century* 23 (June 1888): 918–26.

Smith, Jane S. "Plucky Little Ladies and Stout-Hearted Chums: Serial Novels for Girls, 1900–1920." *Prospects* 3 (1977): 155–74.

Smith-Rosenberg, Carroll, and Charles Rosenberg. "The Female Animal: Medical and Biological Views of Women and Their Role in Nineteenth-Century America." *From "Fair Sex" to Feminism: Sport and the Socialization of Women in the Industrial and Post-Industrial Era.* Ed. J. A. Mangan and Roberta J. Park. London: Cass, 1986. 13–37.

Ticknor, Caroline. "The Steel-Engraving Lady and the Gibson Girl." *Atlantic Monthly* 88 (July 1901): 105–8.

Vertinsky, Patricia. "God, Science and the Market Place: The Bases for Exercise

Prescriptions for Females in Nineteenth Century North America." *Canadian Journal of the History of Sport* 17.1 (May 1986): 38–45.

Warde, Margaret. *Betty Wales, Sophomore.* Philadelphia: Penn, 1909.

———. *Betty Wales Decides.* Philadelphia: Penn, 1911.

Webster, Jean. *When Patty Went to College.* New York: Grosset, 1903.

"Women and Basket-Ball." *Mind and Body* 7 (May 1900): 60.

SALLY MITCHELL

Girls' Culture: At Work

Through most of the Victorian period in England, gentry and middle-class girls were expected to stay home until they married. Inside her father's house, the girl was exhorted to "create feelings of greater . . . love" (Wynne 19) and "pay her way by filling in the little spaces in home life as only a dear daughter can, by lifting the weight of care from her mother, and by slipping in a soft word or a smile where it is like oil on the troubled waters of a father's spirit" ("Between School and Marriage" 769–70). By the early years of the twentieth century, however, advice manuals and mainstream periodicals used the language of moral imperative in precisely the opposite direction: when a girl leaves school, she "must find work," either paid or unpaid, which will provide regular duties and teach her essential skills and habits that she cannot learn in the shelter of her family (Chesser 132). No matter how wealthy she may be, insists another conduct book, "every girl by the time she reaches eighteen must know how and where she may place her talents in order to earn money, position and content" (Curnock 110).

Over the space of a single generation, the public ideology about a girl's place, role, and occupation had shifted. It is important to understand that there was no change in the real numbers. Three-quarters of all unmarried English females over the age of fourteen had been in the labor market ever since the census began asking. During those very mid-Victorian years when the "ideal woman" lived in decorative leisure, that life was possible because one-third of all girls between fifteen and twenty were working as domestic servants. The change is one of perception, attitude, expectation: in 1905 it was seen as usual for girls—those girls visible to the man or woman doing the writing—to work outside the home; in 1880 it was seen as unusual.

This essay explores the shape of that change in expectation. How does the idea of paid work affect the culture of girlhood? Looking at advice manuals, popular fiction, and especially girls' magazines in the period between 1880 and 1915, I have identified a number of contested and conflicting messages. The feminine ideal of service and self-sacrifice is reconstituted to encompass women's employment. The independence required in a public role encounters the "sweet dependence" of femininity. There is an imaginative reshaping of courtship and heterosexual companionship. Personal relationships at home are ambiguously distinguished from business relationships in the workplace. Feminization alters certain occupations and affects wages. The very concept of "the girl" interacts with all of these changes.

In middle-class advice manuals, the alteration was just becoming visible in the 1880s. According to Phillis Browne (Sarah Sharp Hamer), author of *What Girls Can Do,* many people still look down on the "young person" at work as opposed to the "young lady" at home, but girls themselves feel "respect and even . . . envy" for "their companions who are busy, independent, and self-supporting" (307).

The vocabulary is fairly easy to unpick: "young lady" is the stereotype of leisured femininity, particularly the newly idle dependents who had become a status symbol for middle-class men. "Young person" is drawn from the Factory Acts. Those laws defined children, whose work was increasingly regulated, as under fourteen, and men and women as those nineteen and over; the "young person," aged fourteen to eighteen, was in an intermediate and partially protected category.[1] In fiction of the period, the latter term is an insult, a class marker much resented by pupil teachers or apprentice dressmakers.

The class label of "young person" also erases gender; one of the magic ways that nineteenth-century stereotypes manage to ignore women's labor is by overlooking the sex of female workers. The medical books that recommend avoiding physical activity during the six months that mark the "transition from girl to woman" and instruct adolescents to "give up all violent exercise"—as well as "excessive intellectual work"—during "those few days each month when . . . special care is called for" (Chesser 48, 55, 58, 54) are not intended for the thirteen-year-old down in the kitchen who works a sixteen-hour day.

But if "young person" and "young lady" are reasonably transparent concepts, "girl" is not. The word became enormously popular in the last quarter of the nineteenth century. "Young lady" and "young person"—like "lady" and "woman"—had class referents; "girl" is inclusive. It takes in work-girl, servant girl, factory girl, college girl or girl graduate, shopgirl, bachelor girl, girl journalist, and office girl. It includes schoolgirl as well, but she is not a child; a "schoolgirl," in Victorian usage, is probably over eleven.

The "girl," then, is neither a child nor a (sexual) adult. As "young person" unsexed the worker, so, in a somewhat different sense, did terms such as college girl, girl graduate, working girl, or bachelor girl unsex her middle-class counterpart. The "young lady" at home is on the marriage market, but a "girl" is not husband-hunting. The ascription of immaturity and liminality gives her permission to behave in ways that might not be appropriate for a woman.

At the same time, the understanding that "girls" could—indeed, should —earn their own livelihoods released them from an obligation to remain childish. In the 1860s, even a feminist such as Jessie Boucherett of the Society for Promoting the Employment of Women could write that if a father wanted his daughter at home "to amuse . . . and cheer him," it was her duty to obey (50). By the end of the 1890s, however, the *Monthly Packet*—a high church and conservative magazine for young women— reported that fathers who had formerly "scraped together" an annuity so their "unmarried daughters might pinch out an uneventful existence" were now investing the money in training so the daughters could support themselves (March-Phillips 502).

Was it, however, acceptable for a girl to work if she did not need the money? "Conscientious girls," Evelyn March-Phillips continued in her *Monthly Packet* series, "are deterred . . . by the accusation that . . . they are 'taking the bread from out their starving sisters' mouths.' " Why is it, she wondered ingenuously, that "We do not hear it said of a young man that because he has £500 a year, or £5000 for that matter, he is guilty of unfair competition, if he goes into the Army or is called to the Bar[?]" (502–3).

This debate surfaces frequently from the 1890s on. In almost every case, the answer is the same: it's perfectly all right to take the job, provided girls understand their "real moral obligation" not to "sell their labour below the market-price" ("Editor's Chat" 655). Clementina Black enlisted religious rhetoric in teaching girls to demand fair pay:

> To do work at a price by which we could not live, because we happen to be otherwise supported, is to make it impossible for some other unsupported woman to live by work of that sort. If actions are to be measured by the sufferings they cause, few actions are more wicked than those which tend to lower the payment of labour; and such an action is committed by every woman who lets herself be ill-paid for her work. (45)

The language of suffering and virtue, however, is only one part of the story. Money in the pocket also leads to feelings that had been suppressed or denied when "sweet dependence" was the ideal. These subversive emo-

tions are found more often in fiction than in essays. One example, plucked
out of many: In a story from an upper-middle-class girls' magazine, a
widow—that is, someone who has been not only a daughter but also a
married woman—says to a newly orphaned girl, "If you will believe me
(and I speak from experience), the bread we earn for ourselves is sweeter
than other people's money buys for us" (Hodgkinson 639).

The idea of earning one's own bread was, clearly, increasingly attractive to girls of all social classes. "Career novels" were a new genre toward
the end of the century. A selection of titles gives an idea of the kinds of
work that appealed: *Miss Secretary Ethel* (Ellinor Adams, 1898), *A Woman
of Business* (Mary Bramston, 1885), *A Ministering Angel* (Ellen Clayton,
1895), *A Girton Girl* (Annie Edwardes, serialized in *Temple Bar* 1884;
3 vols. 1885), *The Probationer* (Amy Irvine, 1910), *Dr. Janet of Harley
Street* (Arabella Kenealy, 1893), *Pickles: A Red Cross Heroine* (Edith C.
Kenyon, 1916), *Catalina: Art Student* (L. T. Meade, 1896), *Mary Gifford,
M.B.* (Meade, 1898), *The Medicine Lady* (Meade, 1892), *Nurse Charlotte*
(Meade, 1904), *A Sister of the Red Cross* (Meade, 1900), *Elizabeth Glen,
M.B.* (Annie S. Swan, 1895), *Mrs. Keith Hamilton, M.B.* (Swan, 1897),
Mona Maclean, Medical Student (Graham Travers [Dr. Margaret Todd],
1892), *The Newspaper Girl* (Alice Williamson, 1899).

There are far more books about doctors than about schoolteachers,
though by 1889 a grand total of seventy-two women physicians were on the
British Medical Register. (Their names are listed in the *Englishwoman's
Review;* see "Registered Medical Women.") Aside from the drama of
women's recent struggle for entry, medicine could be described (in the language of sentiment and service) as "one of the best openings for women"
because "it is a useful occupation" and "provides full employment for
all a woman's faculties both of heart and head" (Maxwell 113). Note the
order—heart first. And one could almost miss the next sentence, tagging
along with less emphasis: "There are very few, if any positions open to
women where they can so soon make themselves independent as in the
practice of medicine" (113).

The cross currents generated by the older ideal of service and the newer
ethic of self-sufficiency are also evident in the *Girl's Own Paper,* which
was the first broadly successful magazine for girls. At a price of one penny
a week, its ascribed audience was lower middle class. The letters column,
however, shows that servant girls read it, and autobiographies reveal sub-
scribers also among professors' daughters and others from the professional
classes. The *Girl's Own Paper* (like the *Boy's Own Paper*) was published by

the Religious Tract Society (RTS) in order to provide the increasingly liter-
ate young people who benefited from the 1870 Education Act with healthful alternatives to the romantic novelettes and blood-and-crime "penny
dreadfuls" that were the most easily available cheap reading matter. In a
daring and rather controversial move, however, the RTS deliberately kept
the new publications almost entirely free of overt religious instruction,
concentrating instead on interesting and entertaining articles about topics
that appealed to young people, and on fiction that demonstrated approved
social values within an exciting narrative. The formula evidently worked:
in an 1888 poll of one thousand girls between eleven and nineteen, almost
a third listed the *Girl's Own Paper* as their favorite reading (Salmon 22).

In the 1885–86 volume of this periodical, five stories center on girls
who earn money and seven on girls "at home." None of the working girls,
however, is really in the world of commerce—there are three varieties of
governess, a dressmaker who does pin-money work for friends, and an
aspiring novelist who becomes a children's writer after conquering her inappropriate desire for fame. Likewise, the domestic girls are not wholly
confined to the private sphere. The "Stay-at-Home Girls," in a serial of that
title, look after their invalid mother and do charity work; the story is really
a lesson, through fiction, about how to set up a penny bank, start a Band
of Hope, and so forth. In this volume from the mid-1880s, many essays
provide information for working girls, but the weight of emotional energy
in the fiction lies with home and unpaid community service.

A decade later, the volume for 1894–95 has, numerically, quite similar
proportions of paid versus volunteer workers. The working girls, however,
are far more evidently out in the world—they include a hospital nurse,
an elementary teacher, a telegraph clerk, and a shopworker. Furthermore,
almost all of the home girls would have been called employed by the census
of 1871 (which still had a category for unpaid household work). One man-
ages her brother's estate, one has been running the farm since her father's
eyesight failed, another is raising an orphaned step-family, yet another is
an overworked secretary for her brother the scholar. Indeed, these "non-
working" heroines would be better off with the regularized duties and free
time of a paid job. Their physical and emotional labor at home, performed
with little recognition or reward, may be valorized by its appearance in
fiction—but it no longer glows with peace and happiness.

In the earlier decade, paid work had been meliorated through a homelike
setting that emphasized emotional service, imitated family relationships,
and provided a shield against public visibility in the role of worker. In the

1890s, by contrast, the fiction explicitly teaches girls to put a businesslike detachment between their personal lives and their work lives. One young woman who has first worked as a companion and later in a shop explains that though her social status was "lowered" she much prefers the purely " 'money' bond": "When Lettice and her mother were unkind to me, it always hurt me because once I had been their friend." In her sales job, however, "From ten till six I am at [Mr. Jobling's] orders, but all the rest of the time I am independent, and I needn't feel grateful to him, because my salary is fairly earned" (Hodgkinson 638).

I have so far been looking primarily at middle-class readers and middle-class work—this being the arena in which the change of outlook was most visible. What about girls who had always expected to support themselves, as had their mothers before them? A new phenomenon from the 1890s was the halfpenny weekly paper for working-class girls. These are eight-page tabloids, often on pink or green paper, with such titles as *Girls' Best Friend, Girl's Friend, Girls' Reader,* and *Forget Me Not.* Purely commercial enterprises, the halfpenny weeklies featured serials, horoscopes, and contests to generate circulation; they had none of the underlying educational and religious purpose that sustained the *Girl's Own Paper* and the middle-class monthly magazines such as *Atalanta* and the *Girl's Realm.* Many of the halfpenny papers were published by Alfred Harmsworth, later Lord Northcliffe, inventor of the mass media conglomerate—and the fortune and peerage to be made from it. Harmsworth was a marketing genius who used contests, clubs, and advice columns to find out what readers wanted and even what language to cast it in.

In middle-class fiction, serving in a shop is respectable only if the shop sells toys or old lace or art goods or very expensive hats (presumably because the customers are largely female and upper class). Office work is a little suspect—the "secretaries" are generally private secretaries (working for a scholar or statesman at his home, with his wife in evidence), and the girl in a business office is apt to find the conditions fairly sleazy. In the work-girl papers, however, "business" has entirely favorable meanings. The columns providing advice about training and opportunities use "business" where middle-class magazines would describe the same work as a "career" or "profession." The jobs in a *Girls' Best Friend* series "Businesses for Girls" include telegraph learner, post office sorter, and "typewriting girl in Parliament"—a position established two years earlier, according to this 1898 article, for which one must take shorthand at 120 words per minute and type 80 words per minute on a Remington typewriter.

The titles of the novels cited earlier showed us that middle-class girls, who would probably become typists and teachers, were fantasizing about medicine and art and journalism. Girls who read the halfpenny papers—which sold sewing patterns to make "overalls for shop and factory" and nursery maids' dresses sized for ages twelve, fourteen, and sixteen—had a comparable fantasy in the idea of office work. But popular fiction also finds ways to cast a haze of glamor around the work we actually do. Just as the middle-class typist has an exciting persona in a novel about a statesman's private secretary, the work-girl papers offer glamorized versions of domestic service in serials about the shipboard stewardess, the "Complexion Specialist," the waitress in an elegant tea shop, or the detective under cover as a lady's maid.

The halfpenny papers also contain an extraordinary number of stories about circus performers. I'm a little puzzled about what to make of them. Is it the tomboy appeal? The performance and public attention—without the insistence on having the right accent to be an actress? The courage? The "Queen of the Ring" in the first volume of the *Girls' Best Friend* turns out to be the long-lost daughter of the Countess of Chippenham. At the conclusion she is "happy in the love of her mother . . . so happy that she has already refused to listen to the importunities of her many suitors" (142).

That makes us stop to consider the fourteen-year-old sent away to live-in domestic service. Many of the work-girl serials are "family romances," in the Freudian sense, that discover good parents elsewhere, but more simply they're also about being restored to a family, and they make us see how young these working girls are. Indeed, it is not so much restoration to a nuclear family that provides the emotional fuel of these tales (and of the otherwise puzzling stories set in "convent schools" where girls have been sent for punishment) as it is a longing for mother. Fathers may well be unmentioned; a good mother's embrace supplies the happy ending.

For all this emphasis on the security of the mother-child bond, however, the fiction in work-girl papers often has a delightful physical energy. Girl detectives grapple with muscular (although female) suspects. In "Emma Brown of London, Or, The Girl Who Defied the Kaiser," which began in *Girls' Reader* in January 1915, working-class feistiness has national significance: a servant runs away, gathers a band of nondescript Frenchmen and her trusty bulldog, and leads them to victory against the Germans.

It may be more raucous in the work-girl papers, but with the independence and self-confidence that come from work, a barely covert rebelliousness enters all kinds of writing for girls. Take a didactic book such as

M. H. Cornwall Legh's *An Incorrigible Girl* (1899), in which a drunkard's daughter is sent to a county council rescue home where "wild girls could be . . . tamed, and the daughters of 'undesirable homes' rescued from them just in time, and all be turned into, what everybody said were so much wanted, well-trained domestic servants" (124). Narrative doubt wells up in the rhetoric—"undesirable homes" is in quotation marks; irony tinges the interruptions of "just in time," "what everybody said were so much wanted."

That tone becomes even more marked after the turn of the century. Although the lines of influence are impossible to trace, it is evident that the sassy smartmouth manner of the working-class girl is on its way to becoming a degree of acceptable "smartness" in *any* girl, a mark of her self-assurance—and a mark of the distance between the new "girl" and the old feminine ideal. L. T. Meade, one of the writers most popular among girls whose families could afford to keep them at school during their teens, explained in a 1903 article that her readers "love a naughty heroine," one who is fearless, daring, and "a little imperative to her elders" ("Story Writing").

Self-assurance and independence, however, could cut both ways. When girls entered the workforce, the perceived social ranking of the various jobs open to them was only tenuously related to pay. Once the value of board and lodging is taken into account, real earnings were probably highest in domestic service on the one hand and in factories—particularly unionized textile mills—on the other. Yet these two kinds of work had the least desirable image. Girls found domestic service demeaning because of the supervision, the dependence, and the irksome rules about "no followers"; yet many of the same girls saw the factory as "not genteel" because of the independence it promoted.

Ladies who did social service thought factory work was dangerous because girls and men worked in the same shops (and could be seen larking around when they poured out of the gates). They tended to overlook the risks of privacy in domestic service. When religious tracts show a servant girl endangered by "rude" behavior, it's usually the footman who is to blame, not the man of the house (see, for example, Freeman). Mainstream publications for working girls were less reticent. *The Girl's Encyclopedia* (1909) provides a section on employment law that tells the young worker that "cruelty, violence, impropriety or familiarity (such as a kiss) done to a girl by one of the other sex against her will" is punishable, and gives the address of an agency for the protection of women and children (Barnard 172).

Among working-class girls, both dressmaking and shop work seemed more attractive than domestic service or the factory. Yet both had poorer wages and working conditions. One young dressmaker wrote: "The girls are kept working till half-past ten or eleven, day after day, through the best part of the season. . . . You can think what the air is in July, when we have all been working in it for twelve hours" (March-Phillips 162). Shop work also meant long hours, close supervision, fines that ate the wages, and (in the most desirable stores) the expense of dressing well. "Why," the *Monthly Packet* asked, "do so many women crowd into it? First, there is the fact of social status. . . . The shop assistant all her life belongs to a higher caste, so to speak, than the domestic servant." She wears better clothes, has a better chance of marriage, and "looks forward to having her free Sunday. . . . The idea of a number of young people, all working and living together, is lively and amusing" (March-Phillips 270–80).

Status interacts with questions of gender, sexuality, and the ideology of difference. Emily Pfeiffer pointed out in 1888 that men use an arsenal of sentimental arguments in order to protect girls against "unwomanly" callings—that is, "precisely such as offer the highest rewards in money" (8). The *Girl's Own Paper* reported a "widespread feeling, especially amongst the lower middle-class, that a woman becomes unwomanly when she enters into the same field of labour as a man, in direct competition with him" ("Women's Work" 51). This is certainly one reason why the new occupations created in the 1880s by the typewriter and the telephone were particularly welcome. They were almost immediately labeled as women's work. Typing solved "the problem of finding suitable employment for ladies" because it was "suited for their nimble fingers" ("Type-Writer" 745). The telephone receptionist needed a clear speaking voice; employment guides said it was especially suitable for "the daughters of professional men who have received few educational advantages" (Grogan 84).

Did a girl's social position come from her own work or from her father's occupation? The case of elementary teaching suggests that the latter may have been more common. The elementary schoolteacher was likely to be the daughter of a tradesman or even a laborer. Usually herself from a state-supported school, she began at fourteen as a "pupil teacher"—but after passing an exam at eighteen, she went to a training college and, later in the period, sometimes to a university.

The social class of young teachers created a dilemma for the Girls' Friendly Society (GFS), an Anglican organization designed to provide "friendship" between "young ladies at home" and girls from the working class. The people on its rolls were listed as either "associates" or "members." (The members were the working girls.) Elementary teachers were insulted if they were put in the member category and tended to withdraw. But according to one of the clergy wives who organized the GFS: "It is only necessary to go once to any 'Centre,' where large numbers of pupil-teachers of both sexes gather for lessons . . . to realize how very much the tone of these girls needs raising" (Girls' Friendly Society 11). Compare that comment with the recollection of a pupil teacher: "All of us were desperately anxious about qualifying, getting to College, getting jobs in a wider world . . . this idea . . . of success and independence made us capable of living laborious days and nights and shunning most of the delights of youth" (Eyles 152).

What we see here is one example of the problems in recovering the history of girlhood: virtually all of our information comes from adults, who may well be unreliable or at least selective in what they observe or recall. The class bias in the language of the GFS report is evident. In objective terms, pupil-teacher centers were essentially coeducational Saturday high schools; the pupils were boys and girls between fourteen and eighteen who worked all week as classroom aides. They probably did talk to each other, without much restraint—they were teenagers, after all, who had many experiences in common. Yet memoirs by those who were once pupil-teachers emphasize seriousness, ambition, and the real bliss of having adequate teaching and of learning with other students who cared about the same things. On the other hand, almost all of the autobiographies and memoirs about life as a pupil-teacher were produced by women who remained single, had long careers in education, and did their writing in the 1950s after they had retired as superintendent of curriculum for Liverpool or headmistress in Camden Town—a self-selected group of bookish and ambitious girls who perhaps didn't join in whatever rowdiness and flirting there may have been.

One final suggestion about the "tone" that shocked the clergy wives: virtually every recollection of pupil-teacher life in the last decades of the nineteenth century that I have discovered mentions—with bated breath and great excitement, as a thrilling, liberating, and highly secret experience—reading Olive Schreiner's Story of an African Farm (1883).

As the fascination with Schreiner's novel suggests, heterosexual relationships clearly stood on a piece of the contested ground that was reshaped by the impact of work on girls' culture. Both fiction and essays exposed the fear that independence made girls less willing to marry and less attractive to men. A particularly poignant example appears in "The Girls of To-Day, by One of Them," in the Girl's Own Paper for 2 December 1899: "If we do not work . . . we are told that we cannot make good wives; and if we do work, that we shall be unable to make our husbands happy because they want companions more or less frivolous when they have been at work all day" (131).

On the other hand, as the middle-class work ethic came more and more to mean paid work, a certain distaste attached to the "young lady" whose exclusively social life could be seen as open commerce on the marriage market. The novels about students and bachelor girls celebrate comradeship between women and men. Because it is less artificial than "courting," it will ultimately promote healthy marriage.

Nevertheless, these characters have a "detached Amazon look" (Tynan 135), the look of someone who is not thinking about men and sex. Girlhood's innocence is invoked to permit their unprotected independence. To an extraordinary extent, heroines are described as boyish—but there seems to be no disparaging overtone. "Girl" suggests prolonged latency rather than inappropriate masculinity. The lack of erotic tension enables wholesome working relationships with men; and by calling her a girl, fiction evades the "danger" that a woman with economic and social freedom might prefer not to marry.

Paid work also enabled physical separation from home. The earlier advice manuals were sometimes blindly naive in their insistence that girls stay in the parental dwelling. The author of *Girlhood* commented in 1869:

> Many working girls, as soon as they earn a few shillings . . . leave their homes, and go into lodgings. We know that there is some excuse for this—that too often their homes are not happy places, and that they can really be more comfortable, as well as more independent, in strange houses. And yet, would it not be better—if not for themselves, yet for their brothers and sisters . . . if they remained with them, and tried to make the home better and more comfortable? (Farningham 108)

Charitable ladies who actually worked with the poor recognized that both girls and their mothers knew that a one-room or two-room cottage was not a suitable place for housing teenagers of both sexes (especially given the additional presence of the father). This was one of the primary reasons that mothers wanted their daughters to go into domestic service instead of other work—it got them out of the house.

In fiction, working girls discovered the pleasures and responsibilities of a latchkey or a shared flat. Series in *Young Woman* and the *Girl's Own Paper* gave instructions for cooking on a hotplate and sharing chores. Novels

coach through example: how to make cupboards from cheese boxes, where
to get stamps for the lease, ways to conceal the bed when using the room
for other purposes. In the process, social and moral standards underwent
another vast but almost unremarked change. In fiction of the 1890s, working middle-class girls can and do invite men friends into their rooms as
long as it's clear that there is no romantic involvement. The seventeen-
year-old heroine of *A Home Ruler*—one of the many novels about gently
raised young women who take to self-support after becoming penniless
orphans—responds to the family doctor's criticism of her unchaperoned
friendships by telling him that she is "a working woman and an artist. It is
only rich idle people who have time for . . . all those sort of things" (Young
and Trent 160).

I have found no mention of the political reason for leaving home: after
the local government reforms of the 1890s, unmarried women occupiers—
even if they had only one room as a separate dwelling—were eligible to
vote in school board and county council elections (*Englishwoman's Year
Book, 1899*, 177). However, listen to the resonance in this halfpenny serial
called "Handsome Harry, the Girl-Man," which ran in *Girls' Home* from
19 November 1910. Harriet Nash is fired for resisting the manager's sexual
harassment and is unable to find another job. Discouraged, hungry, looking for something to pawn, she pulls out the box that her brother left
behind when he went to sea . . . nothing but clothes. Oh. With her brother's
wardrobe and her hair chopped off she discovers that life is much more
pleasant. She enjoys freedom of movement, the absence of insults from
men, a very good job as a trolley driver, and some healthy competition
with her workmates in an athletic club.

The fear that a massive realignment of gender roles lurked in the offing
was muted, in the middle-class fiction and even in "Handsome Harry,"
by the insistence on the youthfulness of girls. Real career work that pays
a decent income must be justified by invoking other powerful traditions
to provide reassurance that the worker has some good reason to remain
single. The doctor in Meade's *Mary Gifford, M.B.* (1898) takes up the East
End practice begun by the man she loved, who has died; the social worker
in Ethel M. Forbes's *Daughter of the Democracy* (1911) also remains single
because of her lover's death. Family tragedies or eugenic imperatives require other admirable professional women to live solitary lives.

While the stereotype of femininity as equivalent to service and self-
sacrifice was partly reshaped by the culture of work, attitudes about certain
kinds of work were simultaneously reshaped by women's entry. We might

call this something like "frontlash"—as women move into a new profession, the conception of that profession is altered to show how it serves the womanly ideal. The woman physician, for example, "will have the delightful consciousness of being useful to her fellow-women . . . and the satisfaction of making herself independent, so as to be able to stretch out a helping hand to those that need it" (Maxwell 123). Notice the instant melioration of financial independence with yet more service. Likewise, the character of schoolteachers changed markedly when the profession was feminized. The number of elementary pupils almost tripled between 1875 and 1914 (Holcombe 34). To create a national system of schooling, make it compulsory, and extend its length at both ends required vast numbers of new teachers—at wages that could not attract adequately educated men. Teaching became a job requiring cheerfulness and love of children (*Leng's Careers* 53), though as a man's profession it had needed intellect, system, order, and force of character.

Much the same thing happened with clerical work. The number of female clerks exploded from 6,000 in 1881 to 125,000 in 1911 (Holcombe 34). Early in the Victorian period boys who began as clerks might expect to rise into management, but as businesses and civil service expanded, clerical work was subdivided and made routine; upward mobility became rare; and the pay eroded to working-class levels. While this was happening, the description of clerical work became more and more aligned to the feminine ideal. The "lady clerk," according to an article in the *Young Woman*, "must learn *to do exactly what she is told*" and "to *work in silence*" (1:262; emphasis in the original). Advice to boys taking up clerical work had emphasized brains and energy, alertness, confidence, and seeking opportunities to take the initiative (Anderson 43 ff.). The value of obedience (or lack of initiative) comes in with women.

As has become evident, although the number of unmarried females in the workforce did not change significantly, the proportion working in white-collar jobs—as teachers, nurses, shop assistants, clerks, civil servants—underwent dramatic gains between 1881 and 1911 (Holcombe 216). Compulsory and longer schooling gave bright working-class girls the literacy to enter these occupations. It would seem also that they brought some of their values about independence, sexual responsibility, and economic self-interest with them, into the culture of white-collar "working girls."

Furthermore, as is clear to us if not to many Victorians, the mid-Victorian "ideal" of womanhood (fragile, dependent, protected) had excluded three-quarters of the unmarried female population, who labored in factories, on farms, in workshops and private houses. As work became part of girls' culture, however, girlhood was increasingly conceptualized as an age class without reference to economic status. When the middle class began to approve of paid work for its own girls, "going to work" was seen as a temporary stage, a learning experience. The fact that work provided "training"—for one thing or another—made it acceptable. The concept of the worker as a girl, not a mature woman, removed her from the sexual marketplace and bought her a new freedom in social and living arrangements. The culture of work promoted a girl's self-dependence, provided a new estimate of her capabilities, and reshaped her romantic expectations.

These gains, however, had their corresponding cost. To think of the worker as a girl is to emphasize lack of maturity, lack of skill, need of supervision, emotional (rather than intellectual) labor. It encourages separate job categories, impassable barriers to advancement, de-skilling, separate pay scales. Thus even in the 1890s, Black was protesting that wages were depressed by the assumption that "girls" were working. She reported that many female employments "offer no opening for the future. For instance, shop girls, nurses, and teachers of all sorts are preferred moderately young; after a certain time of life they have a difficulty in finding fresh employment and their earnings tend rather to diminish than to increase" (42).

The social and economic forces that encouraged occupational segregation and the habit of paying females less than a living wage were not created by the working girl, and they continued to hold sway long after she had learned to call herself a woman. Yet although it was economically damaging to see "going out to work" as merely a transitory phase, the world of work was indeed one of the key components that created a culture of girlhood as a distinctive—and extended—passage between puberty and marriage.

NOTE

1. "Factory Acts" is a generic term used to describe the legislation passed by Parliament (from 1802 on) to regulate the hours and conditions of work. The *Englishwoman's Year Book* (an annual published between 1881 and 1916) provides convenient and regularly updated summaries of employment laws that affected women, children, and "young persons" during the period under discussion.

WORKS CITED

Adams, Ellinor. *Miss Secretary Ethel: A Story for Girls of Today.* London: Hurst and Blackett, 1898.

Anderson, Gregory. *Victorian Clerks.* Manchester: Manchester UP, 1976.

Atalanta. October 1887–September 1896.

Barnard, Amy Beatrice. *The Girl's Encyclopedia.* London: Pilgrim Press, [1909].

"Between School and Marriage." *Girl's Own Paper* 7 (4 September 1886): 769–70.

Black, Clementina. "Typewriting and Journalism for Women." *Our Boys and Girls and What to Do with Them.* Ed. John Watson. London: Ward Lock, 1892. 35–45.

Boucherett, Jessie. *Hints on Self Help: A Book for Young Women.* London: S. W. Partridge, 1863.

Bramston, Mary. *A Woman of Business.* London: Society for Promoting Christian Knowledge, [1885].

Browne, Phillis [Sarah Sharp Hamer]. *What Girls Can Do.* London: Cassell, [1880].

"Businesses for Girls." *Girls' Best Friend* 1 (1898–99): 38ff.

Chesser, Elizabeth Sloan. *From Girlhood to Womanhood.* London: Cassell and Company, 1913.

Clayton, Ellen. *A Ministering Angel.* London: Dean and Son, [1895].

Curnock, Mrs. George. *A Girl in Her Teens, and What She Ought to Know.* London: Cassell, 1907.

"Editor's Chat." *Girl's Realm* 3 (1900–1901): 655.

Edwardes, Annie. *A Girton Girl.* 3 vols. London: Bentley, 1885.

Englishwoman's Year Book, 1899. London: F. Kirby, 1899.

Eyles, Leonora. *The Ram Escapes.* London: Peter Nevill, 1953.

Farningham, Marianne [Mary Anne Hearne]. *Girlhood.* London: J. Clarke, 1869. Also revised edition, London: J. Clarke, 1895.

Forbes, Ethel M. *A Daughter of the Democracy.* London: Cassell, 1911.

Forget Me Not. November 1891–6 April 1918.

Freeman, Flora. *Polly: A Study of Girl Life.* Oxford: Mowbray, 1904.

Girl's Friend. 17 June 1899–24 January 1931.

Girls' Friendly Society. *Report on the Conference of the Department for Members in Professions and Business.* London: Girls' Friendly Society, 1886.

Girls' Home. 5 March 1910–27 February 1915.

"Girls of Today, by One of Them." *Girl's Own Paper* 21 (1899–1900): 131.

Girl's Own Paper. 1880–1917.

Girls' Reader. 29 February 1908–27 January 1915.

Girl's Realm. November 1898–October 1915.

Grogan, Mercy. *How Women May Earn a Living.* Rev. ed. London: Cassell, 1883.

Hodgkinson, Florence. "The Adventures of Joan." *Girl's Realm* 10 (1908): 555ff.

Holcombe, Lee. *Victorian Ladies at Work.* Hamden: Archon, 1973.

Irvine, Amy. *The Probationer.* London: S. W. Partridge, [1910].

Kenealy, Arabella. *Dr. Janet of Harley Street*. London: Digby, Long, [1893].

Kenyon, Edith C. *Pickles: A Red Cross Heroine*. London: Collins' Clear-Type Press, [1916].

Legh, M. H. Cornwall. *An Incorrigible Girl*. London: Religious Tract Society, [1899].

Leng's Careers for Girls: How to Train and Where to Train. Dundee: John Leng, 1911.

March-Phillips, Evelyn. "Women's Industrial Life." *Monthly Packet* n.s. 13 (1897): serialized in six parts.

Maxwell, Mrs. M. A. "Medicine for Women." *Our Boys and Girls and What to Do with Them*. Ed. John Watson. London: Ward Lock, 1892. 113–23.

Meade, L. T. *Catalina: Art Student*. London: W. and R. Chambers, 1896.

———. *Mary Gifford, M.B.* London: Wells Gardner, 1898.

———. *The Medicine Lady*. 3 vols. London: Cassell, 1892.

———. *Nurse Charlotte*. London: John Long, 1904.

———. *A Sister of the Red Cross*. London: T. Nelson and Sons, 1900.

———. "Story Writing for Girls." *The Academy and Literature* 65 (1903): 499.

Monthly Packet. 1851–98.

Pfeiffer, Emily. *Woman and Work*. London: Trübner, 1888.

"Queen of the Ring." *Girls' Best Friend* 1 (1898–99): 25 ff.

"Registered Medical Women for 1889." *Englishwoman's Review of Social and Industrial Questions* 20 (1889): 65–69.

Salmon, Edward. *Juvenile Literature as It Is*. London: Drane, 1888.

Swan, Annie S. *Elizabeth Glen, M.B.* London: Hutchinson, 1895.

———. *Mrs. Keith Hamilton, M.B.* London: Hutchinson, 1897.

Travers, Graham [Dr. Margaret Todd]. *Mona Maclean, Medical Student*. 3 vols. London: Blackwood, 1892.

Tynan, Katherine. *Kitty Aubrey*. London: J. Nisbet, 1909.

"The Type-Writer and Type-Writing." *Girl's Own Paper* 9 (1887–88): 745–46.

Williamson, Alice. *The Newspaper Girl*. London: C. A. Pearson, 1899.

"Women's Work: Its Value and Possibilities." *Girl's Own Paper* 16 (1894–95): 51–53.

Wynne, May. *Life's Object, or Some Thoughts for Young Girls*. London: James Nisbet, 1899.

Young, Amelia, and Rachel Trent. *A Home Ruler*. London: W. H. Allen, 1881.

Young Woman. 1892–1915.

LYNNE VALLONE

"The True Meaning of Dirt": Putting Good and Bad Girls in Their Place(s)

"That's the reward for your services," said Mother Holle, and closed the door. So then the lazy girl went home, but she was all covered with pitch and when the rooster on the rim of the well saw her he crowed:
> "Cock-a-doodle-doo,
>   Our dirty girl is home anew."

And the pitch refused to come off, and it stuck to her as long as she lived.—"Mother Holle," in *Grimms' Tales for Young and Old: The Complete Stories*

It is sublime work to save a woman, for in her bosom generations are embodied, and in her hands, if perverted, the fate of innumerable men is held. The whole community, gentlemen, personally interested as they are in our success because the children of the virtuous must breathe the atmosphere exhaled by the vicious, will feel a lively sympathy for you, in your generous endeavors to redeem the erring mothers of the next generation.—Bradford Peirce to the Massachusetts Legislature, 1857; quoted in Brenzel, "Domestication as Reform"

In *Some Practical Suggestions on the Conduct of a Rescue Home* (1903), the late-nineteenth-/early-twentieth-century social reformer and co-leader of the National Florence Crittenton Mission (from 1896), Dr. Kate Waller Barrett, defines "the true meaning of dirt" as "matter out of place" (76). This essay argues that this definition of dirt illuminates central ideologies surrounding various aspects of the Woman Question— particularly those of female sexuality and domesticity—in terms of three "institutions" for girls: the rescue home for bad (read "sexual") girls, reformatories for juveniles and women, and the domestic science movement. The cult of cleanliness that informs this "dirt"-seeking organization and salvation has a very clear idea of where "dirt" ought to be placed. For instance, a room open to the effluvia of the out-of-doors is dirty, just as a girl with "lazy" morals or idle habits is dirty (even her breath and her body,

as the epigrams to this essay indicate). Both the room and the girl are im-
pure. Barrett's system allows for the reclamation of dirty girls, however, by
putting them "where they belong" (in a rescue home) and renaming them
"daughters." That some girls are dirty implies an earlier mismanagement
or misplacement of them, an assessment that eventually gives rise to the
conflation of female sexuality with domesticity so prevalent in theories of
gender of the nineteenth century: the place where all girls (women) belong
is in a home.[1] As I will discuss below, that home, whether a female penitentiary, rescue home, or Yankee bungalow, had certain common structures.
And the females who were to live in these places also had qualities in
common.

However, the unselfconscious placement of women in the home became
problematic by the mid-nineteenth century during the fervor over women's
roles created, in part, by the Woman Question debate as it was furthered
by Mary Wollstonecraft, the Grimké sisters, Susan B. Anthony, Elizabeth
Cady Stanton, and others.[2] The eloquent and vibrant voices of these and
other reformers on the subjects of women's rights, suffrage, abolition, and
female education made the argument for separate spheres based solely on
duty—as it had been conventionally rehearsed—sound faint and look pal-
lid.[3] The domestic science movement, led by Catharine Beecher, was able to
animate the separate-sphere ideology by transforming housekeeping into
an important, demanding, and intellectual career that only the female could
fulfill.[4] Kathryn Kish Sklar writes in her biography of Beecher: "Women
in America had always experienced such inequity [between the sexes], but
they had never before needed to reconcile it with a growing ideology of
popular democracy and equal rights" (156). As reformers wrote and agitated for greater participation in the political processes of democracy, the
domestic science movement co-opted what seemed most appealing about
life outside the home—social responsibility, important decision-making,
service to others, paid labor—and then "shrunk" these desires to fit inside
its walls by professionalizing and systematizing the running of the home.[5]

In her highly influential first treatment of the subject of domesticity, *A
Treatise on Domestic Economy for the Use of Young Ladies at Home, and
at School* (1841), Beecher outlined in detail her system of domestic practice:
"Here for the first time was a text that standardized American domestic
practices—prescribing one system that integrated psychological, physiological, economic, religious, social, and political factors, and in addition
demonstrating how the specifics of the system should work" (Sklar 152).[6]
This standardization and systematization of domesticity elevated its moral

and political significance to a "science," and in turn raised the "significance" of the women—young and old—who practiced it. Beecher writes
that "every woman should imbibe, from early youth, the impression, that
she is training for the discharge of the most important, the most difficult,
and the most sacred and interesting duties that can possibly employ the
highest intellect" (144).

As the title of her treatise indicates, Beecher felt that the movement could
best be started and sustained by including domestic science as part of the
curriculum of the new female seminaries springing up in the Northeast
and West (in Ohio, for example).[7] In this way, the concerns of domestic
science were included in the general ideologies of enlightened female education that would properly train young women in the values and ideals of
the new republic: self-reliance, hard work, (relative) egalitarianism, and
independence (within the framework of separate spheres).

A proper education for the daughters of the new republic was *useful*
above all things—the "ornamental" education of accomplishments (drawing, dancing, and music lessons) was sneered at by nineteenth-century educational reformers as wasteful and even harmful. By contrast, the education
offered in *A Treatise on Domestic Economy* enabled a diligent girl to leave
school (at approximately sixteen years of age) eminently qualified to fill
her God-given role as housekeeper, whether it be for some member(s) of
her immediate or extended family or for her new husband.[8] The knowledge that the student of domestic economy gains, Beecher argues, has great
value because of its practical nature. She finds some of the gains made in
the general curriculum of female seminaries shocking in light of what she
understands to be a deplorable ignorance of crucial domestic skills:

> And let the young women of this Nation find, that Domestic Economy
> is placed, in schools, on an equal or superior ground to Chemistry, Phi-
> losophy, and Mathematics, and they will blush to be found ignorant of
> its first principles, as much as they will to hesitate respecting the laws
> of gravity, or the composition of the atmosphere. But as matters are
> now conducted, many young ladies, who can tell how to make oxygen
> and hydrogen, and discuss questions of Philosophy or Political Econ-
> omy, do not know how properly to make a bed and sweep a room;
> while they can "construct a diagram" in Geometry with far more skill
> than they could construct the simplest article of female dress. (46)

A brief list of some of the subjects covered by Beecher in *Domestic Economy* reveals the inclusiveness of her understanding of necessary domestic

knowledge: "the preparation of healthful food," "cleanliness," "domestic exercise," "the management of young children," "the propagation of plants," "muscles; their Constitution, Use and Connection with Bones [with] Engravings and Description," and "the care of domestic animals, barns, etc."

Beecher's various books and speeches on the subject of domestic science established a discourse of domesticity in which nationalism and a kind of proto-feminism became inseparably entwined.[9] In her first two chapters, "The Peculiar Responsibilities of American Women" and "Difficulties Peculiar to American Women," Beecher discusses both the primacy of the United States's form of democracy and the American woman's place in the hierarchy of that democracy's health:

> The success of democratic institutions, as is conceded by all, depends upon the intellectual and moral character of the mass of the people. If they are intelligent and virtuous, democracy is a blessing; but if they are ignorant and wicked, it is only a curse, and as much more dreadful than any other form of civil government, as a thousand tyrants are more to be dreaded than one. It is equally conceded, that the formation of the moral and intellectual character of the young is committed mainly to the female hand. The mother writes the character of the future man; the sister bends the fibres that hereafter are the forest tree; the wife sways the heart, whose energies may turn for good or for evil the destinies of a nation. Let the women of a country be made virtuous and intelligent, and the men will certainly be the same. (13)

Informed by Alexis de Tocqueville, Beecher refers to the relation of women to men as "equal" but at the same time necessarily subordinate, a viewpoint shared by many female reformers of the mid-nineteenth century:

> It appears, then, that it is in America, alone, that women are raised to an equality with the other sex; and that, both in theory and practice, their interests are regarded as of equal value. They are made subordinate in station, only where a regard to their best interests demands it, while, as if in compensation for this, by custom and courtesy, they are always treated as superiors. (9)

According to Beecher, the means by which woman achieves "equality" with man is through her important work in the "home," whether it be a family dwelling, a schoolhouse, a room of one's own, or someone else's house:

The woman who is rearing a family of children; the woman who labors in the schoolroom; the woman who, in her retired chamber, earns, with her needle, the mite to contribute for the intellectual and moral elevation of her country; even the humble domestic, whose example and influence may be moulding and forming young minds, while her faithful services sustain a prosperous domestic state;—each and all may be cheered by the consciousness, that they are agents in accomplishing the greatest work that ever was committed to human responsibility. (14)

The domestic science movement elevated woman's work to the status of nation-building through the "construction" of the nation's citizens and through the management and caretaking of democracy's essentially undemocratic family relationships.

Beecher conflates all women into one group—whatever their class, national origin, or race—and "elevates" them all through separate-sphere ideology that attempts to raise the status of homemaking and women's roles generally. In so doing, however, she elides the very real and significant social and economic distinctions made between women based upon the very differences she is at pains to ignore. As Sklar notes, "by defining gender identity as more important than class, regional, or religious identity, and by ignoring altogether the imponderables of American racial divisions, she promoted the belief that the society's only basic division was that between men and women" (156).[10]

Beecher is able to dispatch breezily any questions about the noticeable differences between the life/work experiences of servants and "ladies" (separate entrances into the household, for example), by naming difference in the service of the all-important "order," and by attempting to convince the servant class that they are actually happier this way:

They [domestics and the lower class] should be taught, that domestics use a different entrance to the house, and sit at a distinct table, not because they are inferior beings, but because this is the best method of securing neatness and order and convenience. They can be shown, if it is attempted in a proper spirit and manner, that these very regulations really tend to their own ease and comfort, as well as to that of the family. (201)

Domestic scientists held that it was important for woman's labor first to be rendered systematic—increasing its value—and then made invisible—dispersing labor's value by denying its existence as *work*.[11] For example, in

her imaginary description of a female seminary's washing-room, Beecher
sentimentalizes the scene of labor by painting it in neo-republican pastels
that elevate washing to all that is enjoyable and artful:

> Let [aristocratic daughters and mothers] see some thirty or forty merry
> girls, superintended by a motherly lady, chatting and singing, wash-
> ing and starching, while every convenience is at hand, and everything
> around is clean and comfortable. Two hours, thus employed, enables
> each young lady to wash the articles she used during the previous week,
> which is all that is demanded, while thus they are all practically initi-
> ated into the arts and mysteries of the wash-tub. (32–33)

Here "washing and starching" become equivalent activities—and sancti-
fied ones—to "chatting and singing."

The powerful ideology of labor, which disguises itself as female duty,
physical exercise, or career opportunity, is delineated carefully in fiction
of the mid-nineteenth century. For example, Harriet Beecher Stowe's *The
Minister's Wooing* (1859), while set in late-eighteenth-century New England, concisely communicates the general rule (which has all the force of
a moral law) that housework should be completed in the morning to allow
for afternoon study, repose, and social obligations:

> Everything [in the kitchen] seemed to be always done and never doing.
> Washing and baking, those formidable disturbers of the composure of
> families, were all over within those two or three morning-hours when
> we are composing ourselves for a last nap—and only the fluttering of
> linen over the green yard, on Monday mornings, proclaimed that the
> dreaded solemnity of a wash had transpired. A breakfast arose there
> as by magic; and in an incredibly short space after, every knife, fork,
> spoon, and trencher, clean and shining, was looking as innocent and
> unconscious in its place as if it never had been used and never expected
> to be. (16)

Stowe's definition of the Yankee term "faculty" contains the magical elements of a romanticized domestic practice: this labor is magical in that it
transforms the worker by virtue of its very imperceptibility—work does
not change the body, clothes do not cost money, labor does not take time
("everything seems to be always done and never doing"). The domestic
woman is not diminished, but accrues excess value through this invisible
work that can then be "spent":

To her who has faculty nothing shall be impossible. She shall scrub floors, wash, wring, bake, brew, and yet her hands shall be small and white; she shall have no perceptible income, yet always be handsomely dressed;—she shall have not a servant in her house,—with a dairy to manage, hired men to feed, a boarder or two to care for, unheard of pickling and preserving to do,—and yet you commonly see her every afternoon sitting at her shady parlor-window behind the lilacs, cool and easy, hemming muslin cap-strings, or reading the last new book. She who hath faculty is never in a hurry, never behindhand. She can always step over to distressed Mrs. Smith, whose jelly won't come,— and stop to show Mrs. Jones how she makes her pickles so green,—and be ready to watch with poor old Mrs. Simpkins, who is down with the rheumatism. (2–3) [12]

Domestic science and reform ideologies thus participate in one of the pre-vailing idealistic notions of post-Revolutionary America: that as a "new" system the new republic's social makeup was perfectible. As Sklar writes: "As a postrevolutionary generation bent on extracting practical benefits from their theoretical innovations, many Americans believed that elementary matters like diet and health should be as susceptible to improvement as anything else in the new age, and that wherever possible they should be made perfect" (154). Beecher and the institutional reformers contend that there is one correct system of household management and one "system" of female character. Of course, both ideologies of female behavior—within the family and within the institution—believe in domesticity as the "per-fect" female lifestyle. In this way we see that the institutions of domesticity are expanded to include not only the domicile of the family, but also the female seminary and, finally, houses of correction for female (usually sex) criminals, prostitutes, and unwed mothers.[13] Those "good girls" who live in houses like Stowe's Katy Scudder's, and who thus have extra time on their hands, are expected (as Beecher carefully points out in her chapter en-titled "Charity") to "spend" that time usefully and charitably in exchanging domestic knowledge, services, and goods in the pursuit of self-satisfaction and happiness.

The ideology of the "social gospel" made current by both men and women in conduct books, sermons, periodicals, and novels from the eigh-teenth century onward stressed that woman, with her differences from man expressed as both saintly and childlike, was especially suited to perform charitable works as an extension of the domestic ideology that contained her arts in the home. Her skills in needlework, food preparation, and education were brought together to help clothe, feed, and educate the poor. Women's traditional charitable activities included visiting the poor and sick; making them clothes and linen; donating money to relief societies; educating children in Sunday schools; and undertaking "rescue" work in homes for prostitutes and "fallen" women, or missionary work by distributing Bibles and religious tracts.[14]

As charitable institutions, the Magdalen Hospital (established in London in 1758 as England's first rescue home) and the National Florence Crittenton Mission of late-nineteenth-century America (1883) both sought to convert girls whose sins were sexual—prostitutes (the particular clientele of the Magdalen Hospital) or seduced and abandoned girls—to Christian values, and to train them in domestic arts such as laundry work and sewing.[15] While both institutions seek, in Linda Mahood's words, to "colonize the poor," [16] a comparison between the two institutions yields significant ideological differences in their structures.[17] The span of years and location that separates them clearly accounts for some of these differences; however, the particularly notable ways in which Barrett's Rescue Home distinguishes itself from institutions such as the Magdalen Hospital, the London Female Penitentiary (1807), or the British Female Penitent Refuge (1829) are in its "republicanisms," or as Barrett calls it, "the democratic spirit of our Home" (26).[18] The girls seeking admittance to a Florence Crittenton Home remain essentially nameless, and stories of their past lives were expressly forbidden by the Crittenton staff as topics for discussion. The Magdalen Hospital also maintained this requirement, and the reasons are easily imagined: dwelling upon a past, sinful life would impede progress in Christian humility and could give rise to unnecessary melancholy or, worse yet, revive desires for the company, drink, clothing, and freedom that the old life either produced or promised to produce. The American Rescue Home, however it might have feared the bad effects of storytelling, nevertheless stoutly believed in the legal right to privacy: "Everybody has a right to discuss, or not, their private affairs, and the world is entitled to know that only which it can find out by watching the actions of persons. The Constitution of the United States asserts that everybody has an equal right to the pursuit of life, liberty and happiness" (Barrett 53).

The success of the National Florence Crittenton Mission was in part due to its leaders' vigilance in detecting vice and publicizing the pervasiveness of its unhealthy presence, thereby rallying support for their institutions that attempted to transform the image of the fallen girl in the eyes of the public from unreclaimed, willful sinner to pathetic victim.[19] One example of this kind of useful propaganda is a choice Barrett once made about the concentration of her bountiful energies; she canceled a trip to the International Council of Women held in Berlin in 1904 in order to tackle a problem in the United States. Rather than talking about the status of women at a conference, she hurried to the World's Fair in St. Louis, where it had been rumored that innocent young girls were being rounded up as prostitutes to service the crowds attracted to the Fair. As Otto Wilson writes in his brief life of Barrett,

> It was their [the Florence Crittenton apologists'] great achievement that they presented the fallen woman not simply as a vessel of sin, a person of mature judgment who had deliberately sold her soul to the devil, but as a human being, sometimes perversely erring but in the great majority of cases merely a child victim of the seducer or of circumstance. (179)

This redefinition also had been the greatest hope and challenge of the British charities of earlier times, but as Sarah Green writes to her niece in *Mental Improvement for a Young Lady, on Her Entrance into the World* (1793), the failure of such charities as the Magdalen Hospital to reform clients was largely due to the penitents "not meeting with sufficient charity and encouragement from the rigidly virtuous of their own sex!" (61).[20]

In the same way that the Rescue Homes of the Florence Crittenton Mission attempted to reflect what the Mission believed to be the strength of American society—the home and family—the Magdalen Hospital replicated the class structure of the outside society inside the institution. Penitents of a higher class were separated from the other girls and given special treatment (better food, for example). The American rescue home, by contrast, self-consciously mixed the girls, the matron and her assistants, and the domestic workers of the home. Everyone ate at the same time, except for those girls whose turn it was to serve the food. Barrett writes: "The most important reason [for everyone to eat together], of course, is that we want to be in a true sense a family, with the matron as the mother, presiding at the head of the table" (21). This artificially created familial structure is explicitly maternal in cast: the matron acts most particularly and closely "as the mother" in the rescue home, while at the same time the middle-class female reformer functions maternally for the young unwed mothers who are the objects of her reformative program.[21]

In *Some Practical Suggestions on the Conduct of a Rescue Home* (1903),

Barrett outlines her understanding of the proper organization of a rescue
home for girls that will house (especially) fallen teenaged mothers. A pervasive ideological feature of her pamphlet, which includes philosophical
ruminations on the behavior of those connected with the Home, as well
as specific organizational advice on issues such as the duties of the trea-
surer, the setup of the kitchen, and "one day in detail," is the means by
which the institution is described as systematically de-institutionalized so
that the Home becomes a "home." While Barrett explicitly discusses some
institutional features that the Home can and should avoid (for example,
the girls are to make many smaller batches of bread using recipes that
could be found in any kitchen, rather than adhering to the "bakery plan"
[107]), in general this de-institutionalization occurs subtly, so that "home"
and "Home" are used interchangeably both semantically and connotatively
within any given sentence. The institution ("Home"), therefore, is invested
with the same emotional/social value as is the dwelling-place of related
persons: "This incident [the story of a girl who had left the rescue home
but who ultimately ratified her training there by gaining a position of trust
in a "respectable" family] had given me much peace, as it proves to me
what an effect a true Home has upon a girl" (94–95). In this way, Barrett
extends the commonplace judgment that a girl's home "makes" her a social
success or failure to the fallen girl who admirably reflects her [h]ome.

In *Literature and Crime in Augustan England,* Ian Bell argues that the
work of the eighteenth-century social reformers, while revisionist in its attempts to change the means of punishment, can also be understood as con-
firmation of the state's *right* to control and to punish: "However, while it is
still possible to see the reformers as instigating a decisive and transforming
break with precedent, it is just as interesting to see them as maintaining
and developing the state's right to punish, albeit presented as the right to
impose punishments which have more utilitarian justification" (150). The
American women's prison-reform movement of the late nineteenth century, led by Josephine Shaw Lowell, participates in a similar kind of moral
conflation of physical incarceration and moral regeneration, in both cases
highlighting domestic skills central to the success of each.[22] As Stanley
Cohen notes in *Visions of Social Control: Crime, Punishment and Classification,* by the mid-nineteenth century, in contrast to the eighteenth-century
practice, institutions became places of "*first* resort, the preferred solution
to problems of deviancy and dependency" (32–33).[23] Interestingly, adolescent chastity offenders not only made up the greatest number of prisoners
incarcerated in the reformed women's penitentiaries, but they also received

longer sentences than those who had committed theft or a violent crime.[24] As Freedman writes in *Their Sister's Keepers:*

> The chastity offenders included young women sentenced for "stubborn-ness" when their relatives could not control their behavior. Sixteen-year-old Eliza L., for example, committed for two years as a "stubborn child," had been "weak and licentious rather than deliberately bad." Another sixteen-year-old who had run away from home was sentenced at her grandmother's request. The length of these sentences reflected officials' belief that the young, promising cases deserved fuller treat-ment. (84–85)

This theory of "incarceration in case" was also a main tenet of the Critten-ton Mission's revised ideology, which sought to contain girls who had made "one mistake" in becoming pregnant, in order to "save" them from prostitution:

> The eyes of the Florence Crittenton workers were more and more turned toward the erring girl rather than the confirmed professional. It was logical, too, that in reaching out a rescuing hand the Mission could accomplish most by coming into the girl's life at that precise point where the old life was most threatened with disintegration through ter-ror and despair—the months when she realized that her misstep must soon become evident to the world. (Wilson, *Fifty Years* 8–9)

The new penology of late-nineteenth-century and Progressive-era female prisons was rehabilitation (Freedman 130). This ideology accompanied the rise of the New Woman in reform activism; women's jobs were increas-ingly paid, professional positions rather than voluntary work. Examples of such professional women include Katharine Bement Davis, superinten-dent of the Bedford Hills reformatory (New York), and Jessie Donaldson Hodder, superintendent of the Framingham, Massachusetts reformatory.[25] These two women were in the forefront of the struggle for anti-institutional female prisons.[26] In her discussion of Davis's Bedford Hills facility (estab-lished on the cottage system in 1901), Freedman describes the doctrine of practical lessons and shared education:

> To make classes more palatable, the Bedford Hills staff adopted Pro-gressive educational methods. All tasks, both in the classroom and outside it, were to be shared by inmates and teachers. The staff was expected to do as much menial work as their charges, and instructors

tried to make subject matter relevant to the lives of the women. Daily
institutional experiences became the subjects of the lessons. (133)

This ideology is shared by the Crittenton rescue homes in their union of
the "family system" with practical domestic training.

Upon admittance to a Florence Crittenton Home (and every [white] girl
seeking asylum was admitted on a trial basis),[27] the girls were told that
the rescue home belonged to them alone "and that all is required of any
is that each one shall do her part in making it a real Home" (16). This
statement privileges Beecher's ideology of "homemaking": participation
in the primacy of domestic duties, the cult of cleanliness, the drive for
self-improvement through the study of the Bible and "good books," and
the romanticization of motherhood. If a girl did not have this knowledge,
however, the rescue home would train her in it. In discussing the training
that the girls received in the Home, Barrett packs and overloads her meaning once again, in a manner consistent with her ability "to get twenty-five
hours out of the twenty-four." That is, by calling the girls "ladies" and then
enumerating the skills necessary to become a lady, she is able at once to
raise the reputations of the fallen girls *and* firmly place the idea of the lady
within domestic, middle-class ideals: "We believe that every lady should
know how to cook, wash, and iron, if she does not know anything else,
and as we expect our girls to be ladies in the highest and truest sense, they
must all learn to do these things, and do them well" (26).[28] The nineteenth-
century British system, by contrast, while mimicking as much as possible
middle-class ideals about female behavior within the home for penitent
prostitutes, did not expect the girls to be transformed into ladies but rather
into improved domestics (Mahood 84). Beecher also confronts the issue of
"lady-like" behavior and domestic work by countering the argument that
labor is degrading to women. Domestic labor, she writes, is for everyone
(female):

> The last method suggested for lessening the evils peculiar to American
> women, is, a decided effort to oppose the aristocratic feeling, that labor
> is degrading; and to bring about the impression that it is refined and
> lady-like to engage in domestic pursuits. . . . But as soon as ladies of
> refinement, as a general custom, patronise domestic pursuits, then these
> pursuits will be deemed lady-like. (39–40)

Barrett's system for the rescue home also trains the girls to be gender-
rather than class-identified. She describes enforced menial labor as a means
to this identification, and as a condition of moral reform and repentance:

If a girl comes to us well dressed and with manicured nails and tells us that she has never been accustomed to do any sort of work in her life, we are sure to put this girl at the wash-tub, because we will never be able to do anything with her until she has learned to believe in the aristocracy of hard hands and the dignity of labor. (37)

In order to establish a Home that will both appear and operate, for all intents and purposes, as a "home" for "ladies," Barrett prefers an extant structure rather than a new building; otherwise, "a great many institutional features are apt to creep in" (7). As Barrett's casual and cheerful claim "no home is complete without a baby" (9) would imply, each Rescue Home's large and commodious nursery is present primarily to mimic the ideal home, rather than to accommodate the illegitimate children who unwittingly make their mother's presence in a rescue home necessary.

In *Practical Suggestions* Barrett reinforces her idea that "bad girls" are no different from unfallen girls and deserve the same love, attention, and strict parental guidance that girls within families should receive: "the training and discipline which is good for our own girls is the best kind to use in a Rescue Home" (*Practical Suggestions*, introduction). Barrett made the transmission of this idea her life's work through writing newspaper articles and speeches and making appeals to town administrators all over the country. (This zeal bled into a second generation, as two of Barrett's children—a son and a daughter—were involved in the National Florence Crittenton Mission after their mother's death). In persuading her readers (the mothers and fathers of the unfallen) of the mission of her charity work, Barrett emphasizes the daughterly role that (any) girl plays in society. One small example of this ideal of the universal daughter is demonstrated by the theory of Home decoration: "When we remember with what fastidious care we try to have our own daughter's room the most attractive in the house, and how we love to think of the purity of the furnishings as emblematic of the purity of her who occupies it, we will understand how necessary it is, when we are dealing with God's daughters, to use the same watchful care in the little detail of their lives" (13–14).

Another telling example of the conflation of daughters effected by the "institution that is not an institution" is that the matron is instructed to refrain from asking the girl seeking admittance to the Home her name, but rather to ask, "What name did you love best for your mother to call you when you were a little girl at home?" (19). The efficacy of using the baby name, or maternal nickname, is that the girl is reminded of her mother and her pure "home self." The recalling of these memories seeks to prompt the girl to better actions in the future and to aid in her redemption. At the same time, Barrett recognizes the limitations of girls—fallen or "upright"—when she comments, "We cannot hope to do more with a girl after she has fallen than it would have been possible to have done with that same girl before her trouble, but we ought to be able to do as much with her" (84). Barrett assumes a "practical" stance in this sentiment, admitting to variations in female conduct for both the pure and the penitent.

Nineteenth-century reform ideology for juvenile delinquents, too, stressed the need to return the erring child to childhood, just as the fallen girls must be restored to the place of the daughter, in order to enable positive behavioral change. The object of juvenile reform expressed by the British reformer Mary Carpenter in *Juvenile Delinquents, Their Condition and Treatment* (1853), not surprisingly, is closely related to that of the Florence Crittenton Homes: in both cases, the inmate must "be gradually restored to the true position of childhood. He must be brought to a sense of dependence by reawakening in him new and healthy desires which he cannot himself satisfy, and by finding that there is a power far greater than his own to which he is indebted for the gratification of these desires" (qtd. in Philips 61). Healthy children and domestic girls are raised in homes; therefore, sexual girls must be placed in Homes to reestablish both their rights as "citizens" and their duties as subordinates.

Of course, no institution can totally succeed in its attempts to disguise itself, whatever its good intentions. While Barrett's leadership in the National Florence Crittenton Mission's establishment of the extensive network of rescue homes (together with that of the Mission's founder, Charles Nelson Crittenton) takes its place alongside the efforts of other inspirational and effective female institutional reformers of late-nineteenth- and early-twentieth-century America—such as Dorothea Dix, Katharine Bement Davis, Jessie Donaldson Hodder, Jane Addams, and Josephine Shaw Lowell—that each rescue home operated as a self-sufficient house of correction should not be overlooked. Certainly, as this essay has attempted to show, a rescue home is like a juvenile reformatory, is like a women's prison, is like a penitent prostitute's penitentiary, is like a lock hospital (for venereally diseased prostitutes—also generally organized as a house of moral correction and as an industrial plant), is like a female seminary where domestic science is taught. Freedman's description of the requirements of the rescue homes thus sounds familiar:

> The Florence Crittenton Homes, originally for rescuing prostitutes, searched inmates on entry, forbade profane or slang language and

coarse jesting, required "family worship" morning and evening, cen-
sored letters and surveilled visitors, and taught "plain sewing and
simple working," table setting and orderly kitchen work. Bible readings
required attendance, as did the "general work of the Home." (198 n35)

The separate "franchises" in the Mission's "corporation" were responsible
for earning money toward their upkeep (donations for the charity, however, were eagerly sought from members of the community and from those
successfully trained girls who left the Home and gained employment elsewhere). The suggested methods of self-sufficiency were laundry work or
sewing, as was the case in the model furnished by the Magdalen Hospital
and other "female" institutions. Such labor was understood to be valuable
for females in general, and for those in need of moral training in particular: "Apart from its remunerative features, the laundry may also be used
as a 'means of grace.' There is nothing that settles a restless, high-strung
spirit, like weariness of the flesh" (Barrett 28). The inmate of the Rescue
Home was compelled to learn a new economy to replace the one she had
"willingly" learned at an early age: from the sale of the (sexual) body in
exchange for money, pleasure, and/or love, to the sale of the (laboring)
body for money, shelter—and, the reform ideology insists—self-respect
and eternal reward.

After two years of training, the now reclaimed Christian girl was expected to leave the Home with her child and take a position as a servant,
thereby becoming independent of the Home (except insofar as she would
like to visit or donate money toward its upkeep). The Homes, however, according to Barrett, are to be relatively forgiving of those girls who either fail
while out on their own or never feel able to leave. Of a girl who desires the
protection of the Home, Barrett writes that "she is our child for life when
once she has come under our care" (51). In general, the Florence Crittenton
Homes, as Barrett conceives of them in her pamphlet, are "humanized"
institutions. The girls do not wear uniforms or a distinctive dress that sets
them apart from ("respectable") society at large; the only clothing requirement is that everyday wear must be washable cotton in order to facilitate
the practical matters of hygiene and laundry work. Barrett is not free from
ideological assumptions about female dress and class, however, as is apparent when she equates the diseases of promiscuity with unwashable fabrics,
and health with inexpensive materials: "There is nothing more depressing
than a number of women, many of whose faces bear the marks of disease,
dressed in woolen clothes that cannot be readily cleansed. . . . On the other
hand, to see a girl dressed in a seven-cent gingham, neatly made, rustling in

its spick and spanness, is exhilirating [*sic*], like a breath of fresh air" (41).
In fact, it is the matron, assistant matron, and workers who wear uniforms
in the Home: the matron dresses completely in white, and the assistant
matron and workers wear a blue gingham dress, white apron, and "dainty
little cap" that is understood to be a "badge of authority" (43).[29]

Regularly scheduled entertainment for the girls was an important feature of Barrett's "humanistic" organization of the Rescue Home. One night
a week was set aside as "Play Night," special foods were served (apples,
peanuts, or candy), and a social event was planned. When Barrett lists
the different committees (some examples are the Educational Committee,
Nursery Committee, and Devotional Committee) that make up the organization of each Home, she describes the Entertainment Committee as the
most "important" (80).

And yet it is exactly "entertainment by committee" that reveals each
Home's insistent institutional nature. The ideological makeup of the "institution that looks like a home" (as well as that of women's prisons and
"domestically enhanced" female seminaries) recalls a kind of idealistic belief in the restorative powers of the loving nuclear family.[30] The institution
must also operate, however, as social apologist for the weaknesses of that
preferred system. While the family rejected its bad girls, the institution took
its place and created a "homelike" atmosphere in the place of the home.
As Barrett writes, the "true meaning of dirt" is "matter out of place." The
Florence Crittenton Mission swept turn-of-the-century "dirty" girls into
its own place (its "Home") and renamed them as its own daughters: in-
heritors of a reformed feminine ideology that both accepted them as ladies
and continued to keep them in place.

NOTES

Portions of this essay were presented at the 1992 Children's Literature Association meeting and the 1993 Modern Language Association convention. I want
to thank Howard Marchitello, Pamela Matthews, and Claudia Nelson for their
thoughts on this essay.

1. In Charles Dickens's open letter to fallen women (1846), he describes the
Home that a "great lady" is opening for the redemption and succor of prostitutes:
"[Angela Burdett Coutts] has resolved to open at her own expense a place of refuge
near London for a small number of females, who without such help are lost for
ever, and to make a HOME for them. In this home they will be taught all household
work that would be useful to them in a home of their own and enable them to

make it comfortable and happy. In this home, which stands in a pleasant country lane and where each may have her little flower-garden if she pleases, they will be treated with the greatest kindness: will lead an active, cheerful, healthy life: will learn many things it is profitable and good to know" (qtd. in Flint 235). Dickens's description of the cozy home is persuasive for its one-two punch: not only does it tempt by way of conjuring up the future home a reformed prostitute might have if sufficiently repentant, but it also harkens back to the memories of a home that she should have had—even if she didn't—as a child.

2. In *Their Sisters' Keepers,* Estelle Freedman discusses Anthony's theory of "Social Purity": "Anthony distinguished between the causes of crime in men and women, claiming that the former acted from 'love of vice,' while the latter acted 'from absolute want of the necessaries of life'" (41). See also Lori Ginzberg's *Women and the Work of Benevolence* for an extended discussion of the history of women's participation in the reform movements and campaigns of the nineteenth century.

3. The "celebration" of difference offered by many female reformers of the nineteenth century accentuated the moral "superiority" of women over men; in fact, men were often viewed as impediments to the creation of a new moral society: "[moral reform] could not be entrusted to man, as . . . he is often the worst enemy of the other sex, and generally has not virtue sufficient to qualify him for the trust" (qtd. in Ginzberg 20).

4. Later leaders in the domestic science movement included the chemists Ellen Swallow Richards and Isabel Bevier, who were among the first instructors of the subject at the university level.

5. For an interesting discussion of the economic implications of "women's work" (its changing treatments in census terminology and classification in Britain and the United States) see Nancy Folbre's "The Unproductive Housewife: Her Evolution in Nineteenth-Century Economic Thought." See also Nell Du Vall's *Domestic Technology: A Chronology of Developments* for descriptions of the technological advances, as opposed to socio-moral practices, of domesticity.

6. Beecher's *Treatise on Domestic Economy* was reprinted nearly every year until 1856. The enlarged and revised version was published under the title *The American Woman's Home,* with Harriet Beecher Stowe listed as coauthor, in 1869. *Principles of Domestic Science; As Applied to the Duties and Pleasures of the Home. A Text Book for the Use of Young Ladies, in Schools, Seminaries, and Colleges* (1870) was another of the domestic science manuals for girls that Beecher jointly produced with Stowe (Sklar 306).

For a discussion of the Beecher sisters (Harriet Beecher Stowe, Catharine Beecher, and Isabella Beecher Hooker) and their writings, personal and professional, see Boydston, Kelley, and Margolis.

7. The first four-year domestic science curricula were established about 1875 in the state colleges of Illinois, Iowa, and Kansas. By 1899–1910, thirty-nine colleges

had departments of domestic science. The term "domestic science" was ultimately changed to "home economics," but domestic science continued to be used as a descriptive term (East 20–24). Emma S. Weigley provides a brief but detailed history of the home economics movement.

8. There are two levels to Beecher's understanding of the practical need for a (middle-class) girl to gain domestic knowledge: the first is that the latter needs this knowledge in order to execute her female role with dignity and skill, and the second is that the lack of "suitable" domestics will force her to undertake some of their jobs (whether in their "proper" training or to make up for their absence). In the second chapter, "Difficulties Peculiar to American Women," which succinctly reveals her racism and xenophobia, Beecher cites the scarcity of female domestics as a difficulty to surmount: "There is such a disproportion between those who wish to hire, and those who are willing to go to domestic service, that, in the non-slaveholding states, were it not for the supply of poverty-stricken foreigners, there would not be one domestic for each family who demands one. And this resort to foreigners, poor as it is, scarcely meets the demand; while the disproportion must every year increase, especially if our prosperity increases" (17).

9. The beliefs of Beecher's major predecessors (Theodore Dwight, Heman Humphrey, Thomas Alcott, and Lydia Maria Child), in contrast to her own, included an assumption of "male control of the domestic environment" (Sklar 153).

10. Consult Noralee Frankel and Nancy Dye's *Gender, Class, Race, and Reform in the Progressive Era* for essays that focus upon the very relationships among gender, class, and race in the nineteenth century that Beecher dismisses.

11. An example of Beecher's organization of household tasks is the breakdown of the week into units of domestic labor: Monday is "devoted to preparing the labors of the week," Tuesday is washing, Wednesday is ironing, and so on (149).

12. See Walter Buehr's *Home Sweet Home in the Nineteenth Century* for illustrations and brief commentary on nineteenth-century gadgets and labor-saving devices for the household. One interesting example of a labor-combining invention that could enable a "literary" housewife to read and complete other tasks at the same time was a portable bookrest that a woman strapped around her waist and shoulders, freeing her hands and arms (56–58).

13. In *The Discovery of the Asylum*, David J. Rothman links the "rise" of the asylum in nineteenth-century America with the abundance of domestic tracts such as Beecher's (216).

14. An ardent advocate of women's managerial work in charity and social causes, the British reformer Elizabeth Fry, wrote: "May the attention of *women* be more and more directed to these labours of love; and may the time quickly arrive, when there shall not exist, in this realm, a single public institution [where women] . . . shall not enjoy the *efficacious superintendence* of the pious and benevolent of THEIR OWN SEX!" (qtd. in Freedman 23). In *Women and the Work of Benevolence*, Ginz-

berg quotes an admiring comment made about reformer Paulina Wright Davis's head (1853): " 'Her strongest moral organ is Benevolence' " (11).

15. See Linda Mahood's *The Magdalenes: Prostitution in the Nineteenth Century* for an excellent extended discussion of the Magdalen charities of Scotland. See also Donna T. Andrew's *Philanthropy and Police* (119–27). A good general discussion of prostitution and reform in America appears in Barbara Meil Hobson's *Uneasy Virtue: The Politics of Prostitution and the American Reform Tradition.*

Begun by Charles N. Crittenton, a successful businessman turned social activist and philanthropist, the Florence Crittenton Homes (named for a beloved daughter who died of scarlet fever at four) attempted to reform prostitutes and unmarried pregnant girls to religious and domestic values. In *Fifty Years' Work with Girls* Otto Wilson provides a complete history of the Florence Crittenton Homes. There were other rescue homes in operation in various cities by the time the Florence Crittenton Mission was first established (1883): the Magdalen Home, the Catholic Protective Society, the Empire Friendly Shelter (for African-American women), the Salvation Army Rescue Homes, the House of Mercy (est. 1865), the Society of the Epiphany.

There were institutions for good girls as well: the Shelter for Respectable Girls was established in New York City in 1874. The Girls' Friendly Society was modeled on the English Society and established in 1877 by female reformers of the Episcopal Church in order to help girls in "the most exposed and trying period of their lives" (Edson 45). The latter two organizations were distinctly separatist in membership, attempting to aid those young female workers who had not (yet) fallen. "No one who had not borne a virtuous character" could be a member of the Girls' Friendly Society (Donovan 85).

16. In *The Magdalenes: Prostitution in the Nineteenth Century,* Mahood writes: "The establishment of magdalene asylums, female refuges, and penitentiaries for destitute and homeless women and girls was the common response to the prostitution problem, which reflects part of a larger movement to 'colonize' the poor. In these homes a 'problematic' segment of the female working class was isolated from the more respectable community, and 'voluntarily' underwent intensive re-socialization, moral education, and industrial training, and was thereby restored to 'respectability' " (62).

17. Under Barrett's direction, the National Florence Crittenton Mission shifted the focus of its reformative program from rescuing prostitutes to sheltering unwed teenaged mothers. In his history of the institution, Wilson writes: "In the public mind the name of Florence Crittenton is no doubt rightly associated with any kind of help to the victims of sexual irregularity, but first and foremost it stands for help to the erring girl in her first mistake" (60).

Like the Home for Deserted Mothers (established in Britain in 1873), which restricted admission to "first time fallen" girls only, the Crittenton Mission was much less forgiving of girls who returned to the Mission again pregnant. While Barrett writes that the matron and board could decide to readmit a girl who had had one child under Christian influence yet returned pregnant out of wedlock, such a readmission would have been rare indeed (*Practical Suggestions* 88).

18. In its most reduced and polemical form, the gender-based ideology of women's prisons, juvenile reformatories for girls, rescue homes, *and* the domestic science movement (as well as women's suffrage, if one ignores race) privileged gender over class within the reform movement. As Freedman writes about prison reform: "The use of sisterhood to describe the relationship of women prisoners and reformers suggests the influence of the ideology of women's separate sphere. Reformers attempted to dismiss class difference and emphasized the common bond of an innate womanly spirit. Moreover, case histories in their annual reports stressed the leveling influence of the home. In 1849, for example, an upper-class woman and an Irish servant, both seduced and abandoned by upper-class men, were given shelter. The former was 'placed on an equal footing' with other inmates, all of whom achieved redemption through penitence and docility" (33).

19. The British model of assigning two separate identities for the nineteenth-century illicitly sexual woman as either seduced or fallen is described by Sally Mitchell in *The Fallen Angel*. The fallen woman, unlike the seduced one, was thought to be "capable of sin and therefore responsible for her own destiny" (x). One of the goals of the Crittenton organization was to enable the figure of the victim to overshadow that of the sexual "criminal."

20. In her stirring fundraising tract *The Helping Hand: Comprising an Account of the Home for Discharged Female Convicts and an Appeal on Behalf of that Institution* (1853), the reformer and women's rights activist Caroline Kirkland calls upon every privileged female to accept her responsibility toward all other women, or be implicated in their misery: "Among the most precious of Women's Rights is the right to do good to her own sex. . . . Sad it is that [the] fallen woman hopes less from her sisters than from her brothers . . . women should consider themselves as a community, having special common needs and common obligations, which it is a shame to turn aside from under the plea of inability or distaste. *Every woman in misfortune is the proper object of care to the happier and safer part of her sex.* Not to stretch forth to her the helping hand—not to defend her against wrong and shield her from temptation—is to consent to her degradation and to become, in some sense, party to her ruin" (qtd. in Freedman 34).

21. Just as nineteenth-century Progressive-era female reformers attempted to conflate the institution with the home, they also agitated for the separation between the factory and the home. Many female reformers, such as Mary Simkhovitch, testified against the practice of tenement homework: " 'I speak of it [tenement homework] as a business rather than a home because we know very well these homes have the form but not the substance of home' " (Boris 75). Home ideology

was critical, as well, to the Women's Christian Temperance Union (WCTU), whose slogan was "Home Protection" (Ginzberg 203).

22. In fact, women's prisons contained domestic science equipment and training similar to that provided in colleges. Nicole Hahn Rafter describes the well-equipped domestic science department of the women's reformatory in Albion, New York, noting that "from [1912] inmates received instruction in: manufacture and source of food supplies, relative cost, and nutritive values; the care of the kitchen, pantry, and dining room; construction and care of the sinks, stoves (both gas and coal) and refrigerators; table etiquette; the planning and serving of meals; and waitress[es]' duties" (296).

In their discussion of Progressive-era juvenile reformatories, Steven Schlossman and Stephanie Wallach cite evidence that the domestic science element in juvenile institutions for girls was used primarily as "propaganda" in the service of its re-form ideology rather than as a field of knowledge: "To increase public regard for the vocational training programs, reformatory superintendents described them as if they were part of the larger home-economics movement that swept the country in the Progressive Era. Actually, the training rarely went beyond the chores necessary for personal hygiene and cottage upkeep, with a cooking class or two added for good measure" (77). See also Barbara Brenzel for an excellent discussion of the first "family-style" reformatory for girls, established in Lancaster, Massachusetts in 1856.

23. Michael Ignatieff notes the insistent nature of humanistic prison reform meant to be persuasive to the objects of reform: "The persistent ideal of prison re-form was a kind of punishment at once so humane and so just that it would convince the offender of the moral legitimacy of the law and its custodians. The penitentiary was designed to embody this reconciliation of the imperatives of discipline with the imperatives of humanity" (87–88).

24. The female inmates of the Western House of Refuge (Albion, New York) were minor public-order offenders, but it was permitted (by the "commitment law") to keep inmates for five years. After an 1899 amendment the length of incarceration was lowered to three years (Rafter 290).

See Hobson for a discussion of W. I. Thomas's book *The Unadjusted Girl* (1923), about female juvenile delinquency seen through the lens of the Roaring Twenties (184–89). See also Schlossman and Wallach for an excellent discussion of sexual discrimination in juvenile delinquency theory in the Progressive era. Chapter 8 of Rothman's *Conscience and Convenience* offers a discussion of the failures of reform ideology in juvenile institutions in the Progressive era (261–89).

25. See Freedman for an extended discussion of Davis and Hodder, as well as other female prison reform leaders.

26. Freedman describes the two primary aims of female prison reform as prac-ticed by Hodder and Davis: "First, they [Hodder and Davis] attempted to transcend

the physical limitations of women's prisons by emphasizing the cottage system, parole, outdoor work, and recreation. Secondly, they pressed against the less-tangible boundaries of domesticity by expanding training to include academic and industrial classes and non-traditional women's work" (131).

27. Admission into the Magdalen charity, by contrast, was offered only to the "cream," to use Andrew's word, of the prostitutes. The admission policies were strict and rigorous: "Each applicant for admission had to face an examination by a board of governors who questioned and scrutinized her in an attempt to discover how deep and genuine her contrition was. This was an important process—it was essential to distinguish those women who were truly penitent from those who only wanted a temporary vacation from all labor" (Andrew 124–25).

It is important to note that the Crittenton Mission also desired the "best" of the fallen to help promote and sustain their charitable enterprise that required philan-thropic support from a critical society in order to survive. A telling example of the Mission's conservative policies even in the face of great social need was the reso-lution of the conflict in the late nineteenth century between a Crittenton Mission in Kansas City and an association of Free Methodists who sought to open a rescue home in the same area. Both sides agreed that two such institutions would be in competition with each other for funds and community support, so they agreed to unite their forces. This idea proved difficult to enact, as "Mother Lee" (a Free Meth-odist rescue worker) writes in *Mother Lee's Experience in Fifteen Years' Rescue Work,* for doctrinal as well as ideological differences between the two groups: the Free Methodists felt that the Crittenton Mission was not strict enough in enforc-ing particular religious principles, and the Crittenton associates disagreed with the others in their admission policies. The conflict was resolved by the superinten-dence of the home by the Methodists with the agreed provisos—mandated by the Florence Crittenton Mission—that the home would remain part of their organiza-tion (with the Crittenton name) and that entrance could never be denied any white girl, while permission for black girls had to be obtained from the president of the Mission (103).

When in 1886 "Mother Benedict" broke with the WCTU's sponsored rescue home ("Benedict House"), her action was a result, she states, of the WCTU's greed for the five thousand dollars set aside for the Benedict House by the Iowa legisla-ture. However, the Union again reported the cause of the separation as the result of a difference of opinion over admission policies. Benedict wanted to minister to any repentant fallen girl, while the WCTU made clear in a letter to its mem-bers that they could not support such standards for many reasons—among them, "Mrs. Benedict desires to have the doors of the Home open to all classes of women who have strayed from the paths of virtue, viz: abandoned women whose undisci-plined lives and drinking habits make voluntary subjection to the discipline of the Home almost impossible, they really needing mild prison discipline, which we are not authorized to enforce" (*Woman's Work for Woman* 167).

28. Stowe's Katy Scudder, when a girl, could perform feats of physical as well as domestic strength—each seeming to take the same degree of courage and skill, and all without harming her status as a lady: "Katy could harness a chaise, or row a boat; she could saddle and ride any horse in the neighborhood; she could cut any garment that ever was seen or thought of, make cake, jelly, and wine, from her earliest years, in most precocious style;—all without seeming to derange a sort of trim, well-kept air of ladyhood that sat jauntily on her" (3–4).

29. In this way the rescue home resembles a hospital where the caretakers—nurses—are identified and "crowned" by their white caps.

Barrett earned her medical degree from the Medical College of Georgia in 1892. While she was never a practicing physician, her knowledge of medicine and status as a doctor "legitimized" her work with the "fallen."

30. The visions of many female reformers—and therefore the practices of their institutions—had to be altered. Freedman describes the "failure" of the new penology in women's prisons: "Despite the founders' self-conscious differentiation of women's prisons from other nineteenth-century institutions, the feminine experiments eventually resembled traditional prisons in many respects. Like other efforts to humanize institutional care, such as the 'soft-line' in juvenile reformatories or 'moral therapy' in insane asylums, women's prisons increasingly relied on traditional methods of discipline. . . . In both skill training and character building the tension between domesticity and discipline pervaded the internal life of the women's prisons" (90).

WORKS CITED

Andrew, Donna T. *Philanthropy and Police: London Charity in the Eighteenth Century.* Princeton: Princeton UP, 1989.

Barrett, Kate Waller. *Some Practical Suggestions on the Conduct of a Rescue Home.* 1903. New York: Arno, 1974.

Beecher, Catharine. *A Treatise on Domestic Economy for the Use of Young Ladies at Home, and at School.* 1841. Source Book Press, 1970.

Bell, Ian A. *Literature and Crime in Augustan England.* New York: Routledge, 1991.

Benedict, Lovina B. *Woman's Work for Woman.* Des Moines: Iowa Printing, 1892.

Boris, Eileen. "Reconstructing the 'Family': Women, Progressive Reform and the Problem of Social Control." Frankel and Dye, 73–86.

Boydston, Jeanne, Mary Kelley, and Anne Margolis. *The Limits of Sisterhood: The Beecher Sisters on Women's Rights and Women's Sphere.* Chapel Hill: U of North Carolina P, 1988.

Brenzel, Barbara. "Domestication as Reform: A Study of the Socialization of Wayward Girls, 1856–1905." *Harvard Educational Review* 50 (1980): 196–213.

Buehr, Walter. *Home Sweet Home in the Nineteenth Century.* New York: Crowell, 1965.

Cohen, Stanley. *Visions of Social Control: Crime, Punishment and Classification.* Oxford: Polity, 1985.

Cohen, Stanley, and Andrew Scull, eds. *Social Control and the State.* New York: St. Martin's, 1983.

Donovan, Mary Sudman. *A Different Call: Women's Ministries in the Episcopal Church, 1850–1920.* Wilton: Morehouse-Barlow, 1986.

Du Vall, Nell. *Domestic Technology: A Chronology of Developments.* Boston: Hall, 1988.

East, Marjorie. *Home Economics: Past, Present, and Future.* Boston: Allyn and Bacon, 1980.

Edson, E. M. "The Girls' Friendly Society." *Church Work* 1 (1885–86): 45–48.

Flint, Kate. *The Victorian Novelist: Social Problems and Social Change.* New York: Croom Helm, 1987.

Folbre, Nancy. "The Unproductive Housewife: Her Evolution in Nineteenth-Century Economic Thought." *Signs: Journal of Women in Culture and Society* 16 (1991): 463–84.

Frankel, Noralee, and Nancy S. Dye, eds. *Gender, Class, Race, and Reform in the Progressive Era.* Lexington: U of Kentucky P, 1991.

Freedman, Estelle B. *Their Sister's Keepers: Women's Prison Reform in America, 1830–1930.* Ann Arbor: U of Michigan P, 1981.

Ginzberg, Lori D. *Women and the Work of Benevolence: Morality, Politics, and Class in the Nineteenth-Century United States.* New Haven: Yale UP, 1990.

[Green, Sarah]. *Mental Improvement for a Young Lady, on Her Entrance into the World.* 1793. London, 1796.

Grimm, Jacob, and Wilhelm Grimm. *Grimms' Tales for Young and Old: The Complete Stories.* Trans. Ralph Manheim. New York: Anchor, 1977.

Hobson, Barbara Meil. *Uneasy Virtue: The Politics of Prostitution and the American Reform Tradition.* New York: Basic Books, 1987.

Ignatieff, Michael. "State, Civil Society and Total Institutions: A Critique of Recent Social Histories of Punishment." Cohen and Scull, 75–105.

Lee, Martha A. *Mother Lee's Experience in Fifteen Years' Rescue Work.* Omaha: n.p., 1906.

Mahood, Linda. *The Magdalenes: Prostitution in the Nineteenth Century.* New York: Routledge, 1990.

Mitchell, Sally. *The Fallen Angel: Chastity, Class, and Women's Reading, 1835–1880.* Bowling Green: Bowling Green University Popular Press, 1981.

Philips, David. "'A Just Measure of Crime, Authority, Hunters and Blue Locusts': The 'Revisionist' Social History of Crime in Britain, 1780–1850." Cohen and Scull, 50–74.

Rafter, Nicole Hahn. "Chastizing the Unchaste: Social Control Functions of a Woman's Reformatory, 1894–1931." Cohen and Scull, 288–311.

Rothman, David J. *Conscience and Convenience: The Asylum and Its Alternatives in Progressive America.* Boston: Little, Brown, 1980.

————. *The Discovery of the Asylum: Social Order and Disorder in the New Republic.* Boston: Little, Brown, 1971.

Schlossman, Steven, and Stephanie Wallach. "The Crime of Precocious Sexuality: Female Delinquency in the Progressive Era." *Harvard Educational Review* 48 (1978): 65–94.

Sklar, Kathryn Kish. *Catharine Beecher.* New Haven: Yale UP, 1973.

Stowe, Harriet Beecher. *The Minister's Wooing.* 1859. Hartford: Stowe-Day Foundation, 1978.

Weigley, Emma S. "It Might Have Been Euthenics: The Lake Placid Conferences and the Home Economics Movement." *American Quarterly* 26 (1974): 79–96.

Wilson, Otto. *Fifty Years Work with Girls, 1883–1933.* 1933. New York: Arno, 1974.

————. *Life of Kate Waller Barrett.* 1933. Printed with Barrett, *Some Practical Suggestions.*

Contributors

CHRISTINA BOUFIS is completing her dissertation, entitled "Where Womanhood and Childhood Meet: Female Adolescence in Victorian Fiction and Culture," at the Graduate School of The City University of New York.

JULIA COURTNEY holds a bachelor's honors degree in history and a doctorate in English literature, both from London University. She is an Open University Arts Tutor and is widely involved in adult education. Her research concerns representations of nuns in nineteenth-century fiction, biography, and painting.

SHERRIE A. INNESS is an assistant professor of English at Miami University, Ohio. She has published essays on a variety of topics, including girls' culture, gender, British nineteenth-century imperialism, and domestic service, in *American Literary Realism, 1870–1910*, *Journal of American Culture*, *Journal of Popular Culture*, *NWSA Journal*, *Studies in Scottish Literature*, *Studies in Short Fiction*, and *Women's Studies*.

CAROL MAVOR is an assistant professor of art at the University of North Carolina, Chapel Hill. She received her master's of fine arts degree from the University of California, San Diego, and her doctorate from the University of California, Santa Cruz. She has completed a book on utopic theory and Victorian culture, and an article on the feminization of olfaction.

SALLY MITCHELL, professor of English and affiliated professor of women's studies at Temple University, edited *Victorian Britain: An Encyclopedia* (1988). Her earlier books include *The Fallen Angel: Chastity, Class and Women's Reading, 1835–1880* and *Dinah Mulock Craik*. She is working on a study of girls' culture in England at the turn of the century.

CLAUDIA NELSON is the author of *Boys Will Be Girls: The Feminine Ethic and British Children's Fiction, 1857–1917* (1991) and has completed a study of images of fatherhood in British periodicals between 1850 and 1910 (Georgia, forthcoming). She is an assistant professor of English at Southwest Texas State University.

JUDITH PASCOE, an assistant professor of English at the University of Iowa, is at work on a book about poetry and theatricality in the Romantic period. She is also editing the collected poems of Mary Robinson.

JOYCE SENDERS PEDERSEN is lecturer in British studies at Odense University in Denmark. She is the author of *The Reform of Girls' Secondary and Higher Education in Victorian England* (1987) and is working on a study of liberalism and feminism in Victorian and Edwardian England.

LYNNE VALLONE is an assistant professor of English at Texas A&M University, specializing in children's fiction and eighteenth-century literature. She has completed a book on Anglo-American girlhood from 1700 to 1880 (forthcoming).

MARTHA VICINUS, professor of English, women's studies, and history at the University of Michigan, Ann Arbor, is the author or editor of books and articles on Victorian women, popular culture, and the history of sexuality. Her essay in this collection grew out of research for a selection of Florence Nightingale's letters coedited with Bea Nergaard, *Ever Yours, Florence Nightingale* (1989). She is completing a book on the formation of the modern lesbian identity, 1660–1940.

LESLIE WILLIAMS teaches art history at the University of Cincinnati. Her publications include "Visualizing Victorian Schooling" in Patrick Scott and Pauline Fletcher's *Culture and Education in Victorian England* (1990) and "The Womanly Art of Breast-Feeding in Victorian Britain" in *Politics, Gender and Society*, edited by Richard Dotterer (1992).

Index